CW01647713

Mcdoc

Thankyou for your inspiration & support.

It may get tough ahead, but lets find ways to be pro-human.

Best

Rob G

A Wake-Up Call for Every Leader Who Thinks They Have Time

Garlick shows, in plain language, how billions of non-human workers, AI agents, and robots will collide with our current systems—and what Pro-Human leaders must do now to grow profits and people. *AI - Anarchy or Abundance?* is the rare book that makes you both uneasy and deeply hopeful, then hands you a path forward.

—**Dr. Marshall Goldsmith** is the *Thinkers50* #1 Executive Coach and New York Times bestselling author of *The Earned Life*, *Triggers*, and *What Got You Here Won't Get You There.*

Required Reading for Any CEO Who Says, "People Are Our Greatest Asset"

If you've ever stood in front of your organisation and claimed that "people are our greatest asset," this book quietly asks, *Do your AI decisions prove it?* Garlick draws a stark line between leaders who use AI to squeeze labour costs and those who use it to create better work and better organisations. This is a business book that will sit in your conscience as much as your strategy offsite.

—**Professor Ying Zhou**, Director of the Future of Work Research Centre at the University of Surrey

From "Weak Competition" to Strong Leadership

Garlick's long history with technological change underpins his forecasts for what's ahead. The point that humanity has entered a period of "weak competition" with AI is both chilling and clarifying. This book will unsettle some but also embolden leaders who want to win without breaking the social contract.

It's less about fear or hype and more about responsibility. It is timely, balanced, and very insightful.

—**Naveed Sultan**, Professor of Practice at Imperial College Business School and Former Global Chairman of Citigroup's Institutional Business Group

A Playbook for Pro-Human Capitalism

Leaders across private, public and social sectors are navigating extraordinary times. Decisions made over the next few years will have profound implications for how we live and work, and how our economies and societies evolve and transform. Garlick not only argues for a pro-human stance in an AI age, he explores realistic strategies to bend the power of capitalism towards more positive outcomes for people - all those who are alive today and those yet to be born. Anyone with decision-making responsibilities should read this book now to be more equipped to shape a better future for us all.

—**Sarah Gillard**, CEO of Blueprint for Better Business

The BESST™ Framework Is a Gift to Future-Facing Boards

The developments in artificial intelligence are game-changing for many businesses. For directors pulled between shorter-term shareholder returns and long-term system stability, this book gives boards a language and framework to hold that tension honestly. Garlick's BESST™ Framework turns a chaotic debate about the impact of AI on business and work into a simple, sticky tool that boards and C-suites need and can use.

—**Hitesh Thakrar**, Member of the Board of Trustees of Alan Turing Institute, Cancer Research UK, and STFC Council, and Partner at Syncona Limited

A Compass for Governments Standing at the AI Crossroads

Instead of peddling doom or fairy tales, Garlick offers what governments actually need: a grounded, data-rich guide to what happens to wages, jobs, tax bases, and social stability when AI and robots scale faster than our safety nets. His examination of the options provides a handbook on how societies can "vote" on the AI paths ahead.

—**Professor Ian Goldin**, Professor of Globalisation and Development at the University of Oxford and Founding Director of the Oxford Martin Research Programmes

AI – ANARCHY OR ABUNDANCE?

WHY THE FUTURE OF WORK NEEDS PRO-HUMAN LEADERS

AI – ANARCHY OR ABUNDANCE?

WHY THE FUTURE OF WORK NEEDS PRO-HUMAN LEADERS

Rob Garlick

Copyright © 2026 Rob Garlick.

All Rights Reserved. This book contains material protected
under International and Federal Copyright Laws and Treaties.
Any unauthorized reprint or use of this material is prohibited.
No part of this book may be reproduced or transmitted in any form
or by any means, electronic or mechanical, including photocopying,
recording, or by any information storage and retrieval system without
express written permission from the author/publisher.

ISBN: 979-8-89079-463-5 (hardcover)
ISBN: 979-8-89079-464-2 (paperback)
ISBN: 979-8-89079-465-9 (ebook)

01010100 01101111 00100000 01101000 01110101
01101101 01100001 01101110 01110011

01100110 01101111 01110010 00100000 01101000
01110101 01101101 01100001 01101110 01110011

(To humans, for humans)

To my amazing wife, Coral, and children, Lucia, Macca, Jasmine, and Dexter—this book was written in the hope of leaving a better world for your generation.

My thanks to the wonderful people who helped bring this book to life, including my editor, Sarah Busby; Ben Gioia, Chris O'Byrne, and the publishing team at Leadership Awake Press; and Wenyan, Giles, Anuj, Ebrahim, and Madoc. And to all those who have opened doors and shown kind encouragement over the years—thank you.

CONTENTS

Part 3 – Pro-Human Leadership

INTRODUCTION

"Better leaders, Better world."

—Robert Hargrove[1]

When the conditions change, pessimists fret, optimists hope, and procrastinators dither; yet leaders *act* to forge the BESST path.

SWIMMING WITH THE TIDE

It was a beautiful day in August when our son jumped from the back of a boat into the sea. We were laughing as the water gently carried him away. But then he tried to swim back towards us. His smile quickly turned to panic as the current continued to pull him further from the boat, too powerful to overcome. Our laughs quickly turned to anxiety—then horror—as he was overwhelmed by the tide and dragged backwards.

Thankfully, the episode ended well. Another boat was nearby, and they were able to pull him out of the water. But there are parallels between this incident and the subject of this book: how artificial intelligence (AI) will impact work and leadership, and how we can thrive within this changing landscape.

The biggest lesson I've learned from over three decades in business, investing, and work is to try and find the strongest currents—those swim lanes that can carry you towards more work opportunities, more pay, and more fun. They can be the reason some people find themselves in "the right place at the right time." However, the opposite can also be true. If you swim against the tide, it can not only get exhausting but also jobs, pay, and fun can move further away from your grasp.

How does this relate to AI? We are experiencing one of the most significant technology trends the world has ever seen. AI is a powerful tide that will sweep through businesses over the next few decades, carrying many along with it, particularly in relation to company profitability and investor returns. Unfortunately, most workers will find themselves swimming against an unstoppable current. Employment shapes not only livelihoods but also lives, so this has dramatic downstream implications.

AI is not new, of course, but a series of recent AI tipping points have pushed us into unprecedented territory. They are coming together to transform AI from useless at many tasks to useful and, eventually, superhuman. There is little debate about the fact that we have entered a new technological revolution, but what comes next is a work revolution that will disrupt most jobs. As economist Tyler Cowen has said, "If you are not scared of AI, you are not paying enough attention."[2]

While it's clear that AI will bring many benefits, we also need solutions to make sure these outweigh the risks: the disruption caused by a continued quickening in the pace of change, job losses for both white-collar and blue-collar workers, graduate unemployment, falling wages, rising inequality, winner-takes-most economics, datafication, and a gap in necessary skills and education. Indeed, in the worst-case scenario, we could be looking at an economic singularity in which incomes could collapse, with knock-on impacts on consumption, taxation, and asset prices. This could lead to a large-scale worker backlash, strikes, and political change.

However, this is not a book about an AI-driven future dystopia. It's a book about how to mitigate the negatives and move towards the many positives that AI can bring to the world of work. A book about what to ask of leaders as they invest in AI. A book about how leaders can make the right choices at this critical moment in time, so the upsides exceed the downsides.

Queen Elizabeth II asked a simple, brilliant question after the 2008 Financial Crisis: "Why did nobody see it coming?"[3] AI will also have a seismic effect on society. Given we can already see elements of the impact AI will have on work, the question we need to ask ourselves is, *What are we going to do about it?* This is a leadership question, not a technology question. It is about being proactive and pro-human.

I felt compelled to write this book for this reason: to explain the trends that are coming, to surface the solutions we need to consider, and to urge action rather than burying our heads in the sand. We must be proactive if we want as many people as possible to benefit from this AI tidal wave—if we want to swim with it, not against it.

A RINGSIDE SEAT

By design—and a little luck—I have found myself at the centre of the debates on AI and work.

I have had a ringside seat at most new areas of technological innovation over the past 30 years, whether it was going to Netscape's IPO in 1995, being part of Google's IPO in 2004, starting Citi's Disruptive Innovation series in 2013, or becoming head of innovation and technology at Citi Global Insights. When it became clear that the world of work would be disrupted by AI and robotics, we partnered with Oxford's

Carl Benedikt Frey, one of the world's experts on technology at work and someone I've published many papers with since 2015.

From theory to practice, as an investment banker and fund manager, several thousand meetings with C-suite leaders and top investors across the globe gave me the best business education I could have ever wished for. It was a hands-on lesson in how businesses are run, how capital markets work, what CEOs and investors really care about, how technologies are implemented, and how they disrupt. As a manager for over 20 years, including running Citi Research, I've gained an understanding of the trade-offs and tough decisions that leaders must make. To help me coach executives, I added a master's in behavioural change along the way.

This book comes from a combination of these experiences and a passion for helping people grow. Now, let's dive into what this book covers and why—a taste of the journey you're about to embark on.

A GUIDE TO THE CHAPTERS AHEAD

Have you ever been caught in square waves? This rare phenomenon occurs when two swells collide with each other, creating powerful and unpredictable rip tides that can be dangerous for swimmers, surfers, and boats alike. We are entering a decade of square waves in the world of work, with several digital megatrends colliding—including AI, robotics, and digital labour—that could leave many needing lifeboats. Part 1 of this book delves into these threats so we can confront reality in order to move forward.

As physical AI grows, our world will start to look very different, as we'll discuss in Chapter I. In mid-2024, when forecasting how big the robot market could become, I had an aha moment. Actually, it was more like a *holy shit* moment. I realised that the payback period for investing in humanoid robots, meaning the time it takes to earn your money back, could be merely weeks—not years or months. As we will discuss, the economic implications of this alone are huge, but remember that humanoids will only make up 650 million of the 4 billion robots forecast to be moving around us by 2050.[4]

Chapter II explores the cognitive work that AI will impact: the AI industrial revolution. This "unseen AI" impacts white-collar jobs in a similar way to how automation has impacted blue-collar jobs over the last five decades. This might sound hyperbolic, but I explain why this really is different from previous technological revolutions and far more radical. Part of this will be an enormous wave of new AI agents coming to help you, learn from you, and replace elements of what you do.

This combination of AI agents and AI robots means that human workers will be competing with billions of new non-human workers in the years ahead. Non-human workers will go from less that 1% of the workforce today to exceeding the size of the human workforce in the next two decades. As I said previously, this really is a tidal wave, but it does not stop there.

Chapter III explains that AI will accelerate the use of digital labour, which involves those working for others via digital platforms that allow them to be based anywhere in the world. It will increasingly connect millions of smart workers in low-cost locations to companies looking to take advantage of this wage differential. For example, an accountant in Manila might cost 5% of what one in New York does. This will only increase competition between human workers looking for work. There are already over 250 million NEETs around the world in search of jobs—young people not in education, employment, or training.[5]

The combination of the trends above and the declining costs of AI will not only create more job competition and substitution but also falling wages for many. Chapter IV goes on to explain a risk that could be existential for our current economic systems: an economic singularity in which human wages collapse. We need to discuss this threat and seek solutions quickly, given that artificial general intelligence (AGI)—AI that can emulate human intelligence across a wide range of tasks—is approaching faster than anyone expected just a couple of years ago.

Of course, what might be bad for workers could be great news for company margins and investor returns as labour costs fall. Despite the common refrain you hear in business that "people are our most important asset," Chapter V argues that data could take that crown very soon. Indeed, data should already be classified as the "fifth factor of production," and our lives are being datafied as we speak. This has implications for both individuals and countries, as it drives winner-takes-most economics and an increase in the concentration of businesses.

Chapter VI concludes Part 1 of this book by warning that these trends could cause backlash and anarchy if we do not take thoughtful action. Anarchy is defined as "without a leader"—the exact opposite of what this book asks for in pro-human leadership. Here, we look at tipping points in technology and society, the history of unemployment and unrest, and the current canaries in the coalmine, resulting in high and rising youth unemployment.

I recognise that the problems surfaced in Part 1 of this book will be an uncomfortable read for some, but they lead us into the search for solutions in Part 2. We are after solutions.

Moving away from dystopian worries, Part 2 starts with the utopian concept of AI abundance in Chapter VII, including what it is, why it could be great, and areas in which abundance may appear. In theory, AI could create so much growth and wealth that you may not even need a job. Abundance is a North Star to aim for in the AI age, but we must also separate ambition from reality. The abundance theorists need to acknowledge that there is a high probability we'll see an abundance of non-human workers and AI dilemmas at first. Pain before gain.

Chapter VIII examines the argument that technology creates new jobs to offset those lost and the evidence for this trend throughout history. It is good news that there are three big megatrend areas that will produce new opportunities—technology, sustainability, and care roles—plus a likely wild card around creativity and innovation. Aging demographics—the idea that we will run out of workers before we run out of jobs—will help here, but it is a don't-worry-ism that we must not overplay. Given the difficult history of technological transitions in the world of work and the rapid pace of change today, more job augmentation and enhancement, rather than job substitution, would create a helpful bridge. If we are moving from a knowledge economy to a caring economy, we should also think about how society values care roles.

Chapter IX looks at an exciting opportunity for AI to enhance our roles, but this also requires a critical eye. Better jobs *must* be a primary goal in the AI era, but having a *better* job is conditional on *having* a job. And we need to increase the dreadfully low employee engagement levels in the workplace. Reducing mundane tasks is an easy suggestion to make, but Chapter IX also explores more controversial debates on shorter working weeks and more rights in the AI age.

Chapter X explores how the upskilling and reskilling of workers to help them move from old to new era jobs—essential to mitigating the risks of AI—is not happening quickly enough. While everyone agrees it's important, we have an investment problem, and we need to create the space—or "room"—to reskill. We also tackle the question, "Upskill to what?" and look at the risk of "humans getting dumber," explore the problems AI creates for young people, and consider what the solutions are.

In search of solutions, Chapter XI highlights the key difference between human workers today and the fate of unemployed horses when tractors and cars took their place: humans get to vote for the future they want. What, then, will they vote for as AI sweeps through work? We discuss 25 options to demonstrate that there are plenty of choices, even if some may be challenging, initially, for leaders to embrace.

Most democracies were born out of worker backlash during the First Industrial Revolution, and it is entirely possible that we will see employees forcing change once again. Unwilling to accept the new status quo, they may seize more control over companies, moving voting rights and leader incentives away from the doctrine of shareholder primacy that has been dominant since the 1970s. This potential dramatic change is explored in Chapter XII, along with other ways in which workers could get more say in the direction of AI at work, such as trade unionisation or more HR influence in C-suites and at board level.

In Part 3, the final section of this book, we look at the role of leaders in this transformation. They must become bridges between the problems raised in Part 1 and the solutions in Part 2. AI could either raise anxiety over jobs or make them better; leaders must choose which. Indeed, it can be used as a catalyst to debate how we improve positive engagement at work. Nine pro-human solutions are offered in Chapter XIII that we know can work, along with a simple habit that can nudge us towards a better place.

The penultimate chapter of the book takes a longer-term lens and asks how we *want* work to change during the AI age. It should be the responsibility of each generation to leave the world in a better place for the next generation. What should we aspire towards? Looking at lessons from the past and what we imagine might happen in the future, three options are offered, with an explanation of how we can measure and improve outcomes. It's about making it a race to the top, not the bottom. A race that everyone can win.

Chapter XV finishes with the BESST™ Framework: a simple model that brings everything together, shaping how AI impacts work to benefit most. It proposes we engineer **B**etter jobs and **E**nough jobs, ensure a **S**ay in the outcomes, provide **S**afety nets for those left behind, and drive debate on the **T**ilts needed to support people in this new reality. For example, taxation will probably need to tilt away from labour and towards taxing technology, corporates, or wealth. We likely need to tilt towards the areas we want to see abundance in, rather than relying on capital markets to drive where AI flourishes. And capitalism itself could tilt towards its next iteration: Capitalism 4.0.

The chapter finishes with what you can do to adapt as AI sweeps through the world of work. Importantly, leadership in this context is not just about leading businesses, society, or technology; it is also about self-leadership. We all have a part to play in shaping the future of work in this AI age.

Given that the aim of this book is to help many, I have attempted not to be overly technical. You don't have to understand how AI works to understand how it will impact us. ChatGPT proves that. I have also tried hard to be objective and apolitical, but we are all biased by our very nature. I do know my primary bias is that I care about how we direct AI towards benefitting as many people as possible, and so I'm doggedly in search of solutions. To that end, I make no apology for the multitude of ideas I propose, as the aim was to show we do have options. To provide some focus and clarity in Part 3 of the book, I narrow these down to five primary solutions and one key habit.

WHAT IS NOT COVERED

While this book covers a lot of ground, it is, of course, impossible to include everything. Given that it is about how AI impacts work and leadership, there are many important AI topics that are beyond its scope. For example, regulation is only discussed in relation to the work context. Some of the amazing new potential discoveries and benefits of AI are touched on, but it is not the primary focus. Finally, while it's important to recognise there is a vast melting pot of concerns that could create a bigger backlash against AI—as discussed in Chapter VI, "AI Anarchy"—I can't cover all of these here, whether that's its impact on warfare and climate change or its contribution to the creation of a post-truth society. Suffice to say, there are big existential risks if AI cannot be controlled or aligned with human values.

Although I have had three global roles in my career, I've spent most of my time looking at US trends, and I live in the UK, so the data included in this book is concentrated on those two countries. AI will permeate every sector and every region, but impacts and timings will differ. Technologies, businesses, and leadership are also context specific, with the devil often being in the details. This book generalises by necessity, but it's worth noting that this simpler perspective sacrifices some of that context and nuance. There are no perfect solutions, and predicting the future is not easy, but predict we must, to prepare for different scenarios and attempt to shape outcomes.

CREATING RIPPLES OF HOPE

I ask you to please hold three things in your mind as you read this book.

Firstly, while we have entered a new and important phase of change in the AI era, Amara's law suggests we usually overestimate the impacts of technology in the short term and underestimate them in the long term. AI will take time to become fully embedded in the workplace, but don't use this lag as an excuse to assume that big changes are not coming. They are, and solutions *will* be needed.

Secondly, later in the book, I highlight President John F. Kennedy's view that if we have the ingenuity to invent technology that can put people out of work, we also have the capability to invent solutions to make technology benefit most people. This is about our priorities and the way we incentivise the use of AI, not a question of what AI is capable of.

Thirdly, we would do well to remember Albert Einstein's plea after the nuclear bomb was invented: "We appeal as human beings, to human beings: Remember your humanity, and forget the rest."[6] I feel confident that, with careful forethought, we will move in the right direction with AI, but I am very concerned there could be much pain before the gain. By heeding Einstein's words, leaders can help smooth the path for millions of workers.

So, just three things:

1. It may take time, but we *have* entered a new era (Amara).
2. Solutions are needed that help as many people as possible to thrive, and we do have the ingenuity to create them (Kennedy.
3. But only as long as we have the humanity to do so (Einstein).

Einstein's plea is discussed more later in the book. Having worked on this subject for over a decade, my position has moved from being deeply worried to being a conditional optimist and now a proactive optimist. We must create ripples of hope; it is both a pillar and a fuel for life.

As a conditional optimist, I felt I needed to see certain things happen to ensure AI was a positive for many in the workplace. For example, more supportive upskilling needed to take place, and the *right* skills needed to be taught. But what I realised is that we can't just watch from the sidelines. We need to be proactive to make sure these pro-human conditions are built. If we just sit back and allow capitalism's drive for profitability to shape how technologies progress, workers will be left behind, finding themselves swimming against an overwhelming tide.

Instead, we need leaders to create friendly, swimmable waters, and we all need to be proactive to make this happen quickly. That includes me—and you. This book is designed to explain why and how—why the waters will get very difficult and how we create ripples of hope and positive outcomes for the many. Most importantly, how to become a change maker and not a passive change taker.

PART 1

Work WITHOUT Human Workers

1

THE RISE OF AI ROBOTS

"Everything that moves will be robotic one day."

—Jensen Huang, CEO of NVIDIA[7]

"Computers have already achieved ubiquity in human society. In the future, robots will, too."

—Daniela Rus, Director of the MIT Computer Science and Artificial Intelligence Laboratory[8]

MORE ROBOTS THAN HUMANS

What will your reaction be when you meet a humanoid—a robot that resembles a human in shape—for the first time in a real-world setting? It could depend on context:

- You might think *that's cute* as a four-foot-five-inch robot host escorts you to your table in a restaurant.
- You might appreciate a robot bringing an item to your hotel room or a delivery to your house.

- You might feel envy as a humanoid serves you food and drink at your rich neighbour's house.
- You might say, "Put one of those on my wish list" when you see a robot doing chores, such as cleaning or laundry.
- You might realise how helpful it would be for your parents when you see a humanoid help an older person get up, walk, take their medication, and stay in their house for many more years.
- You might feel perturbed as an eight-foot security robot patrols an area, asking, "Is that even legal?"
- "Holy shit" might be all you can say as you see an armed nine-foot military robot coming towards you.

While these scenarios may seem like the stuff of sci-fi movies, they're not as far away as you think. Humanoids can already walk at a pace that exceeds the average human, carry more than the average human, be pushed over and get up on their own, do backflips and parkour, and have the dexterity to thread the eye of a needle. They can see better than humans, take verbal instructions from humans and execute tasks, recognise human emotions, operate 22 hours a day, and change their own battery in three minutes. There is even one that can fold itself up to fit into a cupboard. These capabilities weave together several AI advances in the last 15 years, called multi-modal AI, that have enabled humanoids to leap from theory to reality.

Robots are not new, but AI innovations are supersizing the opportunity. There are over 50 humanoid versions being developed by companies around the world, and in my previous role as head of innovation and technology at Citi Global Insights, we modelled how big this market could be in the years ahead. The conclusion was 650 million humanoids by 2050 and a market value of more than $7 trillion. This is from next to nothing today.

Some of this generation's greatest technology entrepreneurs are enabling these developments in AI robots. Elon believes we will eventually see more robots than humans in the world and has said that, over time, Tesla's robot business could become bigger than its car business.[9] The CEO of NVIDIA, Jensen Huang, recently said, "The next wave of AI is here. Robotics, powered by physical AI, will revolutionise industries."[10]

While the Citi estimate for humanoids may appear large, at 13 million in 2035 and 650 million in 2050, it pales in comparison to others' predictions of 10 billion by 2040.[11] There are also many other forms of AI robots that are already here and will be moving around us in the years ahead. Indeed, I led an analysis modelling nine main areas for AI robots, of which humanoids were just one, the highlights of which were published in a December 2024 Citi GPS report titled "The Rise of AI Robots."[12] We forecasted 1.3 billion AI robots by 2035 and just over 4 billion by 2050, and that was a conservative estimate, as the numbers we were getting were huge. For context, the world's labour force was 3.7 billion in 2024.[13]

It is clear that we are entering a new era. A huge non-human market is being born. We are at the bottom of the S-curve for AI robot adoption, similar to where we were with smartphone adoption in 2008. The good news is that they are coming to help you. To do so, they will need to learn from you. Given that they get better when they have more data, learning what you like will increase personalisation and their value to you. The bad news is that they will also replace some jobs. This latter point is the primary focus of this book.

So, when you do start to see robots moving around humans, it will likely evoke a wide range of emotions, from intrigue or amusement at the start to desire and wonder, and then perhaps to worry and suspicion. Eventually, the novelty will wear off, and they will become ordinary. But our world is going to change, whether we like it or not.

ROBOTS ARE ALREADY HERE

While robots have captured our imaginations for centuries, it was not until 1969 that the first computer-controlled robot, the Stanford Arm, which sprayed paint in manufacturing, was produced. In keeping with Amara's law, the tendency to overestimate the pace of change in the short term, progress has been building slowly. The International Federation of Robots count just 4.3 million units[14] worldwide currently, and most of these are static, contained in controlled environments, such as manufacturing plants and factories. The global average robot density reached 162 units per 10,000 employees in 2023, and while this had doubled in seven years, it is still very low compared to the changes that are coming. Korea has been leading the charge with 1,012 robots per 10,000 employees, highlighting the significant upside ahead for most countries.

Static robots will continue to improve and grow, and these are not included in the 4 billion estimate above. For example, some 10,000 da Vinci robot systems have been installed globally in hospitals to support surgical processes. And when you are out of the hospital, the bar-tending robot Kime can mix you a drink. Getting robots to move safely among people in non-controlled environments has been a hard problem to solve, but one of the reasons why robot numbers have doubled in the last seven years is that collaborative robots, or co-bots, can now work alongside humans, rather than in cages or segregated areas.

One of the first areas that introduced moving robots was mining, in the form of autonomous vehicles (AVs), because it was a low-risk environment that required little interaction with people. Another low-risk, early adoption area has been cleaning. Twenty percent of US households and 12% of Chinese households already have robot vacuum cleaners whizzing around their floors. The advanced ones use AI to understand human instructions and navigate around objects without getting stuck. A recent review tested a whopping 94 different robot vacuums currently available, evidence of how this market has exploded. You can buy an iRobot Roomba vacuum for just $250 today. Most households will likely have one over time, and some will have more than one, echoing the rise of the electric washing machine from the 1950s onwards.

These home cleaning robots will largely save people time, whereas commercial cleaning robots will take some people's jobs away. You can already see robots cleaning the streets in Asia or in airports around the world. This will expand into offices, hospitals, schools, and beyond. When you're next in a city, look up. You may see Skyline Robotics' Ozmo cleaning skyscraper windows. This dangerous job has a growing labour shortage, and robots can already clean three times faster than traditional window cleaners. Labour costs can be reduced by 75%, and safety improved. It's a good example of a logical swap.

Indeed, one of the key arguments for the use of robots is to reduce the risk of dangerous jobs for humans. For example, robots are used in nuclear facilities to inspect reactors without exposing workers to radiation. In chemical plants, they are used to detect leaks without exposing workers to toxic substances. In firefighting, robots can already conduct search and rescue operations and assist in battling blazes.

From the dangerous to the mundane, robots are also increasingly transporting goods. You can already see them moving items around factories and warehouses, and this will become the norm. Autonomous mobile robots (AMRs) are forecast to grow from 2.4 million in 2024 to 181 million by 2050.[15] On a more personal scale, go to a hotel in China today, and you may find that when you order room service, the delivery is made by a robot.

Drones are offering a whole new dimension when it comes to transporting goods, providing speed, efficiency, and access to difficult locations. In war situations, they can transport bombs, but they can also carry lifesaving medical supplies, vaccines, or blood that are time sensitive. Some operate underwater to clean or repair boats, and others spray crops, inspect hard-to-reach areas, or even transport people. Given the critical nature of their emergency deliveries, the US Federal Aviation Administration allows the company Zipline to use drones to deliver beyond the line of sight of a human overseeing their progress. They can fly 140 miles in a single trip and drop packages with one centimetre accuracy. Indeed, if you want to enter drone racing competitions, autonomous systems have already beaten human champions. Other, larger drones can already travel 4,500 km. Some of these, often known as "flying donkeys," can carry 400 kg, delivering goods over inhospitable terrain or into disaster zones. For a particularly spectacular example of how far this technology has advanced, watch the 2025 light show in China that used 11,787 AI-linked drones, a world record. Robot swarms are already happening in the air and could extend to robots on the ground, working with each other.

WHAT'S COMING NEXT?

As impressive as some of these developments have been, there are many more coming.

In restaurants, robots will increasingly welcome and seat customers, take orders, serve food, and clear tables. In supermarkets, robots will stack shelves, help customers locate items, and carry their shopping. In hotels, they will carry people's luggage and help clean rooms. They will provide a service to you as a customer but will also replace you as an employee.

A growth area for human workers over the last two decades has been jobs delivering packages or food, but robots will start doing more of this over time, starting with the easier environments. For example, the company Starship has already made more than 6 million deliveries on college campuses. Soon, delivery robots will deliver coffee or food to meeting rooms in office buildings, or to your desk. Later still, they will help with outdoor deliveries. Similarly, although construction sites are messy and difficult to navigate, robots are already starting to lay bricks, paint, and move items.

There's reason to believe that the 4 billion moving robots that Citi estimated would exist by 2050 is conservative, as several big potential markets were not included. For example, many robots will be used in the military, security, safety, and agriculture. Robots are already used in security, for tasks such as inspecting properties or predicting threats. Indeed, the autonomous security robot Knightscope K5 has already been used in some police departments. Weighing in at a hefty 190 kg, it includes 360-degree video recording and thermal anomaly detection that allows it to see in the dark.

In military settings, robot dogs are already being used to transport equipment to the front line in Ukraine or detect issues. At a cost of just $6,000 each, wouldn't you want a robo-dog sent into a conflict situation rather than your son or daughter? I was being deliberately provocative when I asked you to imagine being confronted by a nine-foot armed military robot at the start of the chapter, but it's not a complete hypothetical. Humanoids are traditionally built to be shorter than average human height to aid acceptance and adoption, but they could be built much bigger and in vast quantities if that were a country's desire. It's scary, but it's technically possible. The use of autonomous weapon systems warrants serious debate—and new laws—but the capability is already with us.

Given that robots can take multiple forms, why we bother creating humanoids is a fair question to ask. It turns out the primary reason is incredibly simple. They can slot straight into our man-made world without the need for significant infrastructure change. They fit into homes, offices, streets, and factories. The second point is that, like humans, they are flexible and can be trained to perform multiple tasks. The rise of humanoids is another step in the evolution of robots from static, caged machines that can only perform one task to ones that can effectively mimic human work.

While in the long term, the biggest adoption of robots will be in people's houses, as butlers and cleaners, the initial trials and best economic use cases for humanoids are in factories. Here, they will do repetitive tasks in contained environments, such as assembly or inventory restocking. Lots of challenges remain before humanoids can take off here, mostly related to efficiency and building a low-cost supply chain, but a multitude of opportunities are driving capital and innovation in this sector. Look at the highlights from the World Robot Conference in China in 2025, and you will see that what you thought was science fiction is already becoming reality.

WATCH OUT TAXI DRIVERS

While we are still very early in the humanoid journey, after years of speculation, an inflection point has been reached in the adoption of driverless cars, or autonomous vehicles (AVs), as they are more commonly known. This is an example of Amara's law in action. In technology, people get excited and tend to overestimate the short-term effects of innovation, but when an inflection point is reached, the tendency is to underestimate the long-term impact.

The first DARPA driverless car challenge took place in 2004. One car made it 11.78 km. One year later, five cars drove 212 km. Citi's first "Car of the Future" GPS report was published a decade later, in 2014, but progress has taken a long time—and with good reason. The risk of driving a 2,600kg car without supervision at national speed limits, among other cars on the road and pedestrians on the sidewalks, clearly comes with life-threatening risks. And without enough proof points when it comes to safety, regulators have been understandably cautious. AVs need to be much better than human drivers.

The big AV catalyst came in August 2023 when a landmark decision in California allowed Waymo, an AV ride-hailing service, to drive without human operators in San Francisco. By the third quarter of 2024, Waymo was conducting 100,000 rides per week without any human driver in the car. This was up tenfold from the year before. By December 2025, this had jumped to 450,000 trips per week.[16] Waymo had driven over 100 million miles autonomously by July 2025.[17]

In contrast to human drivers, who can drive wherever and whenever they want after they pass their tests, AVs use layering as a safety protocol. Regulators can stipulate driving conditions, such as AVs only operating in contained areas, in certain weather conditions, or within certain speed limits. For instance, at the start, they may only be allowed to drive between 2:00 a.m. and 5:00 a.m., in dry conditions, on certain roads, at 20 mph. Over time, the boundaries get extended. Regulators can also insist that backup teleoperators intervene if problems occur.

Vehicle automation is classified into six levels, from no automation (Level 0) to full self-driving with no human assistance in any condition (Level 5). Many cars already have Level 1 or 2 automated features, such as emergency braking, adaptive cruise control, lane departure, or collision warnings. To help move us towards higher levels of autonomy, companies such as Tesla provide software updates, so in theory, entire fleets can be enabled for higher autonomy levels as soon as regulators ease off the handbrake. In other words, cars can have automation capabilities switched on as soon as it's legal. This will help adoption hockey stick upwards, and it's one of the reasons Musk forecasts Tesla will have 10 million AVs on the road in just "a few years."

As more real-world evidence is collected that AVs are safe, more countries and cities are gradually opening up AV testing, including the UK, Norway, Germany, the UAE, Singapore, South Korea, Japan, and Australia. However, the biggest experiments, momentum, and market opportunities can be found in China. Sixty Chinese cities had issued AV road test licences by the end of 2023. Beijing opened 700 miles of public roads to 18 companies. Baidu, another ride-hailing service, which operates a fleet of around 1,000 Apollo Go AVs, gave over 1.4 million driverless rides in the first quarter of 2025 alone. China appears to want to take a lead in this AI area.

Autonomous lorries are not far behind. For example, Aurora Innovation, which works with Volvo, Uber, and FedEx, has been making progress with driverless lorries in the US. Similar to the layering system for cars, it is possible for lorries to travel vast distances without a driver and then collect one at the end of the trip to handle the final delivery process.

Can taxi drivers push back against this move to automation? Maybe, but there are several significant reasons why AV adoption is the future:

1. AVs save lives: 1.4 million lives are lost to traffic accidents each year,[18] and human error accounts for 90% of accidents. AVs have faster reaction times and do not get distracted, enraged, drunk, or tired. Moving from theory to reality, Waymo data, based on 71 million miles driven, shows AVs had 78% fewer injury-causing

crashes than human drivers. One common cause of death on the road is drivers not obeying traffic rules. For example, 4.4 million Americans jumped red lights in 2022, according to NHTSA data. AVs not only follow traffic rules better than humans, but new rules can be transmitted simultaneously across AV fleets, updating their knowledge in real time.

2. AVs save money: While AVs cost more than normal cars today, costs are falling. For example, while Baidu's latest robo-taxi costs around $28,500, this is half the price of its previous version.[19] For ride-hailing companies, the most obvious cost savings are from not paying a human driver. For individuals, there are several other appealing financial benefits: insurance premiums should be lower, and parking costs will be reduced. People can also rent out their vehicle when they are not using it, earning an income on an asset that is otherwise parked and depreciating. On a societal level, there will also be considerable costs saved from the reduction in traffic accidents.
3. AVs save time: One of the big appeals of AVs is that they will free up previously wasted time. Americans spend 5 billion hours a year stuck in traffic. AVs also free up time spent parking. And as Benjamin Franklin noted in 1748, "Remember that time is money."
4. AVs increase mobility: For those who cannot drive, such as the infirm, disabled, young, or elderly, AVs may offer a more accessible or affordable lifeline than taxis. They will also appeal to the inebriated or people who are just worried about who they are getting in a car with. As sad as it is, some already trust robots more than humans when it comes to driving.

Given the reasons above and the tipping point we've reached in AV miles driven, how quickly could widespread adoption take off? There is a famous photo of Fifth Avenue in New York that compares the street in 1900 and 1913. In 1900, all you see is people in carriages pulled by horses. In 1913, all you see is people driven in cars. In 2025, all you see is cars bought for human drivers. By 2040, cars will be bought for robot drivers.

A TECHNOLOGICAL INFLECTION POINT

The pace of automobile adoption in New York between 1900 and 1913 was surprising. It is more common in technology to see false dawns and over-optimistic predictions, and we have seen this happen before with AI. AI started in the 1950s and has already gone through two AI winters. Robots are not new either. Since robots first emerged in the 1960s, they have been slow to reach the 4 million that exist today. In this context, the 4 billion moving AI robots forecast by 2050 might seem unlikely. So, what has changed?

Several technological advances have taken place in the last 10–15 years that have transformed what is possible. They've enabled AI robots to see, learn, move, communicate in natural language, turn verbal instructions into code, and take actions.

The big breakthrough in vision came in 2012, and computers can now see better than humans. Building on this, an emerging field of spatial intelligence is being used to train robots to act in our 3D world.

Progress in deep learning has enabled computers to learn without supervision using unstructured data. So far, this has led to computers winning every game they have played. Next up is training them how to do tasks by watching videos of humans doing those tasks.

Big breakthroughs in the last decade in natural language processing (NLP), transformer models, and generative AI (GenAI) are helping AI robots understand instructions, execution of tasks, and two-way communication with humans.

The use of simulated data, known as synthetic data, is also helping with what has been a chicken-and-egg problem for AI robots. To work in the real world as a robot, you need data to prove that you can operate safely. But unless you can operate safely, you cannot create enough of this data. Isolated beta tests, or the use of sandboxes, try to solve this, but they can take a long time to build. A simulated data approach, on the other hand, allows you to generate multiple scenarios to test robots in rare but critical circumstances before they are released into the wild. For example, in addition to actual miles driven on roads, Waymo trained its AVs on over 20 billion miles of simulated data by 2024.[20] For comparison, you might drive a million miles in your lifetime.

We now also have the ability to transfer new learnings, new laws, or new upgrades across an entire fleet of robots simultaneously, similar to how most smartphone software is updated today. Going the other way, the ability of robots to self-diagnose and report problems allows for quicker maintenance. While most of the recent attention has been on AI developments in large language models (LLMs), such as ChatGPT, progress has also been taking place in small language models (SLMs), which use much more focused datasets. These are used in edge cases, such as moving robots, where connectivity to the cloud could be challenging. For instance, you would not want to rely on the internet for processing and instructions if you were in a driverless car. These smaller AI models are more customisable, cheaper, and quicker to deploy, so they can be used in robot operations.

In parallel to AI advances, there have been improvements in dexterity, allowing robots to carry out useful tasks such as moving objects. Some robots can already operate at a far higher precision than human hands are capable of, even, for example, stitching a kernel of sweetcorn.

As amazing as these advances are individually, the ability for all these elements to fit together is what is making AI robots possible. Multi-model AI is allowing artificial intelligence to become embodied. It's moving from the theoretical and the virtual into our physical environments, providing genuinely useful tools. This, in turn, is driving lots of capital into the sector, which is driving more innovation—a virtuous circle.

A HUGE ECONOMIC OPPORTUNITY

History shows that technological advances usually lead to cost reductions, which accelerate adoption.

The positive spin that robot companies often give is that they are providing solutions to areas that have labour shortages, such as manufacturing, construction, or care. Like many don't-worry-isms, this is partly true. However, the benefit of robots to investors is less about plugging gaps and more about making money. Labour accounts for over 50% of GDP globally and over 60% in North America,[21] so if robots can do tasks more cheaply than humans, this could be a huge boon for company margins and investor profits. This substitution of labour represents one of the biggest market opportunities ever.

To make this more tangible, let's look at an example. Tesla is looking to price its humanoid robot, called Optimus, at about $25,000. We'll assume it can work for 16 hours a day to allow for charging time and six days a week to allow for maintenance. If the robot were paid the equivalent of a human worker earning the lowest US minimum wage of $7.25, then the payback period would be just 36 weeks. There are elements to this you could dial up or down, but 36 weeks is unbelievably attractive.

For example, the average factory wage in the US is $28 per hour, making the substitution of workers even more attractive. If you think $25,000 is far too optimistic, think again. You can already order IX's humanoid Neo in the US for $20,000[22] or buy Unitree's G1 humanoid in China for $5,900.[23] It will take time for these robots to increase in efficiency and for prices to come down, but in time, both *will* happen.

If a huge market opportunity and attractive economics are not enough, then the emerging field of robots-as-a-service, or RaaS, will also help mass adoption. RaaS models allow companies to rent robots by the hour for as little as $2–8. With little up-front expenditure, upgrades taken care of, and lots of flexibility to deploy robots depending on need, RaaS is another attractive way for companies to experiment with embedding robots in their business. In a world where governments increasingly try to appease their human electorate with restrictive immigration policies and the reshoring of production, the reality is that more factories and warehouses will be operated by robots.

THE SUBSTITUTION OF HUMAN WORKERS

There is much to celebrate in the progress taking place in AI robots. Lower costs will mean better prices for consumers, and arguably, it will lower interest rates in economies. Investors should benefit from higher margins and returns. More people will be supported by robotic cleaners, chauffeurs, butlers, and even carers. These will contribute to the betterment of life, freeing people up from mundane tasks to spend more time on other activities. This has happened in previous industrial revolutions, when running water, flushing toilets, washing machines, and cars gave people more freedom. Robots will also do more dangerous, dull, and dirty jobs that humans don't want to do, like the previously mentioned cleaning of skyscraper windows and bomb disposal.

The downside is that this progress also means tasks currently carried out by humans that provide employment will disappear. We will explore the counterarguments to this in subsequent chapters, such as the growth of new or better jobs, but history shows us that technology *does* displace people.

In the first UK census, in 1801, a third of workers were employed in agriculture. In 2023, only 1.4% were.[24] And one tractor did not substitute one worker or one horse. James Watt originally used the measure of horsepower to compare machines versus the power that a horse could sustain for an extended period. The largest tractor today, Big Bud 747, has 760 horsepower.

Similarly, in 1861, 40% of UK workers toiled away in manufacturing. This fell slowly at first, dropping to 30% by 1960. Then the pace quickened as automation took hold. In 2021, the share of human workers in manufacturing had fallen to 7.3%.[25] Again, one machine did not replace one worker. An MIT study concluded that each robot replaced 3.3 workers in the US between 1990 and 2007.[26] And don't believe the political rhetoric that it was China taking most manufacturing jobs rather than automation. Research shows that most of the substitution came from machines. For example, an analysis by Ball State University concluded that automation led to the disappearance of nine in 10 manufacturing jobs.[27]

Of course, the rate of substitution varies greatly by role. One computer did not replace one secretary, nor did one ATM replace one bank, but it is very possible that if a robot can operate 22 hours a day, without holidays, it will replace more than one worker. Replacement rates also depend on economics, but we know that computing gets cheaper over time. Robot costs have fallen by 50% since 1990,[28] while wage costs have increased materially during the same period. This makes the relative payback of investing in robots over humans much more attractive.

So, which areas are most exposed? Note that the 4 billion robots forecast by 2050 includes a number of household robots that will free people's time rather than substitute paid work. But there are several areas of work that are vulnerable.

Robots in factories and warehouses have already taken many human jobs, but given the estimates for the explosion in AMRs and humanoids, much more substitution is likely.

Professional drivers are particularly exposed as AV adoption increases, just as horse and cart drivers were in 1900. This is a big market. Uber alone has over seven million drivers and couriers,[29] and Lyft has 1.3 million.[30] Data from the International Road Transport Union suggests there are roughly 43 million professional truck drivers worldwide.[31] Many of these roles could be automated. Moving into a career as a driver today is like buying a horse and cart in 1900.

The technology for robot deliveries is still a work in progress, but the number of people who now earn their income from delivering e-commerce packages or takeaway food around the world is substantial. Over time, many of these will become vulnerable. Delivery of food and goods in restaurants, hotels, and other hospitality venues are also areas that robots will invade. They will also expand into shops and, in time, construction.

Robots cannot entirely replace cleaners, but they can do a good portion of their work in terms of hoovering and mopping. There are an estimated 6 million janitors in advanced economies and 33 million in emerging markets. Conservatively, a third of these tasks could be substituted over time.

It is too early to tell how security or military personnel, agricultural workers, or care providers will be affected. The outcome will partly depend on how well policies support this change. As an example, policy has driven electric vehicle penetration in Norway to levels 10 times higher than those in the

US.[32] On the other hand, at this point in time, it seems highly unlikely that cheap Chinese humanoids or AVs will be allowed in US homes, streets, and factories in the long term.

Looking to the future, the scale of the threat is huge. There were approximately 3.7 billion people in the global labour force in 2024,[33] and it's clear that a number of areas with the highest concentration of workers will see growing competition from robots over the next couple of decades: agriculture (1.1 billion workers), retail (500 million), manufacturing (450 million), construction (350 million), hospitality (320 million), delivery (138 million), professional drivers (61 million), and janitors (39 million). These eight sectors alone total almost three billion workers; if only a third of these roles become susceptible to competition from robots, a billion workers would be exposed. Given work supports families, that is a huge number of people who will be impacted and concerned.

We started this chapter with Huang and Rus's views that robots will become ubiquitous, following in the footsteps of computers. As they do so, the impact of physical AI on jobs could be enormous. However, this is just one part of the story, and even bigger changes are coming in non-physical AI. In the next chapter, we turn to the revolution in cognitive AI that is impacting knowledge work—a metamorphosis that has already begun.

II

THE AI INDUSTRIAL REVOLUTION

"We are not living an era of change but a change of era."

—Pope Francis[34]

"I knew I had just seen the most important advancement in technology since the graphical user interface."

—Bill Gates[35]

THE CHATGPT TIPPING POINT

On 30 November 2022, ChatGPT 3.5 burst onto the scene, and AI changed forever. The underlying transformer technology from which large language models (LLMs) such as ChatGPT are built was first formed in 2017. Earlier versions had seen significant improvements, but ChatGPT 3.5 shook the world with its capabilities. As noted by Bill Gates in the quote above, this was a step change. The CEO of Microsoft, Satya Nadella, said we had reached "a real inflection point." Google CEO Sundar Pichai claimed, "We are at a tipping point."[36] People around the world seemed to agree, and ChatGPT surged to become the fastest-adopted consumer product of all time, reaching 100 million users in just two months[37] and 1 billion monthly active users within three years.[38]

One key thing that changed was that ChatGPT put a simple-to-use interface on AI. You no longer needed to have a computer science degree to interact with it. You could just ask it questions, like you would a colleague, and answers would magically appear—instantaneously. And not just any answers, but increasingly smart answers. ChatGPT went on to pass more exams than any human reader of this book can. It quickly reached PhD level, and it scored 148 on IQ tests, nearing Einstein's IQ of 160. As captivating and useful as ChatGPT was, what most people recognised was that, for the first time in history, they were seeing a new form of intelligence that could surpass us.

While new technology takes time to finesse and implement, the development of AI that helps with cognitive tasks is unprecedented, similar to the impact the wheel had on transportation or machines had on manufacturing. Using healthcare as an example, Hippocratic AI quickly passed over 100 medical exams,[39] reaching expert doctor level, and can provide services at less than 20 cents per hour. It is difficult for people to compete at that cost, yet it's not just about money. Microsoft has already built an AI medical tool that it claims is four times more accurate than human doctors.[40] The CEO of Microsoft AI, Mustafa Suleyman, said this is "not just a little bit better, but dramatically better," as well as being faster and cheaper. Other tests have shown AI can also be more empathetic than human doctors.

AI has clearly entered a new era, but perhaps more importantly, humanity has entered a new era: the age of AI.

THIS TIME IT'S DIFFERENT

It is often foolish to claim: "This time it's different." But having experienced every technology cycle over the last 30 years—and studied previous ones—there are four primary reasons why I believe this one *is* different.

The first is the pace of change. Not many will argue with this. It took 50 years for the telephone to reach 50 million users. It took seven years for the internet to do the same. It took ChatGPT just one month.[41] Widening this example to eight key technologies, from electricity emerging in the 1870s to the mobile phone in the 1970s, they took an average of 36 years to reach 50 million users. This quickened to 4.75 years in the internet era when products such as YouTube and Facebook proliferated and accelerated again to less than a year for four of the biggest current AI systems. If things feel quick, that is because the current pace of change is over 36 times as fast as previous industrial revolutions.

We are experiencing a period of exponential growth in the capability of AI systems, such as LLMs. In periods of linear growth, the rate of change is constant, showing a straight, diagonal line on a graph. During periods of exponential growth, the growth rate is proportionate to size, so it is increasingly rapid over time, illustrated by a J-curve on a graph. To illustrate, in a linear world, moving 30 paces forward takes you from one to 30. In an exponential world, you'd move from one to two and then to four, eight, and 16. Eventually, as the number keeps doubling, you'd reach 1 billion in just 30 steps.

In his book *The Economic Singularity*, Calum Chace uses a different example that helps illustrate how numbers can get very big very quickly during periods of exponential growth. Imagine a football stadium is sealed to make it waterproof. One drop of water is added every two minutes. Every two minutes, the number of drops doubles. After 45 minutes, the stadium is 7% full of water. After just 49 minutes, the stadium is 100% full of water. This is what we're currently dealing with when it comes to AI.

And why does this matter? The bigger AI models have become, the more useful they are. On the upside, this provides us with better tools to work with. On the downside, it provides companies with better tools that humans have to compete with. The combination of improving capability and exponential rate of growth means AI will far surpass humans in several areas.

In 1965, Gordon Moore, the co-founder of Intel, observed that the number of transistors on microchips in computers doubled every year. Although this was later revised to every two years, this model, dubbed Moore's law, predicting the speed of technological development, has mostly held true during the computer revolution. For example, the modern smartphone is 100,000 times more powerful than NASA's computing power during the Apollo moon landing in 1969.[42] Improvements in AI far outstrip Moore's law, and the pace of change is more rapid than even the most optimistic experts expected just a few years ago.

There are healthy debates in technology about the sustainability of this exponential growth, also called the law of accelerating returns, in which innovations cascade and progress is made in shorter time periods, and about scaling laws, in which AI performance scales with computation, data, and model size.

As AI explodes, more people and capital are being drawn to the opportunities it provides, fuelling growth. Some of the smartest people on earth are working on improving algorithms, hardware, and data integration. Machines have been good at pattern recognition for some time, but the ability to use unstructured data that has not been labelled, such as images or audio, was a previous bottleneck that has now been unlocked. Data can also be collected in real time, with feedback loops allowing for rapid problem-solving and updates. Unlike the messier process of training human workers, AI models only need to be trained once, and upgrades can be deployed to many globally in one go. This allows for rapid diffusion of new AI systems.

A second reason that this time it's different is the level of productivity AI enables, which is transformative, particularly from generative AI tools, like LLMs. You only need to use an LLM for a few minutes to understand the speed and capability it offers across a range of tasks, from writing to image generating and coding, but a wide range of academic studies confirm this potential:[43] a 55% improvement in coding, a 40% improvement in the speed of writing, a 14% productivity improvement in call centres.

Indeed, these revolutionary improvements in AI and its ability to transform productivity mean that investment is flowing in from businesses and investors. The ChatGPT moment caused a ripple effect through every boardroom and C-suite. For some, the disruptive effect of AI could cause entire business models to collapse. For others, AI could significantly improve margins and returns. No one wants to be left behind, so most companies are adopting AI at the same time, and this mass adoption accelerates its uptake and the pace of change. Venture capital (VC) investment in AI had already gone up 100-fold in the decade before ChatGPT.[44] According to Pitchbook, 2024 VC AI investment rose 52%, meaning 36% of all VC deal value globally was going into AI that year.[45] Countries don't want to be left behind either, given AI's potential impact on wealth, power, and military capability. This scramble to adopt and invest across the board is creating an AI arms race.

In addition to the pace of change and productivity, a third reason why this time it's different is the scope of change. AI is a general-purpose technology, or GPT, that will impact every division of every company, in every sector, in every country. Like the steam engine, electricity, or the computer, the wide scope of GPTs to impact society will be profound. GPTs do not come around very often in a lifetime. To put this into context, Sergey Brin, the co-founder of Google, has said that "AI will be vastly more transformative" than the internet or the mobile phone.[46]

A fourth reason why this time it's different is the nature of AI. It differs from previous technologies in its ability to be truly independent of human direction, whether that's in relation to learning, decision-making, or creating. In other words, we now have "thinking machines." Some forms of AI have self-learning capabilities that have enabled them to improve without human teachers. For example, deep learning techniques have allowed AI systems to win at every game they have ever played: Backgammon (1992), Checkers (1994), Chess (1997), and Go (2016). For those carefully watching AI's rise, an inflection point was move 37 when DeepMind's AlphaGo beat the human world champion of Go. AlphaGo had played 1.3 million games against itself over several weeks to learn how to win, and move 37 was a winning strategy that no human champion had ever used.

Indeed, learning at a superhuman pace and processing at a superhuman scale enables some AI systems to become independent decision-makers. While we may try to insist on keeping a "human-in-the-loop," we will increasingly outsource decisions and actions to smart AI agents. You can already send your AI avatar to an online meeting where it will take notes and do a summary for you while you sit back on the beach reading a book on AI and its impact on the future of work.

Technology systems, including AI, have historically been good at processing rote, routine, and repetitive tasks. They still are, but generative AI (GenAI) tools demonstrate their ability to go beyond this to create new content. The downside is that this can produce incorrect or misleading answers, known as hallucinations. The upside is that GenAI can produce new ideas, which can be useful for brainstorming, creativity, and innovation, as long as they're filtered carefully by a human eye. AI systems known as digital twins, an advanced type of digital simulation, can also help iterate ideas and scenarios by linking the real and the virtual world, in the design of products and processes, for example. Add in new AI agents that can research and action ideas, and a new wave of innovation is probable, allowing it to leap far beyond the rote task automation of previous years. This AI is not only a thinking machine; it has created the potential for a revolution in the way *we* think, create, solve, and decide.

A COGNITIVE INDUSTRIAL REVOLUTION

The term artificial intelligence was first coined in 1956, and after years of experiments, developments, false dawns, and AI winters, what is happening now is not just the emergence of new areas of innovation but the commercialisation of AI across economies.

AI has been used widely in finance for many years, and this sector is forecast to be the most impacted in the future. This is partly because finance is full of data and data is the lifeblood of AI, and partly because of the commercial opportunity to use this data to make money. AI extends the use of modelling, machine learning, and automated systems used in finance in relation to areas such as analysis and forecasting, risk management, portfolio optimisation, robo-advice, cyber security protection, and the need for compliance and governance to provide trust. Most stock market transactions already come from automated trading algorithms. Indeed, by 2019, more than half of global assets under management (AUM) were handled using simple rules-based strategies rather than via human active fund managers.[47] AI will only accelerate these trends. Technology continues to drive finance to be faster and cheaper—good news for finance customers but bad news for finance workers. In one of my old firms, while the volume of equity trades had risen significantly since 2000, the number of traders employed fell 90% as their roles were taken over by machines and algos.

Yet AI is sweeping across most areas of knowledge work, not just finance. It often determines the loan you get and the adverts you see. It routes taxis to you and determines your driving route. AI is used to book your flights and then assists in flying the plane. AI shows you job opportunities and is part of the process of determining whether you get hired for a job.

Taking on human-like attributes, AI can already hear via chatbots; it can talk in multiple languages, via translation apps; it can write, using LLMs; it can produce original scenarios and avatars, using digital twins; it can inform, such as which train route to take or road works to avoid; it can decide, setting insurance rates or filtering job applications; it can see, using facial recognition; it can move, as seen in driverless cars; and it can create images or songs. Only a few years ago, in a 2019 report, I asked 50 experts which areas they thought humans would maintain a competitive advantage in versus machines.[48] Many highlighted creativity as a key human skill. That is now up for debate.

Many of these nuanced skills have only been perfected by AI recently. For example, in 2011, AI was not good at recognising cats in a picture. A breakthrough in 2012, AlexNet, enabled AI to become better than humans at image recognition by 2015, a useful function that now allows it to find photos on your phone. In a commercial context, AI can track goods placed in shopping baskets in an Amazon Go store. This function has even been used on a governmental level in Iran for facial recognition of women wearing veils, a frightening example of how constant AI surveillance could develop in the future.

What is not up for debate is that AI can chew through problems much faster than humans can. The same transformer technology that underpins LLMs, such as ChatGPT, can also be used to model DNA, RNA, or proteins. Mapping one protein used to take a PhD-level expert over a year, but in a major breakthrough in 2022, DeepMind's AlphaFold predicted the structures of 200 million proteins in just a few months.[49] DeepMind estimated they saved over 1 billion hours of research, and this capability will undoubtedly improve science and health outcomes for humanity in the years ahead. This is an example of the impact of the cognitive industrial revolution we have entered.

THE RISE OF AI AGENTS

As crazy, exciting, or horrifying as some of these developments are, this is not the endpoint. The next stage is the rapid development and improvement of AI agents.

Researching LLMs in 2022, it became clear that they would turn into large action models (LAMs), allowing them to act independently as well as understand. At the time, this was called AutoGPT, and we wrongly titled a report "AI Assistants" in mid-2023, rather than "AI Agents," as they are more commonly known today, but the premise was correct.[50] Instead of just talking to a machine, you'd instruct it to carry out useful tasks for you.

The LLM interface allows all humans to have a two-way dialogue with a machine. Another useful function of an LLM is coding. Put these two together, and you can issue a command that the system turns into code to then carry out an action. For example, imagine you are travelling to London and would like to find appropriate flight, hotel, restaurant, and tourist site recommendations. Your AI agent researches these for you, communicates its findings back, and then links to the appropriate sites to book your choices. This might extend, for example, to the use of one-click purchases on a website using Apple Pay, where you no longer need to input your payment or delivery details. There is still some development needed to make agents work seamlessly, but this is the direction we are headed in.

AI agents are also able to link multiple AI systems together. In driverless cars, for example, you communicate where you want to go using a natural language interface, the best route is calculated using another AI system that understands real-time traffic flows, AI vision technology allows the car to see, and software updates digest new speed restrictions.

In some industries, AI agents will even become non-human customers. Using the car example, AI will diagnose a fault, find a place to fix it, and book it in. In finance, your AI agent will search for the best deals for an upcoming insurance or mortgage decision and move the funds across. Today, a lot of money is left on the table as people are too busy to do tedious searches for better rates and make the switch to a new company. This inertia creates a stickiness for financial services and profits for incumbents. AI agents could be far more efficient, changing this pattern. The same could happen for the procurement of supplies for a business or for consumers doing their shopping.

The idea of non-human customers is not something many businesses are thinking about yet, and several steps need to be taken before this is possible, but progress is being made. In 2023, programmers could already complete coding tasks 56% faster using AI-powered coding assistants.[51] Mark Zuckerberg, CEO of Meta, has said that AI will be able to code as well as a mid-range software engineer by 2025, meaning that lots of Meta's AI will be generated by AI engineers rather than human engineers.[52] In 2025, Anthropic said 80% of its code was being generated by AI, without the involvement of a human programmer.[53] AI is already producing more AI.

Towards this end, two significant AI milestones happened in 2025. In July, an AI system achieved a gold medal at the International Mathematical Olympiad.[54] This is important not only because it highlights big leaps in machine reasoning but also because math underpins most areas of science. Then, in September 2025, two AI models outperformed human competitors in the International Collegiate Programming Contest (ICPC) World Finals.[55] This is the world's most prestigious coding competition, known as the "coding Olympics," and it includes developing new solutions. This is very significant because AI can create new AI at a level that exceeds human capability, without human involvement. This implies that recursive self-improvement, where AI systems autonomously create better versions of themselves, is getting close.

Unlike human engineers, agents, or assistants, AI agents can be replicated quickly around the world and at low cost. It took WPP almost 20 years to go from 27,000 employees in 1999 to 134,000 in 2017. Since then, their human headcount is down 23,000 to 111,000, while in early 2025, they had more than 29,000 AI agents.[56] Looking further forward, the CEO of NVIDIA, Jensen Huang, said he can envision a future in which the company's human headcount grows from 32,000 to 50,000 while the AI agent headcount approaches 100 million.[57] It is worth pondering how dramatic AI agent proliferation and impact could be. In December 2025, OpenAI reported that their latest model matched or beat human experts over 70% of the time when completing tasks.[58] The outcomes across 44 occupations were judged by human experts. On average the human's undertaking the tasks had 14 years of experience and the AI responses were 11 times faster and 99% cheaper than the humans.

One of the aims of multiplying AI agents is to better serve customers. Another is to save costs by replacing existing human workers, as we discussed in Chapter I – The Rise of AI Robots. Another is to speed up productivity and innovation. How much extra work could you achieve if you were gifted 10 new AI interns? The AlphaFold example above suggests that, in the right hands, innovation could explode. And when AI agents create and interact with other AI agents, this multiplication proliferates further.

Most companies are at a very early phase when it comes to using AI agents, but the steep part of the technology S-curve of adoption will come. AI is taking place in stages. Stage 1 is human-first, where current workers are assisted by machines. In stage 2, workers will become augmented using increasingly capable AI tools. It will be the co-pilot, or the smart intern, that gradually takes on more tasks. And along the way, AI will learn from the human worker and collect more data. In stage 3, work will become AI-first, with rising autonomy for AI agents, or robots, and reduced human oversight. The AI intern gets promoted, and the co-pilot becomes the pilot, with human workers signing off on their work or moving off to other areas. Over time, AI agents will check the work of other AIs, leaving humans out of the equation altogether, and improving quality and reliability. This is already happening to some degree. The new Microsoft diagnostic tool discussed above uses an "orchestrator" of five AI agents to interact with each other to produce superior results to human doctors.

Most companies are just entering stage 2. Co-pilots are being rolled out and experimented with. However, given the disruption integrating AI agents will cause to existing processes, let alone the difficulty of dealing with non-human customers, some new companies are jumping straight ahead to AI-first processes in an attempt to take share from slower moving incumbents. This, in turn, perpetuates the arms race.

ARTIFICIAL GENERAL INTELLIGENCE AND BEYOND

In 1997, the world chess champion, Gary Kasparov, lost to IBM's computer Deep Blue. He made a comment that is worth reflecting on. Kasparov said that humans had entered a period of weak competition in which computers were only going to get better and better. And he was right. As of 2025, the highest human chess rating achieved is 2,882. The highest computer rating comes from the AI chess engine Stockfish at 3,645. And it's not only super smart; it costs nothing to use. For those hoping that humans working with computers, known as cyborg or centaur chess, would beat the best computer, I am afraid that has not been the case for the last decade.[59] Rather than enhancing AI, humans drag down the performance.

We are in AI's weak competition period. AI will exceed us in many cognitive areas, and some believe it will drive intelligence costs towards zero. The point at which AI exceeds humans across many economic tasks is known as artificial general intelligence, or AGI, as I mentioned in the introduction. There has been a lot of heated debate about the exact definition of AGI and its timing. As Dario Amodei, CEO of Anthropic, has said, AGI is "an imprecise term which has gathered a lot of sci-fi baggage and hype," but he believes that we could have AI tools by 2026 that are "smarter than a Nobel Prize winner across most relevant fields."[60] Progress is leaping forward in some areas and is slower in others, so AGI may not be one light switch moment, but the ability to connect different AI systems together helps.

In the 2010s, the medium estimate from AI researchers for when AGI would be reached was in the second half of this century.[61] While Amodei's forecast is on the more aggressive side, the whole AI community has accelerated its views since LLMs burst onto the scene. Nobel laureate Geoffrey Hinton, one of the "godfathers of deep learning," changed his view in 2023 from 20–50 years to 5–20 years.[62] One of the best places to find up-to-date expert predictions for when AGI will occur is on the website Metaculus, and at the time of writing, at the end of 2025, the median estimate was June 2033.[63] If so, enjoy this period of weak competition. It won't last long.

While there will continue to be lots of debate on when AGI will be reached, and how we can know it has been, in the meantime, computers will gradually do more and more across multiple fields. Those areas that are easy to automate and where the economic incentive is greatest will be impacted first. The harder to automate and the niche areas will follow in time. This is similar to how physical AI has progressed, from domestic hoovers today towards humanoids completing more complex tasks in the future, as discussed in Chapter I.

However, another problem for human workers is that AGI is not the endpoint; indeed, it's just a waypoint on the journey. Quantum computing developments are happening in parallel and will come quicker and be more impactful than most people think.[64] Quantum computers, the fifth generation of computing, will allow the processing of enormous datasets much faster than conventional computers, and importantly, they will be used to supercharge AI progress. In this way, AI and quantum will work together. Quantum computers also scale at a "doubly exponential rate," so according to Google's Hartmut Neven, "It looks like nothing is happening, nothing is happening, and then whoops, suddenly you're in a different world."[65] The pace of change won't slow.

The next stop for AI post AGI is ASI, or artificial superintelligence. Definitions of ASI differ, but in an ASI era, AI will far surpass human intelligence and will be able to self-learn, self-improve, and self-evolve without human supervision. Even in our current AI era, AI systems are often black boxes, and programmers do not truly understand how they arrive at answers or how new capabilities emerge, so just imagine how impossible this will be in an ASI era. ASI will also invent new AI systems, agents, and robots, cutting humans out of the process entirely. This is not a new concept. In 1965, Irving John Good said that as "ultra-intelligent machines could design even better machines, there would unquestionably be an intelligence explosion."[66] This vision of our future makes addressing how we control AI and how we ensure it aligns with our goals and values even more urgent. Many want to keep pushing innovation forward without putting the brakes on, so AI can help humanity solve more problems, hoping we will figure these problems out along the way.

Some people have spoken about the possibility of an AI singularity when AI surpasses human intelligence. Borrowed from physics, this term describes the point at which developments become even more rapid, unpredictable, uncontrollable, and beyond human comprehension. Change speeds up rather than slows down. For workers, there is also a potential economic singularity: as AI does more at lower prices, the human job market and wages collapse. This idea is explored more in Chapter IX – Better Jobs.

Indeed, Mo Gawdat, who ran Google X, has said that AI will become a billion times smarter than the smartest human by 2049, so "your intelligence, in comparison to that machine, will be comparable to the intelligence of a fly in comparison to Einstein."[67] This is why Stephen Hawking and others have warned that the creation of a true thinking machine "could be the biggest event in the history of our civilisation... but it could also be the last—unless we learn how to avoid the risks."[68] To understand the inflection point taking place, including the risks involved, there are some parallels here with nuclear bombs. The largest nuclear test ever conducted, the Tsar Bomb in 1961, had more than 16 times the explosive power of all the bombs that were dropped in World War II combined.[69] So, rising capabilities come with rising risks as well as a greater responsibility to find and implement solutions.

THE IMPACT ON WORKERS

As this all demonstrates, a cognitive industrial revolution will fundamentally reshape work, particularly white-collar, knowledge-based jobs. Opinions and analysis differ widely on the impact of this revolution on workers, so let's explore four primary points.

1. AI Will Disrupt Jobs, Fast

    Everyone agrees that AI will cause an enormous amount of disruption for workers, and quickly. An IMF study estimated that 60% of employment in advanced economies was vulnerable to AI.[70] OpenAI CEO Sam Altman has said, "Jobs are definitely going to go away, full stop,"[71] whereas Microsoft AI CEO Mustafa Suleyman has called AI "fundamentally labor replacing."[72] More forcefully, Anthropic CEO Dario Amodei has warned that AI could replace half of all entry-level white-collar jobs.[73] Matt Beane, in his book *The Skill Code*, estimates 2.7 billion workers will need to relearn and reskill due to AI.[74] Whatever happens, roles will change for many people imminently, and this is leading to anxiety.

    Optimists often cite the World Economic Forum's *Future of Jobs Report 2025*, which concludes that although 92 million jobs will be displaced by 2030, 170 million will be created.[75] A net 78 million positive seems like a double helping of optimism, and it's a more complex picture when you look beneath the surface. The biggest growth areas forecast by the WEF include farmworkers, delivery drivers, shop salespeople, food processing workers, drivers, and educators. This doesn't cover many knowledge-based areas, so it'll require a drastic change in career for people pushed out of those roles. And AI and robots will still impact these jobs in time.

Optimists also point to previous transitions, like the Victorian Industrial Revolution, which worked out in the long term as new jobs were created to employ millions. Yet they don't acknowledge how those changes negatively impacted millions of people for decades. A second problem with drawing on past transitions is that there is a high probability that, as we've discussed, *this time it's different.* The accelerating pace of change increases confusion for people and lowers their ability to transition smoothly.

2. AI Efficiency Will Reduce Jobs for Humans

   AI will move through several phases of development: 1. improving efficiency; 2. increasing personalisation; 3. offering incremental services; 4. forming entirely new industries. As an example of AI in stages 2 and 3, Hippocratic AI uses LLMs to phone patients and check they are taking their medicines, if they are having side effects, and whether they need a follow-up appointment. They do so at a cost of less than $1 per hour. In comparison, a human nurse makes, on average, $45 per hour.[76] So in this case, AI can provide useful incremental and personalised services that were previously uneconomic, given the wages paid to people.

   The opportunities to use AI to raise revenue partly depend on the elasticity of demand, the extent to which lower prices induce more demand, and the need for more workers. Healthcare, for example, has a high elasticity of demand as lowering the costs of prediction and prevention will increase demand for screenings to avoid health problems. Law, on the other hand, is demand inelastic. Someone either needs a will or they don't, and they only need it once, so halving the price won't double your demand. Efficiency gains, or cost-cutting, will be higher in sectors with low demand elasticities.

The biggest revenue growth opportunities have historically come in stage 4 when entirely new industries are created. Some of these are emerging today, such as AI robots or AI audits. However, new industries take time to form; most of the impact of AI in the next decade will be in stage 1: doing existing tasks more efficiently. Indeed, investors and companies will need a reasonably quick return on the enormous amount of capital that's going into AI, and one of the easiest opportunities is reducing current overheads. Concerns that AI is not generating enough new revenue could just be a matter of looking through the wrong lens. Cost-cutting is often part of how AI solutions are sold to companies, with some LLMs already reducing the time to complete a task by 50%. Given that labour is one of the biggest overheads for companies, part of this cost reduction will include substituting workers. Ambidextrous leaders may tell employees that they are the company's most important asset while also telling investors that there are opportunities to reduce headcount using AI.

There is an important nuance here. In stage 1, in many cases, AI will impact tasks rather than whole roles. Consider the bank teller when the ATM arrived: part of their job was automated, but they did far more than just hand out cash. This is a far cry from the complete obsolescence of the lift operator when automated lifts came in. However, just because AI only does 10% of a role does not mean that workers are safe. Managers can cut 10% of the workers and distribute their work among the rest, so those "lucky" to be in the 90% do more. Unless new revenue streams are found, this process gets repeated as technology progresses, with another 10% cut, then another. Using finance as an example, a recent UK finance report found that most current AI deployments target efficiency gains rather than increasing sales.[77] This drive for efficiency will disrupt and substitute existing jobs.

3. The Impact Will Be Pervasive

   Above, we spoke about the enormous scope of change when it comes to AI. It will touch almost every industry, which means that it will impact a huge percentage of workers. One study of 19,265 tasks in 923 occupations suggested 80% of US workers are exposed to LLMs, and 19% may see at least 50% of their tasks impacted.[78] A later Brookings Institute paper on GenAI estimated even higher exposure.[79] LLMs are, of course, just one area of AI, and as shown in Chapter I – The Rise of AI Robots, there are many blue and white-collar jobs exposed to AI variants. One of the best and most cited studies in this area was published by Carl Benedikt Frey and Michael Osborne from the Oxford Martin School. Examining 702 blue-collar and white-collar occupations, they estimated 47% of US jobs are susceptible to computerisation.[80]

   Since Peter Drucker coined the term "knowledge workers" in 1959,[81] over a billion workers have flocked into this category. AI is now pointing directly at white-collar roles in customer service, sales, marketing, translation, journalism, analysis, investing, insurance underwriting, design, coding, legal services, administration, back-office roles, and beyond.

This is not just theory. Tech firms have slowed hiring as they use more AI. In finance, J.P. Morgan reportedly instructed managers to pause hiring and use AI instead.[82] Customer service roles have already been impacted, as seen at Klarna. IBM's CEO said that a third of back-office roles could go in five years because of AI and automation.[83] Amazon CEO Andy Jassy has said AI will lower costs and "reduce our total corporate workforce."[84] It is not difficult to find examples across industries, and more will come. As the CEO of Walmart, the largest private employer in the US, recently said, "It's very clear that AI is going to change every job" before caveating that "maybe there's a job in the world that won't change, but I haven't thought of it."[85]

4. Over Time, AI Will Only Take on More of Our Work

You can debate how long it'll take us to get to AGI, but it is difficult to deny that it will happen. We know that AI will progressively and incrementally take on more tasks that humans do today. With GenAI, we can already see a step change into areas that were difficult for computers, such as writing, two-way communication, empathy, programming, and creativity.

Optimists are correct that AI tools currently augment human intelligence, yet this is likely a temporary phase in which human workers train AI workers on the way to AGI and ASI. Bill Gates has said that within 10 years, humans won't be needed "for most things." He acknowledged mixed feelings: "It's very profound and even a little bit scary—because it's happening very quickly, and there is no upper bound."[86] This phrase, "no upper bound," is important, as it underlines that AI's progress does not appear to have a ceiling. In contrast, our brains have an upper limit on their size that is governed by the dimensions of human birth canals. Progressive AI requires progressive solutions, which is the focus of Parts 2 and 3 of this book.

There are, of course, many factors that could still slow AI adoption, including issues around business implementation, talent, governance, technology, power, and economics. It is also very possible that an AI bubble is being formed and that we repeat the up-down-up technology cycle we saw into and post 2000, when expectations of the internet boomed and burst, after which real-world internet applications were implemented. If so, AI and economic downcycles could be painful for many and could also accelerate job substitution using AI as companies look to cut costs and save money in economic downturns.

Despite these caveats, it's clear AI offers significant cost-cutting opportunities across many sectors, at a pace we have never previously experienced, creating strong currents for workers to swim against. Looking ahead, AI's relentless pace of growth and progress towards AGI suggest the currents and churn will grow, not ease. Given the cognitive industrial revolution taking place for white-collar work discussed in this chapter and the robot revolution taking place in many blue-collar areas discussed in the previous chapter, there are few places to hide in this new AI-driven world. Unfortunately, the threats to workers do not stop there. The next chapter looks at the rise and risks of digital labour.

III

DIGITAL AND REMOTE WORK

"Geography is destiny."

—Attributed to Napoleon[87]

"We are now entering a third phase of globalization based on trade in services."

—Carl Benedikt Frey[88]

THE RISE OF REMOTE WORK

If you want to age yourself, ask your team for their first memory of an event of global significance. Many entering the workforce today were not alive for 9/11. Many will be too young to remember 2008's Financial Crisis. One shared memory will be 2020's pandemic, from the horror and fear of seeing patients on breathing machines in hospitals to the isolation of being locked up at home with no known end in sight, or the feeling of community and collective support engendered when we clapped for key workers.

The pandemic was an example of exponential growth and was a game-changer for digital connectivity. Telemedicine in the US saw a 3,000-fold increase during the pandemic.[89] Education was forced online. E-commerce saw five years of growth in the US in one quarter. In the UK, online food deliveries doubled. Online art sales also doubled.

One of the biggest changes it caused—and one of the most enduring trends—was the rise of remote work. At one point during the pandemic, two-thirds of US economic activity was being done remotely; it was an amazing feat of adaptation and one that should give us all confidence that humans can adjust to changing circumstances. The levels and types of government support for workers differed by country, but in general, we should also take comfort from political leaders' support for workers in the furlough schemes. Governments know they are elected by voters.

Necessity forced collective adoption at speed, so while it took eight decades for the steam engine to take hold, the move to enable remote work happened rapidly. While it literally swept across companies and nations overnight, in time, it was vastly improved and embedded. This accelerated the use of technology and innovation in this arena, whether it was adding more robust digital infrastructure in companies; more home offices and logins; cloud connectivity; messaging channels, such as Slack; video calling, such as Zoom and Teams; surgery carried out at a distance; or VR glasses for remote repairs. Previously, analogue activities, such as team meetings, became virtual and digital by default. This move to the digital creates new data, and this data feeds and improves AI systems. Then add in new AI innovations and functionality to improve outcomes, such as team meetings being transcribed, translated, recorded, and summarised.

The rise of remote work also showed employees and employers what was possible in terms of working experience.

Like many others, my three hours of commuting per day disappeared. Commuting is not just time sapping but stress inducing. More importantly, less commuting allows for more time with family. I'm blessed with four children, yet for 20 years, I almost never saw them during the week, given I left before dawn and arrived back late. Everyone's circumstances differ, but in general, more flexible and autonomous work was embraced by employees who could see the benefits in terms of wellbeing and a feeling of improved agency. This topic has been polarising, as some bosses prefer to see workers physically at their desks, but research suggests remote work can actually enhance productivity.[90] Some rightly feel it provides a lack of opportunity to create togetherness and team spirit as well as learn from others, but studies show that collaboration at a distance isn't just possible but can be additive.[91] For most organisations, this led to a striking change. Some level of working from home went from being culturally unacceptable pre-pandemic to the norm post-pandemic. Society went through a one-way door into a new world of remote work.

This paradigm shift has been described by Carl Frey as the "third phase of globalisation" because if a job can be done remotely, it can be done from anywhere. In the first phase of globalisation, the steam engine started moving goods around the world. In the second phase, the computer revolution enabled ideas to move around the world, so supply chains were reconfigured. For example, the iPhone may have been born in California, but it was subsequently made in and shipped from China. Moving people, however, remained a bottleneck. Executives jumped on planes to meet in person or commuted to cities to work together. In this new era, that's all changed: meeting online has become both possible and acceptable. The cost of moving people around the world has fallen to almost zero. Yet there are even bigger cost savings that lie ahead from the use of digital workers.

DIGITAL WORKERS

There are a multitude of factors that drive whether remote work is used or not, not least the preferences of clients. Economics and the availability of talent are two important considerations; in other words, whether it'll save money and whether it'll give you more access to people with the right qualifications and experience. While there is often a differential in the cost of workers doing the same role *within* countries, there are much bigger differences *between* countries. A 2023 Citi GPS report cited the average salary for an accountant at one of the Big Four firms as $75,709 in New York versus $3,010 in Cairo. Google engineers of the same level were being paid over 20 times as much in New York as in Manila and 16 times as much as in Delhi.[92]

This wage arbitrage will be too wide for some employers to leave on the table. In the same way that manufacturing was offshored to lower-cost locations in the second phase of globalisation, companies will employ more people in locations with lower wages over time.

This is not just about cost. The talent pool in some of these markets is enormous. China and India both produce over twice as many STEM graduates as the US per year.[93] Indonesia produces double the number of graduates that the UK does. In 2020 alone, India graduated 13 times as many students in STEM subjects as the UK did.[94] A 2024 Stanford University AI Index report also ranked India at the top in AI skill penetration.[95] Notably, over 55% of workers in the US with a PhD in science and engineering are immigrants.[96] These deep talent pools allow new clusters of work to grow, starting with the outsourcing of simpler or more repetitive tasks and gradually taking on more complex and value-added tasks to move up the work food chain.

In addition to offering a large quantity of smart people and low costs, the work ethic and average hours in many of these countries are also high, partly out of necessity.[97] There is arguably already an excess of graduates worldwide entering the workplace, creating a very competitive environment. Unfortunately for them, this is happening just as AI is beginning to consume more knowledge work opportunities. The problem is already very acute in some regions. The average NEET—someone not in education, employment, or training—rate for 15–24 year olds in low-income countries in 2023 was 28.7%, compared to 10.4% in high-income countries.[98] The NEET rate is particularly high in North Africa at 31%, and South Asia is not far behind at 26%. When we look at absolute numbers rather than percentages, the problem is even more stark, with 137 million NEET in Asia and 53 million in Sub-Saharan Africa, versus 5.6 million in North America and 8.6 million in Europe. Without work or the tools to improve their skills through education or training, young people will be keenly aware that they have few prospects and even more anxious to find a job, wherever that job happens to be.

This is where digital labour comes in, and it has already taken off. One index measuring digital labour suggested it grew 63% between 2016 and 2021, with 70% coming from Asia.[99] And this is likely just the beginning. The same Citi report estimated that 52% of jobs could, in theory, be done remotely, and 26% could be offshored. In contrast, just 5% of US jobs were remote pre-pandemic. While immigration policies are becoming more restrictive and manufacturing is being reshored, the move to digital labour is allowing firms to find great talent anywhere in the world. And guess what? Technology is helping facilitate this trend.

DIGITAL WORK PLATFORMS

The phrase "geography is destiny" is attributed to Napoleon, and it was very true in his era; where you were born often dictated many things, including work opportunities, but is this still true today? After graduating from MIT, Alex Bouaziz and Shuo Wang posed a question: Was it fair that they, and other highly qualified people born in countries other than the US, could not get good jobs in Silicon Valley because of local labour laws and visa restrictions? To solve this problem, they explored how technology could help companies hire anyone, anywhere in the world, for a role. The result was Deel, a platform they started in 2019 that enables companies to pay international workers without needing to set up local entities. Their timing was perfect, with the pandemic driving the adoption of remote work just a few months later, and demand soared. In 2024, just five years after it was founded, Deel's average recurring revenue had grown to $500 million, making it one of the fastest growing start-ups in history. By mid-2025, Deel had reached a $1 billion revenue run rate, and with over 35,000 customers, "hiring from anywhere" has become mainstream.[100]

Deel is set up as an "employer of record," or EOR, allowing it to employ and pay workers on a company's behalf. The company decides who to hire and sets the tasks, but the EOR helps hire those people quickly, then sorts out the onboarding, payroll, local tax, benefits, terminations, and complex compliance and legal requirements needed in each country. In some circumstances, a new worker contract can be set up in just 10 minutes. Deel offers this service in over 150 countries, saving companies significant costs, and they adapt to the latest changes in each country in real time. Deel also provides a free tool that estimates the cost of a worker in each location.

Services like this, that simplify the process and make it more transparent, are accelerating the move to using digital labour.

While Deel is a market leader, there are over 25 other EOR companies, and the market is expected to grow from $4.5 billion in 2024 to over $7 billion by 2031.[101] Pricing models range from fixed to a percentage of employee salary to customised variations. EORs answer questions from both companies and workers, and the information collected fuels innovation that helps build new AI services, ranging from answering queries to providing organisational charts or creating team reports. This cumulative data is power, and it feeds AI, as discussed in more detail in Chapter V – Data Over People.

ON-DEMAND WORKERS

Digital platforms also connect employers with contractors and freelancers hired on a temporary basis for specific projects. The term freelancer comes from medieval soldiers who offered their "free lance" services to the highest bidders. Today, weapons have been swapped for laptops, and digital platforms link freelancers to jobs from the comfort of their armchairs. This market has boomed. A report from SIA estimates there were 18.3 million contingent workers in the US in 2023.[102] A report by KBV research forecasts the global contingent workforce market could reach $326 billion by 2028, up from $135 billion in 2018.[103]

This growth is being driven by both companies and workers valuing greater flexibility. Work can be broken down into microtasks, offering a transactional relationship, the opposite of a lifelong career with a firm. Every task you can imagine can be contracted out. If you need dog food and don't have time to get it, digital platforms can find someone who will bring it to you. This dog food problem gave Leah Busque the idea for her online company, RunMyErrand, in 2008, which became TaskRabbit in 2010. If you need furniture assembled, help with a home repair, or want something delivered, taskers take care of these for you. It turns out that lots of people are prepared to pay others to do tasks they don't want to or can't do themselves. In 2024, TaskRabbit facilitated the completion of 1.6 billion tasks, saving an estimated 3.5 billion hours for clients.[104]

There are lots of alternative providers of freelance task completion, all with their own twist. PeoplePerHour allows employers to pay for standalone gigs that take a set number of hours, often called hourlies by freelancers. CloudDevs has a pool of over 8,000 senior developers and designers, all with over seven years of experience, who can contribute to tech projects. Freelancer claims to be the world's largest freelancing and crowdsourcing marketplace, connecting over 80 million employers and freelancers globally, from almost 250 countries and territories. Fiverr, which took its name from its original business model, a $5 asking price for tasks, tries to make "hiring freelancers as easy as buying on Amazon."[105] Founded in 2010, Fiverr grew its revenue to $391 million in 2024. Upwork has grown even bigger, reaching $769 million in revenue in 2024, up from $164 million in 2016.[106] Describing themselves as "the world's work marketplace," they now provide over 830,000 clients access to 10,000 skills, and AI helps with search, discovery, and matching. Growth has already been rapid, but AI will likely drive further transformation, and historic work norms will continue to change.

Digital platforms have also been useful for what is known as "drop servicing." This is when a business sells a service to a client, perhaps content creation or app development, and then outsources the work to a third-party provider, such as a freelancer or agency. This is similar to drop shipping, when a store sells physical products that they don't keep in stock. Just as

Uber facilitates drivers finding customers, drop servicing helps workers from anywhere around the world to find customers and projects.

A related concept is the use of "fractional work." This is a model in which someone works part-time for a company, giving the business access to well-qualified talent at a fraction of the cost of a full-time employee. This is particularly appealing for start-ups that may not be able to afford a whole legal expert, chief marketing officer (CMO), chief technology officer (CTO), or chief financial officer (CFO). The number of LinkedIn profiles in the UK that refer to fractional leadership, including fractional CMOs, CTOs, or CFOs, has grown from 2,000 in 2022 to 110,000 in 2024.[107] This flexibility may well suit many individuals, but it will also likely mean fewer full-time roles are needed, and competition from remote locations will increase.

HOW AI WILL ACCELERATE DIGITAL LABOUR

These digital platforms, as well as offering companies lower costs and more access to talent, provide a critical link between businesses and workers across the world. This is a new phenomenon, with many of these platforms only formed in the last two decades, and the pandemic accelerating their adoption. Swelling the supply of available labour reduces prices and increases competition, and this window into labour costs in different countries also highlights the stark differences between high and low-cost locations. Is a computer programmer in New York really worth 20 times what a worker with the equivalent talent in Asia costs? Now it is not only easier to see these differences, but companies can do something about them with straightforward solutions.

So not only will labour be disrupted by the robots and AI agents discussed in previous chapters but also by this linking of talent in low-cost locations to work around the world, cutting out those who have higher wage requirements. Putting these trends together, most US jobs could be automated or offshored. Worse still, 70% of jobs exposed to these two trends are held by women.[108] Indeed, Carl Frey has suggested that advanced economies may become post-production societies in which goods and services are increasingly produced by machines or abroad.

AI will act as an accelerant in all this. Firstly, AI will help gather information about opportunities, then better match workers to work. For example, the same transformer technology that underpins LLMs has been used to build talent intelligence platforms (TIPs) that use AI to find talent or skills across enormous databases of workers around the world. AI can already conduct 90% of hiring tasks, including processing and assessing online applications, one-way AI video interviews, and background checks. Once a worker begins their job, AI will help integrate and assess them, linking people together, with scheduling tools, for example, and measuring KPIs.

AI has also made significant progress in translation, opening huge opportunities for those who need to work in another language. For example, although customer service interactions often begin with chatbots, they usually then move on to online discussion with a human, and then via the phone; translation tools will allow non-native speakers to take on these second and third stages. Indeed, the world's biggest call centre company, Teleperformance, employs some 90,000 people in India and uses AI to neutralise accents in real time.

Another benefit of AI in this arena is in training new digital employees. In a large study of over 5,000 call centre workers, average productivity improved 14% using AI tools, but the productivity of novices improved 34%.[109] The AI tools managed to codify tacit information from more experienced agents and used this knowledge to help improve lower-skilled workers' performance. This is a game-changing development, given that learning practical, experience-based knowledge from others in the moment is invaluable but can be very hard, especially for remote workers.

Using GenAI, non-native English speakers can write fluently, producing professional business reports, client presentations, and marketing copy; poor artists can conjure pictures on demand; and those who need new skills have an always-on personal tutor who will improve their learning outcomes. AI can make a big difference by lifting those who are below average towards average. This will increase competition for tasks and accelerate the opportunities for those in lower-cost regions who will be empowered to add value to work in other locations.

A final simple, yet important, point is worth noting. This chapter started by talking about the pandemic accelerating the digitisation of our lives and work. The AI opportunity is attracting capital at pace, which will only speed it up further. Every time a physical interaction becomes digital, new metadata is created, which helps feed and improve AI systems. This, in turn, helps improve AI tools, digital platforms, and AI robots, as well as driving opportunities to develop more. If you are an investor, this is a virtuous cycle, but it's not if you are a worker whose livelihood is being cannibalised by AI. However, increased human and non-human competition for work will likely have another negative impact: reducing real wages. We turn to this phenomenon in the next chapter.

IV

FALLING WAGES

**"When the facts change, I change my mind.
What do you do, sir?"**

—John Maynard Keynes[110]

"[An economic singularity] would be the single most important event in history, bar none. Working out how to survive it is the most important challenge facing humanity this century."

—Calum Chace[111]

WAGES CAN GO UP, AND THEY CAN GO DOWN

As a thought experiment, just take a few minutes to think about this scenario: How would your world change if you were told that your wages would decline each year rather than go up? Chances are, you would spend less. Would you also try to save more? Would you liquidate some assets? Would you spend less or more on upskilling yourself or on your children's education? How about your year-end review with your boss? How would you feel if the conclusion was: "You have had a great year, so you can keep your job, and we will only reduce your pay by 2% next year"?

Many workers take it for granted that wages rise, but this isn't a foregone conclusion. In 1932, Sir John Hicks, one of the most influential economists of the twentieth century, noted that technological progress can be positive, neutral, or negative for labour. If a technology complements labour, it tends to increase labour demand and wages. When a technology substitutes for human labour, it tends to reduce demand for workers doing those tasks, depressing employment and wages.

In the era before the First Industrial Revolution, known as the Malthusian Age, food supplies were a limiting factor for growth. If you could not produce enough food, you could not feed people, so land was the most valuable factor of production, not humans. Living standards, therefore, largely stagnated throughout this period. During most of the First Industrial Revolution, technology was biased against labour: power looms replaced weavers, and steam power transported goods. Real wage growth was poor, and inequality rose.

In fact, it was only in the latter parts of the First Industrial Revolution and during the Second Industrial Revolution that wages rose, as more skilled labour was needed, and human workers became more valuable. New tools augmented workers, so productivity was boosted by "man plus machine." For example, while combustion engines eliminated the need for horses, they increased the number of roles for people, whether it was operating cars, maintaining them, or building roads. This included new areas of economic activity that never existed before. The transition from labour being economically dispensable to being in demand—indeed, becoming a bottleneck factor of production—led to rising wages as output increased.

Before assessing what might happen to wages in the AI era, it is worth unpacking some of the recent past so we can draw on key trends that might illuminate where things are heading.

LESSONS FROM OTHER TECHNOLOGICAL REVOLUTIONS

Two of the most significant work technologies adopted in the last 50 years have been computers and robot automation.

Technological progress has led to a six-fold increase in robot adoption in the US since 2000.[112] It is now expanding across sectors, but historically, uptake was concentrated in the manufacturing industry. Even in 2024, the automotive industry accounted for 40% of all US robot installations.[113] While robot adoption has been strong, significant growth still lies ahead. In 2023, North America had a robot density per thousand workers in manufacturing of 295, up from 49 in 2000, but this still pales in comparison with Korea at 1,012. [114]

As robot capability has risen, costs have fallen. It is estimated that robot costs declined 50% between 1970 and 1985, while the cost of human labour increased 300% over the same period.[115] Data from the International Federation of Robotics show robot costs fell a further 80%, on average, between 1995 and 2017.[116]

In one of the best academic studies looking at the impact of robots on US labour markets, MIT's Daron Acemoğlu estimated that between 1990 and 2007 each robot reduced employment by 3.3 workers.[117] Notably, the authors also conclude that each robot added per thousand workers reduced wages by 0.42%. The cumulative impact of these trends becomes significant over time in comparison to rising wages elsewhere in the economy.

This has had a disproportionate impact on blue-collar work. The employment participation rate for 25–54-year-old men in the US with no more than a high school qualification fell from 97% in the late 1960s to 85% in 2015. Real hourly earnings for this group fell 18% between 1973 and 2015.[118] This 40-year period of discontent for men with only a high school qualification has impacts beyond unemployment, influencing US politics and contributing to President Trump's rise.

While the automation of manufacturing provides lessons, the proliferation of computer technology across all sectors over the last 70 years has had a much more significant effect on wages. And its impact is more complex, given that computers can substitute work, such as typists; augment work, such as financial analysis; create new incremental work, such as food deliveries; and create entirely new industries that did not exist before, such as cloud computing or the app economy. Here, I'll focus on three primary lessons:

1. The Benefits Have Not Been Widely Shared

   Computers continue to do more and cost less. Most industries have undergone digital transformations over the last half-century, increasing efficiency and transparency and lowering prices for consumers. However, hoped-for productivity improvements were underwhelming in the early stages of the computer revolution, from the 1960s to the 1980s, as Robert Solow famously noted, and this has also been the case for most advanced economies in the last two decades.

   Average US annual productivity growth slowed from 2.5% between 1949 and 1979 to 1.4% between 1979 and 2025.[119] In addition, wages have not kept pace with productivity improvements, with annual wage growth falling from 2.1% to 0.6% during these periods, according to the Economic Policy Institute. There were several policy choices that led to this growing productivity-pay gap—including countries tolerating higher unemployment to reduce inflation, the growing power of shareholders, and the falling power of workers—but technology played a part. During the last six decades of the computer revolution, wage share of income for G7 countries has declined by two percentage points per decade, from a high of 70% in 1970, according to research by Adrjan.[120] Over this period, corporate margins and returns on capital have risen, and a larger share of economic gains has gone to capital over labour. The benefits were not shared. This bias against labour underlines the point Hicks made in 1932 and is similar to the Engels' pause experienced in Britain between 1790 and 1840, in the First Industrial Revolution, as rapid growth in GDP failed to translate to higher wages.

Dive deeper, and you'll see that the returns that did go to labour went to a small portion of the whole. Skill-based technological change has seen a rise in demand for high-skilled labour, such as programmers, whose wages *have* risen. At the same time, the demand for middle-skill jobs, such as clerical work, fell, leading to a stagnation of wages for this majority group. The Economic Policy Institute notes that US productivity grew 60% between 1979 and 2018, yet median workers' compensation grew just 15%. However, the top 1% of workers experienced 160% wage growth over this period, and +345% for the top 0.1%, versus below-average growth for the bottom 90% of workers.[121] It's clear that a long period of rising inequality has taken place during the computer revolution, and also that redistribution was resisted, with the top rate of taxation falling since the 1970s.

2. Digital Disruption Creates Competition and Reduces Wages

The digitisation of industries has accelerated change and disruption for businesses. There have been winners, such as large tech firms, and losers, such as traditional media companies. For example, as online search emerged, yellow page providers disappeared. As online video providers grew, offline firms such as Blockbuster went bankrupt. Chapter VIII – New Jobs examines the net employment effects of this disruption, but there is an important wage-related point that has parallels to declining wages from robot adoption.

First introduced in 1865, taxi drivers in London were required to learn "the knowledge" to operate, effectively memorising London's entire street network.[122] This typically took three to four years of study, creating a significant barrier to entry, which reduced competition and supported higher wages aligned with their skill level. This was no longer needed when GPS technology was introduced, and now real-time AI traffic apps, such as Waze, are often superior to traditional taxi driver knowledge. A second technological change then came from digital taxi platforms, such as Uber, which linked taxi providers to taxi passengers. This was good news for consumers, allowing them easy access to cheap taxis nearby, but it lowered the barriers to entry for taxi drivers. As Uber rolled into new cities, it increased competition, driving down the wages for traditional taxi drivers. Quantifying this impact, a study by Carl Benedikt Frey found taxi driver incomes declined 10% following the introduction of Uber.[123]

As new digital tools improve services across multiple areas of the economy, they will have a similar impact, increasing competition for existing providers and reducing wages.

3. Digitisation Leads to Winner-Takes-Most Economics

Uber has grown to provide 7.8 million active monthly drivers; it made $44 billion in revenue in

2025[124] and is the world's largest taxi company, with a value in excess of $160 billion. Not bad for a company that was only started in 2009.

Digitisation often delivers faster, cheaper, and better solutions to customers, but it also often leads to an increase in market share concentrations, as we've seen across multiple industries: taxis; media, including advertising and TV viewing; social media; e-commerce; computing infrastructure, such as cloud or operating systems; asset management, including the rise of passives and ETFs; and trading, such as in equities and fixed income.

A commonality between these areas is that data gives you power; it has become an ever more important factor of production, as explored in more depth in the next chapter. For companies, control of information has enabled "winner-takes-most economics," in which an increasing share of the returns goes to fewer companies. More data enables more insight, better personalisation, and opportunities for cross-selling. Lower prices increase the importance of scale economics and widen the premium of in-person services, which has an impact on labour. This also affects who earns the highest wages. Research has shown a rising wage premium for occupations with greater control of information.[125] So, as digital technology has spread across industries, we've seen the returns concentrated in winning firms and with winning workers. The other side of winner-takes-most is that everyone else takes less.

With this increasing concentration of power and money comes the rise of monopsony power, in which a dominant buyer of labour in a particular market has increasing power over the sellers of labour. Examples include the NHS, Uber, and Amazon; as some of the biggest players in their industries, with few competitors of their size, they can set wages and working conditions that suit them. As you can imagine, concentrations and monopsonies are good news for shareholders but less so for workers.

Looking at the data behind these trends, Autor and colleagues analysed US sectors accounting for 80% of employment and GDP between 1982 and 2012.[126] They highlighted increasing market share concentrations within industries, noting that it was most apparent in industries "experiencing faster technical change." Most importantly for this chapter, they found a "striking relationship" between increases in concentration and the declines in labour share as a proportion of an economy. The same was true in 11 other developed countries, partly as US superstar firms have also grown their presence internationally.

The computer age has brought many benefits to employers, employees, and society, yet it has also brought increased market share concentration, higher returns to capital than to labour, and higher inequality between workers. Arguably, the disruption it has caused has been more overwhelming than expected, and the productivity gains have been more underwhelming. Unless policy changes, we will likely see the same thing occur in the AI age.

LOOKING FORWARD INTO THE AI AGE

All things being equal, the wage trends driven by the emergence of robots and computers are likely to accelerate with AI.

As outlined in the previous three chapters, human workers will increasingly compete with moving robots, AI agents, and digital labour from across the world.

Let's explore each of these in turn.

Chapter I concluded that 4 billion moving robots could compete with at least 1 billion jobs by 2050. A key point was that the payback period for initial versions of a humanoid robot could be just 36 weeks. If so, the economics would be so attractive to companies that job substitution would definitely occur. There is little question that as AI robots become cheaper and more capable, human wages will fall.

As we've just seen, the opportunity that digital labour offers companies is enormous in terms of both wage differentials and the size of the talent pool. For example, given that Asia's population is so large, there are more people in the top 8% in terms of cognitive ability in Asia than the entire US population. Digital platforms linking this low-cost talent to jobs have grown in the last two decades, and AI will only increase this opportunity. It is plausible that digital labour could reach 500 million workers in time. This will add downward pressure on wages for all jobs that can be completed by digital workers.

The opportunity that AI agents and tools offer companies dwarfs both of these. There are lots of examples of them taking a fraction of the time to do a task and costing less than a fiftieth of the cost of a human. For instance, Vincent, created by legal start-up vLex, can draft legal documents, create litigation pleadings, and do legal research. Novo Nordisk reportedly used AI models to produce clinical documents in just 10 minutes that would have normally taken 10 weeks, reducing resources needed by 95%.[127]

The AI agent market is so embryonic that it is difficult to estimate how many agents there will be, but let's try with some back-of-the-envelope calculations. There are approximately a billion knowledge workers in the world.[128] Some will use more than one agent, but let's assume just one per person. Given that the CEO of NVIDIA used a 2000:1 estimate, 1:1 hardly seems aggressive.[129]

We could stop there, but I think it's reasonable to suggest that half of the world's 5.5 billion internet users will have at least one AI agent doing tasks for them. If you consider how many devices you have that are connected to the internet, or how many apps you have on your phone, this seems conservative. A Citi report estimated 11.6 billion devices had the capability to have a digital assistant in 2022, and that this would grow to 15.7 billion by 2030.[130] The app economy was only born in 2008, and according to Statista, we download over 250 billion apps per year.[131] An AI agent app economy is likely to form.

If we add these numbers together—a billion robots, 0.5 billion AI agents in the workplace, and 2.75 billion personal AI agents—it increases the competition for human workers by at least 4.25 billion. Using the full robot estimate of 4.1 billion would increase the total to 7.35 billion. And that doesn't include the extra 0.5 billion from digital labour. Obviously, this is just illustrative, but it's clear that, considering there are only 3.7 billion human workers today,[132] competition will increase significantly. To put things into context, the agent market is just starting, and the number of robots globally makes up less than 1% of the total working population.[133] And if the potential for the number of non-human workers to grow from less than 1% to over 115% of the number of human workers is not enough, many robots and AI agents will be able to work over double the hours of a human worker.

For most jobs, the impact of this new competition will be incremental. Again, let's estimate cautiously. If we assume it chips away at 2% of your tasks per year, after 10 years, with the power of compounding, that would be 18% of your job transferred and 33% after 20 years. If so, can we assume pay would decline by 18% and 33% over these time periods? This might sound frightening, but the positive counterargument, of course, is that AI tools will allow you to do more, earn more revenue for your firm, and therefore get paid more. For example, turning the 2% decline per year into a 2% gain, compounded over 10 and 20 years, would lead to improvements of 22% and 48%, respectively. The difference between a drop of 33% and a rise of 48% in year 20 is substantial. But how can you know which is the more likely outcome in your job?

These scenarios, albeit theoretical, show the importance of making sure we nudge towards the 2% increase per year rather than the drop of 2%, in other words, AI augmentation rather than substitution. We are in a race to ensure technology allows us to do more, not less. And that it enhances our pay rather than eliminating part of it.

However, consider three other headwinds in this race. Firstly, for all the talk of upskilling for the new AI era, AI can also *deskill* us, much like GPS tools reduce the need for taxi drivers to learn the knowledge, or AI scripts encourage novice call centre workers to recite dialogue rather than develop communication or problem-solving skills. As AI tools lower barriers to entry, this will impact pay.

Secondly, computers are learning how to act like humans; this is a reversal of the trend of the last few decades when humans learnt how to use computers. Experienced workers are teaching these new AI interns what to do, and while they probably deserve a pay raise for doing so, a pay reduction is more likely in the long term as the AI interns take on more and more.

Thirdly, as AI becomes proficient at more tasks, humans will increasingly crowd into the shrinking number of areas that machines cannot master. As an individual, this is a rational move, but collectively, it will lead to a higher supply of labour in non-AI-impacted areas, reducing wages in these roles. To counteract this risk, we'll either need a surge in demand for jobs in which humans hold a comparative advantage or lots of new AI-augmented jobs.

THE DECLINING COST OF INTELLIGENCE

So far, we have discussed incremental change, but what happens if AI's growth continues to be exponential? One aim of leading AI companies is to drive the cost of intelligence down to zero. This might seem fantastical, but it is possible.

If you are old enough, you'll remember a time when an international phone call, or even a domestic mobile call, was expensive. Skype arrived in 2003, and now you can speak via the internet to anyone, anywhere in the world, for free. A similar move towards providing free digital products and services happened for photos, music, maps, and news. Just as Google Search drove the cost of knowledge down towards zero, the same could happen for intelligence.

There are a variety of ways to generate revenue, but LLMs often start by offering intelligence for free to many, as with ChatGPT. In 2023, I interviewed Marshall Goldsmith, the top-ranked executive coach worldwide.[134] In a bold move, he had set up his own free coaching bot that he said already knew more than he did and was available, on demand, 24/7. This might seem strange as coaching is a quintessentially human activity, but Marshall's view was that the value of advice in general will trend towards zero. If so, this has dramatic implications for millions of workers. Free is difficult to compete with.

Sceptics will rightly question this model, arguing that AI has a cost that has to be paid by someone, somehow. But we also know that as technology improves, costs fall dramatically. As Michio Kaku noted in his 2011 book, *Physics of the Future*, "Today, your cell phone has more computer power than all of NASA back in 1969, when it sent two astronauts to the moon."[135] And according to Ray Kurzweil, author of *The Singularity Is Near*, the power of computers per dollar spent has increased 20-quadrillion-fold since 1939. In the short term, the CFO of OpenAI recently noted that the price per token used in their AI models has fallen 99% since ChatGPT-4 was launched in March 2023.[136] The direction of travel for the cost of AI and intelligence will be down.

WHEN AGI ARRIVES ON THE SCENE

Next, ask yourself what happens to wages if AI has another step change in capability and surpasses humans. As Tomas Chamorro explains in the book *I, Human*, "As AI advances, the only thing that sets humans apart is our ability to do a bit of everything, even if AI outperforms us on each of those tasks. It is the inability to develop artificial general intelligence that still makes general human intelligence quite valuable."[137]

As discussed in Chapter II, the debate is not *if* AGI will be reached but when, and this time is rapidly approaching. As mentioned previously, on Metaculus, 2033 is currently the expert consensus, on average. The implications are so profound for human workers that they must be discussed urgently. One of the best economic thinkers on this topic is Professor Anton Korinek at the University of Virginia, who warns that wages could collapse when we reach AGI.[138] Korinek is very optimistic that our output will grow when "the scarcity of labor is no longer a constraint," but he sees machines substituting the vast majority of human workers. His baseline timeline for this is within 20 years, but his more aggressive timeline is within five years.

Korinek argues that many organisations may choose to keep humans employed. For example, they might feel they need to hire human doctors to provide a more comforting "veneer" for AI, or they might hire human lawyers for regulatory reasons, or they might hire human waiters or carers for children based on people's personal preferences. However, the point at which AI can do a cognitive or physical job better and cheaper than a human will be a point of existential risk for workers, employment, and wages.

In some markets, the fall in wages could be a step change to zero, as occurred for those selling physical photos, home phones, and cart horses. Other jobs could follow the linear 2% drop per year described above, similar to how physical shops have lost market share to online stores over the past two decades. If the exponential growth of AI continues on a J-curve, however, that trend could be inverted for human wages. The 2% drop in year one could become 4% in year two, 8% in year three, and so on, until wages disappear altogether in year seven.

Perhaps a doubling in AI's capability each year—and the resultant loss in human work—may be too aggressive, but a doubling in AI's capability every three to five years would be conservative given current predictions. If this happens, wages will fall to zero in 21 or 35 years. As Ernest Hemingway wrote in *The Sun Always Rises*, "'How did you go bankrupt?' 'Two ways. Gradually, then suddenly.'"[139]

Optimists will point out that even if humans cede some share of their work and wages to technology, as the economic pie grows, workers may still be better off having a smaller share of a bigger pie. However, the difference with the AGI scenario is that our share of the pie is falling at a much faster rate than the growth of the pie. Ultimately, zero share of an enormous pie is still zero. If it's true that this time it's different and economic growth occurs only for non-human rather than human workers, pro-innovation politicians may need to have a rethink.

In his book, *Scary Smart,* Gawdat asks why someone would employ a human if machines are multiple times more intelligent, or "the equivalent of a fly relative to Einstein."[140] When we pass the point of AGI, technological unemployment—joblessness driven by technological innovation—could therefore go from possible to probable. Yuval Noah Harari, in *Homo Deus,* warns that as AI pushes people into unemployment and unemployability, we will see the rise of a "useless class," unable to provide any unique physical or cognitive abilities to employers.[141]

Nobody knows for certain how this AGI era will play out, so we should remain open-minded to the forecasts of both boomers and doomers, but the risks are so profound that we have to prepare. One of the reasons we cannot yet predict the outcome is that we could enter an economic singularity, as discussed in Chapter II. Singularity normally refers to the point in a black hole where the normal laws of physics break down. Similarly, in an economic singularity, the normal economic rules will cease to apply, which is why Calum Chace says it "would be the single most important event in history, bar none."[142]

If Chase, Korinek, and others are correct that wages could collapse in this scenario, this has dramatic implications across multiple areas: for personal consumption expenditure, which makes up two-thirds of US GDP[143]; for income tax receipts; for the ways we raise tax; for how government services are funded; for our ability to service government or personal debt; for deflation and interest rates; for wealth, which could rise as company margins soar or fall as people lose their livelihoods, society recalibrates, and people are forced to sell their assets; for the value of education; for how much office space and support services are needed; for what happens to benefits that are tied to work, such as pensions or healthcare; and for leadership, given it is much easier to lead when the currents create a swell of new demand for products and services rather than a collapse demand.

Even if there is a low probability that we'll need a whole new economic system, the reverberations of an economic singularity would be so seismic that scenario planning is urgently needed. In the 2008 Financial Crisis and in the pandemic health crisis of 2020, we experienced how quickly things can change despite the fact that these were driven by known risks. In an AGI era, a job apocalypse could happen quickly, and certainly much quicker than solutions could be agreed on and implemented. And if you still think we have plenty of time, some experts, such as Dario Amodei, the CEO of Anthropic, have said that AGI could arrive by 2026.[144]

Experts in governments, think tanks, and research institutes need to debate, examine probabilities, plan, test solutions, collect data, and form a consensus. Given how many people could be affected, leaders in both politics and business need to tread a careful line between not creating unnecessary panic and irresponsibly hoping it won't materialise or that the problem will be shifted onto someone else's watch.

This book aims to take responsibility by highlighting the issues in Part 1, debating potential solutions in Part 2, and calling on leaders to bridge the gap in Part 3. However, before we get to solutions, if you are not too depressed already, I'm afraid we need to explore another key risk ahead of us: the increasing value of data compared to people. The next chapter warns that you may not be as important as you have been told you are.

V

DATA OVER PEOPLE

"Once men turned their thinking over to machines in the hope that this would set them free. But that only permitted other men with machines to enslave them."

—Frank Herbert, *Dune*[145]

"Have I Told You Lately That I Love You?"

—Scotty Wiseman[146]

INTO THE AIGORACY

Versions of the song "Have I Told You Lately That I Love You," recorded by several different artists over the years,[147] are often popular for the first dance at weddings. They would probably be less popular if followed by the line: "Have I told you there's someone else above you?" But this is increasingly probable in the world of work. Let's dig into why.

Peter Drucker, often called the "father of modern management," said, "People are our greatest asset."[148] This is something that everyone learns, many leaders try to emulate, and some confidently quote to others. But what is said is not always true, and what *was* true can always change.

What has not changed is the need to be more efficient and more productive; this is a constant drumbeat. As Drucker put it, "Efficiency is doing better what is already being done,"[149] and given that he believed "you can't manage what you can't measure,"[150] there has been a consistent drive in business to use data to measure anything useful. In the 1880s, William Legrand Bundy invented a time recorder that gave employers an automatic way of tracking workers. The big efficiency gains at work then happened after Frederick Winslow Taylor published *The Principles of Scientific Management* in 1911. Taylorism broke jobs down into simple and repetitive tasks that could be measured and refined to improve productivity.

While Taylorism was originally applied to factory and blue-collar work, today it is used across all forms of work, including white-collar jobs. We measure everything we can, whether it's how many people have tapped on the smiling face when they leave a public loo to gauge customer experience or the number of likes on a social media post to assess engagement. Rating service output in this way is commonplace, but so too is measuring service input. For instance, in industries such as finance, law, or medicine, time spent with clients or patients is tracked down to the minute. Even the most human-focused areas, such as teaching young children, have become metricised and measured.

The computer transformed Taylorism, and now tasks are mostly organised, managed, and tracked digitally. AI will only accelerate this trend, and increasingly, it will direct the tasks of human and non-human workers. We have already entered an algoracy, or management by algorithm. Employees at Amazon warehouses are guided by routing algorithms that plan the most efficient journey for delivering their parcels. AI also monitors these delivery workers' progress, making sure they hit their targets. Indeed, those workers often fear slow metrics will impact future opportunities, or worse still, lead to them losing their jobs. Cameras in vehicles can even use algorithms to monitor drivers' eyelids to detect drowsiness. There is also talk of trying to monitor workers' heart rates and stress levels, particularly in high-pressure jobs, such as financial trading.

At the office, swipe cards clock you in and out. Some track where you are in the building and even how long you have been in the toilet. The hot desk you use is logged, as is how long you are at it. Camera technology exists that can measure your concentration levels while at your desk by assessing your facial expressions. Your communications—written, voice, or via Zoom—are increasingly recorded and stored, whether you are in or out of the office. One of the reasons many executives carry both a work and a personal phone is that it is possible to track everything on a work device.

In finance, emails and even voice calls are often scanned in real time for compliance breaches. While constant monitoring can feel invasive, these controls do reduce errors. For example, after crediting a customer account with $81 trillion rather than $280, Citi increased its use of automation and AI checks to avoid mistakes from manual processes.[151]

AI is not just used to monitor and control humans but also to monitor and control other AIs. In many organisations, AI is constantly working away to monitor cyber breaches. In other words, AI is used to catch the bad guys while the bad guys use AI to generate cyber-attacks. The volume and speed of attacks mean it's beyond the capability of most cyber professionals to keep up with these problems in real time, so AI lends a hand, and over time, it has become increasingly crucial.

AI can also now drive productivity by capturing tacit information from humans—knowledge based on experience and intuition. It's often hard to pass on this sort of knowledge as it's hard to explain or write down, but in an experiment where AI listened to over 5,000 call centre workers, it managed to extract and share best practices, such as key phrases or tone.[152] This accelerated the process of new recruits getting up to speed, reducing training time from six months to only two, and it increased novice productivity by 34%.

We are increasingly asking experts to teach AI how to think in knowledge work, too; for example, experienced lawyers may assess and guide the answers from AI models. This codification of thinking can then be used to benefit other lawyers, and AI can be used to check their work. The AI student becomes the teacher and the marker. Similarly, some employees leaving their firms have an exit interview with an AI tool that codifies their knowledge and experience by asking them how to do tasks, as is the case with DHL.[153] If you are not willing to train AI to do your job, a whole new industry of hiring freelance subject matter experts, such as lawyers, bankers, or doctors, to train AI systems to do tasks and jobs has already started. According to the Financial Times, one of the leading firms offering this service, Mercor, pays around $2 million per day to 30,000 experts, and despite only being founded in 2023 appears to have raised financing with a valuation of $10 billion.[154]

AI doesn't just monitor and control us. It is usually designed to support workers and those looking for work to increase their productivity. For example, applicants often use AI to help them cope with onerous and voluminous job applications; it is said these days that it is a full-time job to get a new job. Help is also on hand for companies and HR professionals dealing with the rising volume of applications they receive. And 90% of the recruitment of human workers can be handled by AI, from marking applications to online assessments and one-way video interviews. This just leaves the final selection interviews, which are still carried out by a person. The whole process is increasingly data-led, recorded, and measured, reducing the influence of subjective gut feeling when it comes to hiring and the retrofitting of candidate analysis to fit the conclusion the human interviewer has come to.

So, as you can see, digital Taylorism now extends across the job lifecycle, from candidate screening before you start to tracking productivity at work or losing your job due to AI monitoring. This has huge upsides for companies. As Drucker says, "You can't manage what you can't measure." AI turbo-charges measurement at work, helping companies see what's really going on behind the scenes, increase worker accountability and motivation, and take more control of the situation, which all drives productivity and efficiency.

Yet these benefits for companies can come with downsides for workers. According to Gartner, the number of large firms that track employees using workplace analytics, colloquially called bossware, has risen over 60% since the pandemic.[155] Being constantly watched and marked on your performance can be stressful, reducing morale and job satisfaction. Personal autonomy and independence decline, and not just for call centre workers using AI scripts but also for doctors or lawyers whose roles are traditionally characterised by independent decision-making. As workers' actions and customer interactions are increasingly captured as data in systems, they become interchangeable and commoditised because with this information in hand, the next worker can easily pick up where the last person left off. Relationships with clients have moved from being with a person to being with the company. A danger, as we are increasingly measured by machines, is that we become more like machines ourselves.

This dehumanisation of work starts early, from the application process before you have a job. If you do not meet the algorithm's requirements, within seconds of applying for a job, you may get a message like this: "After careful consideration, we regret to inform you that your job application has not been successful at this time." New joiners often get an ID number, or desk number, and these numbers, rather than their names, are used for functions, such as IT support. During the day, remote managers can monitor your array of metrics in real time.

At the end of a performance period, many managers have to mark a worker's performance—called "forced ranking"—using bell-curve rating systems: "Great year, you are a two out of five." Compensation is often based on these ranking systems, with a myriad of underlying KPIs and little management discretion. US government workers received an email from Elon Musk in 2025 asking them for five bullet points listing their accomplishments in the last week. He stated, "Failure to respond will be taken as a resignation."[156] This might sound extreme, but it is unfortunately not as uncommon as you might think for workers to find out, by email, that their job has been deleted. Sometimes the most efficient route is the least human one.

YOU'VE BEEN DATAFIED

We're being datafied at work, whether we like it or not, but many of us are opting to be datafied in our personal lives, too: our analogue habits, actions, and lives quantified into digital information. Like many others, my watch is recording my sleep, my steps, and my heart rate. It senses if I am on a walk, a rower, or an elliptical and asks if I want to record it. It knows the location of our children and our pets and how far from the pin I am on any golf course. If she were to have a fall, my mum's watch would alert the emergency services.

We regularly give up our data when we download free apps or use websites. Google, Facebook, and TikTok have built enormous advertising revenue streams from the data they extract from the free services they offer you. The algorithms behind Amazon, Netflix, and Spotify provide more of what you like to keep you engaged or buying. Many have even outsourced their dating to AI, with algorithms matching your digital profile, preferences, and location to partners. For example, since launching in 2012, Tinder has made over 70 billion dating matches.[157]

As everything becomes datafied, increasingly, it feels like we are drinking from a firehose. Statista suggests the world's data increased 74-fold between 2010 and 2024.[158] It is estimated that 90% of all the data that's ever been generated came in the last two years alone.[159] It is not only difficult for humans to keep up, but the exponential growth of new information dilutes our existing knowledge. As we get outpaced, machines are propelled forward. In comparison, they excel at the ingestion and processing of more data. And data feeds AI and makes it more useful. It's an upward cycle.

In 2006, Clive Humby said, "Data is the new oil," and this analogy offers useful parallels on the change taking place.[160] Energy reservoirs powered the Industrial Revolution. Data lakes are powering the AI revolution. Both are valuable, but they need to be extracted, processed, and delivered, and complementary technologies help us do this. For example, horizontal drilling recently opened rich energy seams that were previously inaccessible. Similarly, the use of unstructured, anonymised, and synthetic data recently opened rich information seams that were previously inaccessible. There are several differences, however. Unlike with oil, the cost of storing data declines rapidly, and the cost of distributing data is almost zero. Oil is rivalrous, meaning once it's used, it cannot be reused; it's made of layers of dead organic matter that have accumulated over thousands of years, and it's then burnt. In comparison, data is inorganic and lasts forever; it can be used and shared multiple times, creating positive network effects. Many layers of data can accrue over time, powering AI systems. So, while oil reserves will one day fall to zero, data gets more valuable as it multiplies.

COMPANIES WANT DATA, NOT PEOPLE

The benefits of data impact work and workers. As workers become datafied, that information is stored and fed to new AI systems to produce insights and actions. Better AI tools also help extract more useful data. As a result, data is increasingly a core foundation on which companies are built.

As I said at the start of this chapter, Drucker, who coined the term knowledge worker, believed people were our most important assets. But Drucker's first book, *The End of Economic Man*, was published in 1939. Similarly, in 1948, the CEO of Procter & Gamble, Richard Deupree, said, "If you leave us all the money, our buildings, and our brands, but take away our people, the company will fail. But if you take away our money, our buildings, and our brands, but leave us our people, we can rebuild the whole thing in a decade."[161] These sentiments have been echoed by countless leaders since, usually to motivate workers, but often with absolute sincerity and conviction. Yet what was true historically may not be true in the AI age ahead—or even today.

One sign that things have changed took place in 2012, when Facebook acquired Instagram for $1 billion. Instagram had 30 million users but just 13 employees.[162] Then, in 2014, Facebook paid $19 billion for WhatsApp, which had 450 million users and just 55 employees.[163] I'm sure these employees were all very important, but Facebook was not buying these companies for the people; they were buying their data, technology, user bases, scale, and first-mover advantage.

The ability to scale quickly without many employees can be seen across many successful firms in the last few decades.

As Martin Ford has noted, Google reached a profit of $14 billion in 2012 with 38,000 employees. In comparison, General Motors had a profit of $11 billion in 1979 with 840,000 employees.[164] At its peak, Blockbuster had a revenue of $5.9 billion and employed 84,300 people.[165] In 2024, Netflix's revenue reached $39 billion, and the firm employed just 14,000 people.[166] There is now a website called *Tiny Teams Hall of Fame* that shows companies with very small teams and very large revenues. At the time of writing, Cursor has $200 million in revenue and just 20 employees.[167] Midjourney has $200 million in revenue and 10 employees. Some entrepreneurs are even talking about creating zero-employee autonomous companies, or zero-employee enterprises (ZEE), populated with AI agents instead of human workers.

To understand whether people are still the most important asset in companies, I looked at how the composition of top firms has changed over time, comparing employee numbers in the 20 largest companies in 1955 and 2025. The median number of employees per firm in 2025 was 125,000, slightly down from 135,000 in 1955. However, revenue generated per employee increased over sixfold during this period, from a $156,000 medium in 1955, inflation-adjusted, to $1 million in 2025. In addition to generating far more revenue per employee over time, the largest 20 companies now give far less back to employees in the form of compensation. In 1955, 36 cents from each $1 generated was paid back to employees; by 2025, this had fallen to just 14 cents. This tallies with the lower labour shares of GDP discussed in the previous chapters. Employees are clearly not valued in the same way they used to be.

One side lesson learned from this process was that disclosure of people's compensation and employee welfare has gone backwards in the last 70 years. It was far easier to find this data about companies in 1995 than it was post-1990s. More recent data often had to be gathered from third-party sources rather than directly from the companies themselves. This seems at odds with claims that people are a firm's most important asset.

Digging further into the data, there has been a significant increase in capital expenditure and R&D in these companies over time. The 2025 medium capital expenditure is 7%, and the average is 10%, up from 5% and 7%, respectively, in 1955. Modern companies have become even more capex heavy than the manufacturing and industrial companies of yesteryear. And an increasing share of employee compensation has been directed towards R&D expense, which is often used to develop new cutting-edge technologies. In 2025, the average R&D expense was 9%. This tells us that technology has driven efficiency and economies of scale so companies can do a lot more with far fewer employees in 2025 than in 1955. In other words, tech is more valued, and people are less valued.

If this has been the trend over the last 70 years of digitisation, without other interventions, it is likely that this will accelerate in the age of AI agents, robots, and digital labour. The substitution of tasks and jobs will lead to a decline in workers. Investment in capex and R&D will likely keep rising, along with declining real wages, driving a shift away from employees. The value of the largest companies on the stock market and valuations of many private AI companies also imply that this trend will continue.

For many years, investors have valued companies with strong recurring revenues and dependable profit streams much more highly than those that have the opposite. Unfortunately, if a company's future earnings depend on people who can walk out the door and never come back, stock market valuations tend to be low. In addition to quitting, workers take holidays, lunch breaks, and sick leave. They might arrive late or leave early, and they need to take time away from work to sleep. Workers also come with peripheral costs, such as offices, parking spaces, healthcare, and pensions. Some join unions and go on strike. For companies needing adaptability, the hardest part of change management is not usually the technology but changing employees. And if a significant leader leaves, this can often cause a ripple effect for teams and cultures downstream, creating disruption. So, as great as workers are, or are told they are, other assets are sometimes preferable.

Let's return to our earlier example. Even though Deupree had an amazing tenure at Procter & Gamble from 1930 to 1959, investors in his company didn't necessarily agree with his belief in the value of people. Instead, they were drawn to P&G's enduring brands, which have far outlived the employees that birthed them, such as Fairy washing liquid (1898), Gillette razors (1901), Vicks cold products (1905), Tide laundry detergent (1946), Oral-B toothpaste (1950), and Pampers nappies (1961). It also appears that P&G's headcount has fallen from 135,000 in 2009 to 108,000 in 2024, while revenue has increased from $77 billion to $84 billion over this period.[168] Revenue up 9%, employees down 20%.

DATA BECOMES POWER

In 2020, China announced that they classify data as the fifth factor of production, the inputs that are used to make goods or services, and it is likely that other countries will soon follow. The fourth factor, entrepreneurship, was added in the first half of the twentieth century to the original three factors of land, labour, and capital.

The simple reason data is so important in the AI age is that when companies gain access to similar AI tools, the data that is fed into these tools will be what differentiates competitors. In the world of AI, bigger is usually better. More data leads to more insight. Take, for example, how much Google knows about you if you use Google Search, Gmail, Google Calendar, Google Maps, the Google Chrome browser, an Android phone, YouTube, or Gemini. This improves cross-selling, targeted advertising, and economies of scale to make products cheaper and better.

The growing importance of data will lead to an important competitive change. Historically, many small companies competed by offering a more personalised service and a more intimate human relationship than larger, more bureaucratic companies. However, when large companies combine enormous amounts of data with AI tools, they will also be able to offer more personalised and bespoke services to people at scale. Being large and more personalised sounds like an oxymoron, but let's take your health as an example. If I have access to your digital data, I might know your heart rate via your watch, that your prescription renewal is due, or that you have recently been searching about a particular health topic. With this information, I can better understand your needs, and I'll be able to personalise products or services for you. The more data, the more insight, the more useful it is to you. Now imagine getting this help or advice in real time, when you need it most, rather than waiting for a human to get into the office and get back to you after they've completed their to-do list.

Take this process and scale it up millions or billions of times, and this is where we are headed, across most sectors of the economy. You are being datafied and fed to the algocracy. Your data is being used to drive useful services back to you and to drive more efficiency, productivity, and profits back to companies. Extending the idea of winner-takes-most economics from the digital age, big companies with more data will get bigger. Smaller competitors with less data and technology will get smaller, losing market share.

Indeed, as we've seen in the examples above, proprietary data will be a core competitive advantage in the AI era, and more companies could be acquired specifically for their data. Some companies will be better at extracting insight and profits from that data than others. Investors don't yet have the expertise to accurately value data, but this will come. As the value of proprietary data rises, so too will ways to protect that data from being used by competitors; copyright lawsuits have already been filed on the use of data by LLMs.[169]

Data matters at a national level as well. It underpins national services, from renewing passports to the military. Countries will increasingly need to offer data protection and transparency, especially for sensitive data, to their citizens. The EU's 2018 General Data Protection Regulation was a big step towards this. Indeed, data sovereignty will become a growing issue, with countries less willing to see foreign competitors transfer, harvest, and profit from their citizens' data. The US cloud computing providers grew up doing just this, and in response, countries such as Germany introduced laws restricting data being transferred to other countries. This could lead to data being owned by national champions chosen by governments.

There is currently a race to build enormous data centres around the world, including the $500 billion US Stargate investment announced by Trump in 2025.[170] These data centres, or "AI factories," are becoming the railroads of the twentieth century, and this has implications for wealth and power. Countries with enormous populations and less onerous data privacy restrictions, such as China and India, already have a big opportunity to feed AI systems and benefit from economies of scale. It would be sensible for smaller countries to own this critical infrastructure and not give away their fifth factor of production.

The use and protection of data also matter for workers. This is not just about worker rights in terms of data protection, transparency about decisions made, or the surveillance levels allowed. Every time an employee's interaction with a customer is datafied, that data is stored and kept by the company. This is a sensible business practice because if that employee is on holiday or quits, others can step in, using that data as a guide. However, it *is* also a transfer of power from the employee to the employer. Every time the employee codifies what they do, they transfer their knowledge to the employer. Every time they train the AI system, they transfer intelligence to the employer's data centres. It is not that workers could or should resist this—ultimately, their work is in service of the company—but we should acknowledge the reality of the process and consider the implications. It is best to discuss the issues now when we are still at the beginning of this worker datafication process.

In 1994, Bill Gates said, "We need banking, not banks."[171] As we move into the AI age, this could be widened to "We need work, not workers." Or perhaps something less catchy but more accurate: "We need your data, not human workers." Gates was a little early with his proposition, but he was right in the long run, as the eventual growth of digital banking has reduced the need for bank branches and bank workers. US bank branch numbers peaked in 2009 at 99,550 and have fallen every year since, hitting a 40-year low in 2023.[172] The fall started earlier and was more dramatic in the UK, with bank branches falling from 21,643 in 1986 to 5,100 by 2023.[173] Digital banking is not only more convenient and efficient but also cheaper. When was the last time you went into a branch or even used cash? Each banking technology shift, from ATMs and phone banking to banking apps and contactless cards or one-click buying, reduces your effort and the need for people. AI will likely follow a similar process in many areas of work, laying one improvement on top of another, with data sitting at the foundation.

Many leaders will still say, with hand on heart, that people are a company's most important assets. That's because this will remain the case in certain human-centred or AI-augmented jobs. It's also because leaders know, in this phase of weak competition, that AI systems are at a developmental phase, and humans are still needed to train them and provide them with adult supervision. Others may say it slightly disingenuously because human workers have to be motivated, persuaded, and inspired; they need to feel like they matter. AI systems, robots, and data repositories, on the other hand, simply do not give a damn about whether they are important.

It's clear that the value of data will continue to rise and the value of human workers will continue to fall. What may have been true for Deupree and Drucker will quickly become less true in the future, unless we alter our course. The rest of this book tries to tackle how we do that, exploring the solutions available to us. The next chapter explores what might happen if we do not choose a path at all—AI anarchy.

VI

AI ANARCHY

"The worst enemy of life, freedom, and the common decencies is total anarchy; their second worst enemy is total efficiency."

—Aldous Huxley[174]

"The roots of the word 'anarchy' are 'an archos,' 'no leaders,' which is not really about the kind of chaos that most people imagine when the word 'anarchy' is mentioned. I think that anarchy is, to the contrary, about taking personal responsibility for yourself."

—Alan Moore[175]

A TIPPING POINT

For the avoidance of doubt, I need to start this chapter by unequivocally saying it is not a call to anarchy. This is a route to be avoided. Part of how we avoid it is by embracing the solutions outlined in subsequent chapters.

The word *anarchy* is adapted from the ancient Greek word ἀναρχία (*anarkhía*), in which the prefix "an-" means "without" and "*arkh*" means "take the lead." Without leadership, disorder is very possible, so we need to think carefully about how this situation might occur and how we can prevent it to protect the future of work. Part 3 of this book focuses on the exact opposite of anarchy: pro-human leadership.

In addition to the exponential growth of AI systems, we have witnessed a series of remarkable AI inflection points in the last two decades: autonomous driving, starting in 2004; recommendation systems from the mid-2000s; self-learning systems from 2010; vision systems from 2012; natural language processing and generative AI from 2017; multi-modal systems in 2023; autonomous agents in 2024; and orchestration systems in 2025. More will follow, including AGI and ASI.

As exciting as these are, workers are having to deal with the greatest change they've ever seen. As the authors of *No Ordinary Disruption* say, "Compared with the Industrial Revolution, we estimate this change is happening 10 times faster and at 300 times the scale, or roughly 3,000 times the impact."[176] Change is not easy for people, and we enter the AI era with the lowest levels of trust in corporate and political leaders we've ever seen. The winds of change are blowing, and we have wobbly foundations.

Add into the mix, as Yuval Noah Harari warns in his recent book *Nexus*, that the invention of new information technology has *always* been a catalyst for major historical changes: clay tablets, holy books, newspapers, and now AI. Harari argues that we underestimate the negative aspects of these changes and warns that we have never had one as powerful as AI. AI that can learn by itself, decide by itself, and produce limitless content by itself. Past changes in information technologies have shaped political and social systems, and it is highly likely that AI will as well. We just don't know how yet.

This combination of rapid change and high levels of uncertainty could lead to a tipping point in how people respond to these developments. As Newton said, "With every action, there is a reaction." Linking this with work, Huxley warned, in his famous 1932 book *Brave New World,* that a drive for more efficiency could create a backlash. Indeed, a minor backlash came in March 2023 when The Future of Life Institute published an open letter from concerned computer science experts who asked for a pause in AI experiments. That did not work, and for various reasons, including the AI arms race between countries, a pause is not on the table. Will a backlash from other groups have more impact? Let's start by looking at some lessons from history.

THE CYCLE OF PROTEST

On 17 December 2010, in the Tunisian town of Sidi, Mohamed Bouazizi set himself on fire. He was protesting the confiscation of his cart and goods. Having trouble finding secure work, 26-year-old Bouazizi had become an underemployed street vendor without a permit. His tragic self-immolation was widely shared on social media and triggered a series of protests in Tunisia, driven by a young population facing high unemployment, limited opportunities, and income inequality.

As the protests escalated, it led to the ousting of Tunisia's President Zine El Abidine Ben Ali, after 23 years in power. Similar uprisings followed in other Arab countries, now known as the Arab Spring. It prompted the resignations of the presidents of Egypt and Yemen. Civil war in Libya, after security forces fired into the crowd, led to the assassination of Muammar Gaddafi in 2011. He had ruled the country since 1969.

While Bouazizi's initial protest served as the spark, it ignited a powder keg of pre-existing socioeconomic and political frustrations that had been building for decades across the

Arab world. Employment in the region ranged from 8–20% at the time, with youth unemployment a worrying 20–40%.[177] And these official figures masked underemployment, with many, like Bouazizi, resorting to unstable work, such as street vending. Despite being educated, the youth could not find good jobs, and they were exasperated, leading to a widespread sense of hopelessness for the future. Just as hope can be a powerful force, so can hopelessness.

History often rhymes. Over 200 years before Bouazizi, fable has it that Ned Ludd, an English weaver, smashed two knitting looms; thereafter, his name was used by others who broke these job-destroying machines, who said, "Ned Ludd did it." As technology transformed the textile industry in the early nineteenth century, and frustrations and unemployment grew, so too did these "Luddite" raids on machines across the country. The government responded fiercely by using an army against the Luddites that was bigger than the army the Duke of Wellington used against Napoleon in the Peninsular War. Sixty Luddites were charged in one trial in 1813, and the convicted were executed by hanging, deported, or imprisoned.[178] Ludd's impact continues to this day, and he's seen as a symbol of worker backlash against technology, as noted in the lyrics from Robert Calvert's 1985 song about him:

> They said Ned Ludd was an idiot boy
> That all he could do was wreck and destroy, and
> He turned to his workmates and said: Death to Machines
> They tread on our future, and they stamp on our dreams.

Similar protests arose in 1830s England against the use of threshing machines, as they threatened agricultural workers. This time, the protestors took on the name "Captain Swing" when they smashed the machines that were taking their jobs.

Riots resulted in 19 labourers being executed, 504 being deported to Australia, and 644 being imprisoned.[179]

A COMPLEX WEB OF FEARS

Fast-forward 200 years to our AI age: is it not likely that concerns about jobs and livelihoods will bubble up into a new wave of Luddites? As AGI nears and the risk of an economic singularity gets discussed, workers may fear that their substitution by AI is both structural and enduring.

The unrest in the Arab Spring and the Luddite protests did not come out of nowhere. Both had been building for some time. Luddite activism grew during a period known as Engels' pause, between 1790 and 1840, when rising output from the Industrial Revolution in Britain brought significant wealth to those at the top, capitalists and landowners, while real wages stagnated or fell for the majority of workers. This continued inequality pushed people to the edge of what they could tolerate.

We may be seeing that cycle come around again; you could argue we have had a second Engels' pause over the last 50 years of automation and globalisation. As discussed in Chapter IV, real wages for US men with no more than a high school education have fallen since the mid-1970s. Real wages for college graduates have also stagnated since 2010.[180] The seeds of disconnect have been growing for several decades, and arguably, they have manifested in recent votes for Trump in the US and Brexit in the UK. When the economy is not working well, unfortunately, foreigners often become scapegoats. We are seeing this happen now with recent calls for onshoring to bring jobs back home, immigration restrictions, protectionism, and tariffs. If these policies do not result in positive growth and more opportunities, greater frustrations will no doubt follow, including against the machines, especially if millions of AI workers are moving around us.

As we've seen, AI will produce many positives for society *and* create many problems. It's high reward and high risk. As Harari's book *Nexus* argues, AI tools could lead to mass misinformation and manipulation, creating a post-truth society in which trust continues to fall; indeed, we've already seen some of this come to pass. AI will also increase cybersecurity risks, which is ranked as one of the top risks the world faces by the World Economic Forum's Global Risk Survey, behind "misinformation and disinformation" at number four.[181] AI can also amplify financial stability risks, impacting asset valuations, defaults, and jobs. Some even argue that the AI boom has parallels with the TMT boom of the 90s and the subsequent stock market crash, when the dotcom bubble burst. Another risk that's emerging is the concentration of data into fewer hands, which could be a boon for authoritarian power, mass surveillance, and the measurement of everything and everyone. Worse still is the rising use of AI in warfare, with and without humans-in-the-loop to control outcomes in real time.

Several of the world's most prominent AI experts and scientists have also warned of existential risks for humanity from AI. The most cited computer scientist, Yoshua Bengio, said in 2025, "The worst-case scenario is human extinction… If we build AIs that are smarter than us and are not aligned with us and compete with us, then we're basically cooked."[182] In 2024, AI godfather and Nobel Prize winner Geoffrey Hinton estimated there is a 10% to 20% chance AI will lead to human extinction in three decades.[183] Elon Musk has said that "AI is far more dangerous than nukes" and is "our biggest existential threat."[184] From one of the world's most successful entrepreneurs to one of the most prestigious scientists of all time, Stephen Hawking told the BBC in 2014, "The development of full artificial intelligence could spell the end of the human race… It would take off on its own and re-design itself at an ever-increasing rate."[185]

Despite these warnings, we are not tackling these risks quickly enough. There is no off switch with AI. We cannot pull a plug out of the wall. There has been a recent trend of billionaires buying boltholes in remote locations as safe houses, a form of "apocalypse insurance." Perhaps actions speak louder than words. Reid Hoffman, co-founder of LinkedIn, notes, "Saying you're 'buying a house in New Zealand' is kind of a wink, wink, say no more."[186] This trend led to New Zealand restricting foreigners from buying property, encouraging the preppers to find other locations in which to build bunkers in case of SHIF (shit hits the fan) or WROL (without the rule of law).[187]

In AI circles, the probability of catastrophic outcomes or doomsday scenarios is known as P(doom), and it rises with AGI and ASI. Despite this, most governments have their foot on the accelerator towards AGI rather than on the brake. Their thinking and actions are heavily focused on the opportunities rather than the risks. Demis Hassabis, head of Google DeepMind, recently said that there needs to be 10 times more effort and research put into the risks and consequences of AI than is taking place.[188] It is worth pausing for a moment to contemplate that the total annual budgets for external AI safety organisations are less than the collective *daily* spend on AI by the leading AI firms.[189]

Without a considered exploration of the risks and robust plans to mitigate them, people's existential fears could fill this vacuum and bubble up into protests. This happened in the 1950s in response to the nuclear arms race. And these were not fringe events. In 1982, 1 million people gathered in New York City calling for nuclear disarmament and bans on nuclear testing. In October 1983, nearly 3 million people across Western Europe protested against nuclear missile deployment. Their fears were not unfounded; in 1983, a machine error almost started World War III.[190]

Yet the risks posed by nuclear bombs are far easier to see and understand. One of the biggest problems with AI is that the risks are so multifaceted, complex, and difficult to contain. The diffusion and proliferation of AI is much harder to stop than the spread of nuclear weapons because it's intangible. It also poses a complicated trade-off between risk and reward that creates confusion; people may not know whether they should be for it or against it. It can be used to find new drugs to treat people or new pathogens to kill people. As there are so many risks that it poses, it could also create vast anti-AI protests that represent a melting pot of concerns. Some people will be worried about bio-terror risks, others about autonomous weapons, AI surveillance in society, AI fraud, AI pornography, or the climate effects of data centres. Others will see it as an existential risk, and so on. For now, let's return to one specific fear: the risk to our jobs.

WORK, AI ANXIETIES, AND RESISTANCE

Our fears about AI's impact on work are also multifaceted, ranging from fairness in hiring, the use of "bossware," IP protection, data privacy, and beyond. The central issues are job security and wages, but even those present a complex picture, as the outcomes range from workers being augmented by AI to it helping shape better, higher paying jobs to a job apocalypse and economic singularity.

You don't have to look far to find concerns from informed experts. The CEO of Anthropic, Dario Amodei, believes executives are "sugar-coating" its impact and that AI could eliminate half of entry-level white-collar jobs in the next five years and raise unemployment by 10–20%.[191] AI investor Vinod Khosla predicts AI will replace 80% of jobs by 2030.[192] The CEO of Klarna believes AI's impact on jobs will lead to an economic downturn. And the CEO of Fiverr told staff, "AI is coming for your jobs… Are we all doomed? Not all of us, but those who will not wake up and understand the new reality fast are, unfortunately, doomed."[193] Even Pope Leo XIV, in his first address to the Cardinals, noted that AI can pose a threat to "human dignity, justice, and labour."[194]

These are strong opinions, but there are several things we know for sure. We know manufacturing automation has had a negative impact on jobs and wages over the last 50 years. We also know the computer era has created disruption, reduced real wages, and increased inequality. We know workers were impacted by austerity and low growth after the 2008 Financial Crisis, and that this was exacerbated by the pandemic, which drove inflation and further belt-tightening. As a result of all these changes, people are increasingly feeling that growth does not benefit them; indeed, analysis from Pola Lehmann shows more anti-growth than pro-growth sentiment in the last decade in G7 political campaigns.[195] Data shows more workers are not engaged at work, or negatively engaged, rather than positively engaged.[196] We also know trust levels in corporate leaders are at an all-time low, and AI anxiety over jobs has been rising. There is a lot of gunk in the melting pot.

After decades of falling trade union membership, these concerns about joblessness raised union activity across many sectors during and after the pandemic. For example, US retail and culinary unions negotiated contracts to protect human workers, while Las Vegas casinos have agreed to union demands to provide more training and severance to combat new technologies. And before introducing drones or driverless trucks, UPS agreed to negotiate with the Teamsters Union.

And strikes have followed, including high-profile ones in Hollywood. It is now technically possible for AI to bring the deceased back to life in films or to use an actor's avatar when they don't show up or are taking time off because of illness. You can make music using a musician's voice without them being present. In fear of AI substitution, actors and writers stopped making movies until they had negotiated higher wages and rules around how the entertainment industry can, and cannot, use AI. Rolling strikes in 2023 cost the industry $6.5 billion—Luddites in 1811, Hollywood in 2023.

In 2024, it was the turn of the International Longshoremen Association, the largest union for maritime workers in the US. While trade boomed, employment of longshoremen had plunged. According to Professor Jean-Paul Rodrigue, employment at the Port of New York and New Jersey fell from 55,000 in the 1950s to about 4,000 in 2024.[197] Facing more job substitution from AI and robots, 45,000 longshoremen went on strike at 36 ports across the US, the first coastwide strike since 1977. Given this impacted half of US ocean shipping and thus supply chains for multiple industries, J.P. Morgan estimated the cost of that strike on the US economy was between $3.8 billion and $5.0 billion per day.[198] Money talks, and the longshoremen were able to secure terms on automation and a 62% salary increase over the next six years, not 6.2%—62%. It may have helped that Trump backed them, saying that automation was not worth the "distress, hurt, and harm" on US workers.[199]

The success of these strikes by Hollywood and the longshoremen could galvanise other unions in their demands or encourage them to take action to secure rights, protections, and a share of the AI spoils. Unions have traditionally been associated with more blue-collar roles, but with AI now pointing at a plethora of cognitive roles, it is possible that unionisation will suddenly take root among a growing number of middle-class, white-collar workers. This is discussed more in Chapter XII – Employees Vote.

With echoes of the Luddite movement, we have also started to see vandalism of self-driving cars in San Francisco. Some AVs have had their path blocked by cones or by people lying down in the road in an attempt to get social media attention. Windows have been smashed or smeared, bodywork graffitied, tyres slashed, and fireworks placed inside; vehicles have even been set on fire.[200] Driverless cars were torched in the LA immigration raid protests in June 2025, when 700 US Marines and 4,200 members of the National Guard were deployed. With no humans inside to deter this level of violence, AVs were sitting ducks. The images of burning AVs went viral, a symbol of anti-tech or anti-capitalist sentiment, or perhaps just a sign of rising frustrations.

If watching burning AVs is not your vibe, search for videos of "The Blade Runners" in action. These British anti-ULEZ activists have posted videos of themselves cutting down "spy cameras" in public places, one of which had over 1.4 million views. Poles or wires are cut, circuits disabled, and cameras spray-painted or stolen. In a game of cat and mouse, the protestors try to take them down as quickly as they can, and the authorities try to replace them as soon as they can. These are not isolated incidents. London's Metropolitan Police recorded 795 ULEZ camera crimes between April and September 2023 alone, and other cities and countries have been "purged" of these cameras by activists "pissed off about the tyranny reigning over us."[201] Presumably, they took their name from the 1982 cult film *Blade Runner*, in which police units, called "blade runners," try to destroy androids, known as replicants. The replicants were meant to aid society, but increasingly went off script and became a danger to humanity.

Borrowing from another dystopian movie, *V for Vendetta*, protestors around the world have begun wearing the iconic Guy Fawkes mask that the freedom fighter V wore in his quest to bring down the government. The UK responded to this in a new Criminal Justice Bill by including potential imprisonment or fines for protestors covering their faces. The National Police Chiefs' Council Lead for Public Order, Chief Constable BJ Harrington, said, "Covering your face at a protest to conceal identity is not acceptable."[202] Laws and prosecutions supporting AI surveillance or protecting robots will no doubt grow, further inflaming resentment.

The point here is that this rising anxiety about how AI impacts us and our jobs isn't occurring in a vacuum; it's just another layer of discontent built on 50 years of rising inequality and an already polarised political environment in many advanced economies. For example, in 2025, nine years after the UK voted for Brexit, the *Financial Times* noted, "The ascent of reform reflects more epochal shifts underway in UK politics. It underlines the restless disenchantment with status-quo politics, driven by a sense that living standards are sliding and 'nothing works.'"[203]

This concept of discontent being built over time, in layers, is important. Research by the IMF on social unrest in 130 countries between 1985 and 2020 highlights that the most important determinant of 350 indictors they examined is "past turmoil."[204] Unrest begets more unrest within countries, but also in neighbouring countries. This matters because AI anxiety can diffuse widely and quickly, just as AI technologies can, given that it will impact all workers in all sectors, in all countries.

Somewhat ironically, digital networks could accelerate the backlash against digitisation and AI. The IMF found that digital access and social media penetration can be influential in social unrest.[205] As seen in the Arab Spring, the ability to easily communicate, coordinate, and gather makes protesting easier today than at any time in history. Most AI-impacted countries have strong digital network infrastructures, and social media algorithms create echo chambers, feeding us content that only heightens our worries about AI. This can amplify emotions, disagreements, and contagion.

UNEMPLOYMENT AND UNREST

Several studies also confirm what we intuitively know: unemployment impacts political action. Giugni showed that unemployment above 5% was a main factor contributing to social unrest.[206] A paper from the International Labour Organization calculated that since the 2008 Financial Crisis, a one standard deviation increase in unemployment raises social unrest by 0.39 standard deviations.[207] It is possible this will only get worse in the future as rising public debt levels mean governments cannot just throw more borrowed money at the problem.

It is also worth leaders noting that not only do poor economies increase the risk of unrest, but unrest can exacerbate poor economic conditions. A 2021 IMF paper found a close link between unrest and a subsequent decrease in GDP.[208] When unrest leads to political instability, it impacts long-term investment. A related IMF paper looking at 156 unrest events in 72 countries shows that stock markets tend to fall after major events.[209]

If we know that AI can cause job losses and that unemployment can lead to unrest, what else can history teach us as we examine potential scenarios? As daunting as recessions can be, they are officially registered as such when we reach just two quarters of negative GDP, so we could experience more of a quick chill than a long, dark winter. Recessions are not abnormal; they are usually cyclical and often prompt governments to add stimulus to induce higher employment.

It's also true that extreme periods of ultra-high unemployment in major countries have been rare. Two obvious examples come to mind: 30% unemployment in Germany in 1932 and 24.9% unemployment in the US in 1933, with a 40% decline in wages between 1929 and 1933. The difference in response was stark. The Nazi party won less than 3% of the vote in Germany's 1928 elections; five years later, Hitler was the leader. In the US, Roosevelt responded with his New Deal and social safety nets, such as the formation of Social Security and unemployment insurance. While unemployment of this magnitude is unlikely, no one can tell you it will not happen in the AI age. However, it's worth noting that unrest could happen at significantly lower unemployment levels.

The historic average unemployment rate in the United States since 1948 has been 5.7%.[210] A rate exceeding 6% is typically recognized as high and has only happened six times in the last 50 years. US unemployment above 10% is even more rare, happening only twice in the last 75 years—once in the 1982 recession (10.8%) and again in 2020, as a result of the pandemic (14.7%). Given these statistics, Giugni's analysis that unrest may occur at 5% unemployment and concerns that AI is only going to get better and cheaper, US unemployment somewhere over 6% *could* lead to a tipping point. A combination of the unemployed, those with friends who have lost their jobs, and those who fear they could one day be out of a job because of AI adds up to a lot of pitchforks.

Concerns about how AI is changing society at a structural level have already emerged. In mid-2025, James Reed, from the Reed recruitment agency, noted, "This is the first time in my 30-year career that I've seen declining job vacancies combined with economic growth. I'm worried that is more serious than a recession—that it's a sort of structural change."[211] Reed fears automation is the cause. In December 2025, on the prediction site Kalshi, which allows large numbers of people to bet on potential outcomes, 90% thought that US unemployment would rise above 6% by 2030, and 37% thought it would rise above 10%.[212]

If rising unemployment and protests are possible, we need solutions. Even more so if we add in AGI and the risk of an economic singularity. We also need to be able to predict when these might happen. For this, we must find ways to accurately evaluate and track leading indicators of AI impacts—the canaries in the AI coalmine.

CANARIES IN THE AI COALMINE

The phrase "canary in the coalmine" is used metaphorically as an early warning sign of trouble ahead. It's based on the practice of using birds to detect dangerous gases in coal mines, used from the late nineteenth century in Britain until legislation was passed in 1986 that ordered miners to replace canaries with electronic sensors. Technological unemployment arrived for the canaries. What early signs could warn us about our replacement?

1. Young Workers

    Youth unemployment often gets amplified in economic downturns. It ranged from 20–40% during the Arab Spring, peaked at 60% in Greece during the Eurozone debt crisis in 2013,[213] and exceeded 64% in South Africa in 2021.[214] New hiring suffers in economic downturns as firms often freeze expansion in an effort to avoid firing existing staff, allowing natural attrition to reduce headcount. This normal, cyclical pattern is now being compounded by AI, which is eating into starter jobs. Also, companies often point their AI investments at the routine and easy tasks first—those that newbies cut their teeth on. The first rungs of the job ladder for human interns are thus now starting to be filled by AI interns, prompting a structural change in employment.

This is a big problem for this large and important cohort. As discussed in Chapter III – Digital Labour, there are currently over 250 million young NEETs—those not in employment, education, or training—globally, which is a troubling starting position even before AI has begun to have an impact. That half of NEET youth in the UK feel "hopeless about their future" is not healthy for them or society, and it points to potential unrest.[215]

Historically, joblessness has been worse for the least qualified. Between December 2007 and January 2010, over 75% of jobs lost in the US around the 2008 Financial Crisis required a high school education or less.[216] Then, from 2010 to 2016, only 80,000 of the 11.6 million jobs added in the US were for those with only a high school qualification. However, in the future, as AI begins to take on higher-level cognitive roles, qualifications may not protect you.

As an early indicator of what might lie ahead, Stanford University's important 2025 study of US payroll data showed that early career jobs, for those aged 22–25, in sectors most exposed to generative AI have already fallen 13%.[217] In the UK, job search site Adzuna has also noted that entry-level job openings have fallen almost a third since ChatGPT launched in 2022.[218]

2. Graduates

Graduates, an important subsegment of young workers, are for the first time ever experiencing joblessness above the overall unemployment rate in the US and beyond. For US male graduates, unemployment has reached 7%. A study by Oxford Economics found that AI substitution was part of the cause.[219] Job search site Indeed has seen graduate-level role advertisements fall 75% in banking and finance and 65% in software between 2019 and 2025.[220]

Concerns from graduates are understandably rising. Desperately searching for a job, Sebastian Bird said, "I'm despondent. I feel I'm not good enough for what I want to do," despite achieving a double first from Oxford University, an MPhil from Cambridge, and multiple prizes.[221]

Given that the number of graduates is rising and graduate jobs are down, it is no surprise that the average number of applications per job has hit an all-time high in some countries.[222] Recently, it was announced that 12 million applications had been made for 1,700 positions in China, a 7058:1 ratio; it prompted a strong reaction from young Chinese hopefuls. Understandably, graduates around the world are getting increasingly frustrated. They have invested several years of their lives, and often considerable money, to gain the skills and qualifications they need to get a good job; to find that this traditionally safe bridge to a stable career is crumbling is a huge shock and disappointment. If it disintegrates further in the AI age, some form of backlash is probable. A piece of street art by Banksy bears the words: "Sorry! The lifestyle you ordered is currently out of stock," capturing this sense of generational disillusionment and betrayal.[223]

3. Tech Workers

Worryingly, another canary in the AI coalmine is an area that you would imagine would be booming in the digital era: technology jobs, especially coders. AI has proved particularly good at coding and will eventually be able to create software on demand. Microsoft's

CEO has said as much as 30% of the company's code is already written by AI, while Meta's CEO expects half of its code will be written by AI within the next year.[224] AI will produce more AI.

Indeed has said that tech job postings are not only at their lowest level in five years, but in mid-2025, they were already 36% below their February 2020 level.[225] And technology graduate hires have declined 50% from pre-pandemic levels.[226] It wasn't that long ago that we believed computer science degrees were meant to offer some of the most in-demand and high-paying jobs for graduates.

It is highly unusual that this booming sector is cutting jobs—unusual and worrying. For example, Microsoft, one of the most successful companies at the forefront of AI, cut over 7% of its global workforce in the first half of 2025.[227] In a normal upcycle, this would be +7%, not -7%. Given that tech companies are also a leading user of technology, AI job substitution does not bode well for job creation in other industries.

4. Administrative Workers

   One of the most obvious target areas for AI is improving the efficiency of administrative roles that are non-customer-facing. An Institute for Public Policy Research study in 2024 suggested 60% of administrative tasks are automatable.[228] And IBM's CEO has said a third of back-office roles could be replaced by AI.[229]

5. Customer Service Agents

   A lot of AI money and development is being put into augmenting or replacing customer service roles. Gartner predicts that AI agents will deal with 80% of common customer service issues by 2029, without human intervention.[230] They expect this to yield a 30% drop in operational costs. Among the first places this will impact are customer call centres and BPO operations in locations like the Philippines, India, and Mexico.

6. Marketers

   New AI tools can help us perform a lot of marketing tasks, such as brainstorming ideas, creating content, and reaching audiences. According to Mark Zuckerberg, Meta is looking to automate the entire advertising process by 2026, from creating ads to targeting, delivery, and monetisation.[231] Pew Research Center estimates 30% of media jobs could be automated by 2035,[232] and this is already underway, with job site Indeed highlighting a 33% year-on-year fall in media and communications job postings in 2024.[233]

7. Interpreters

   Significant AI advances have been made in the last few years in language translation, both in real-time translation and in different content formats. A Microsoft study of 800 occupations found AI could replace 98% of an interpreter's work.[234] A separate paper by Carl Benedikt Frey and team found that every 1% increase in machine translation usage reduced translator employment growth by 0.7%.[235] Frey also notes, "Improved machine translation could significantly boost global services, offering developing countries a new growth pathway for economic growth," which links back to Chapter III on the rise of digital labour and the knock-on effects of AI.

8. Lawyers

   Another area of risk is the legal industry, particularly for junior lawyers and paralegals. The AI tool

CoCounsel, developed by Anthropic and Thomson Reuters, can reportedly save 30–50% of a lawyer's time.[236] It can find relevant cases, edit documents, and analyse closing arguments. Some firms have found that it is 10 times faster than people doing the same role. Separate research by Goldman Sachs estimates 44% of legal work could be automated.[237]

Having been price takers, subject to a historically expensive service, clients will no doubt welcome lower legal prices, and one way to cut costs is by having fewer high-cost junior lawyers. Also, unlike many industries, law has a low elasticity of demand, so reducing prices is unlikely to stimulate enough new business to create more jobs than are lost. AI could also upend the conventional billing per hour approach and encourage value pricing and set fees. The legal industry has always made more money when more time is required, yet AI is a disruptive change that could dramatically cut how long tasks take.

9. Taxi Drivers

   There are several reasons why the adoption of physical AI will take longer, including regulations, but as we saw in Chapter I, autonomous vehicles are coming. We should monitor what happens to taxi drivers in first-mover cities, such as San Francisco, as it is not clear what out-of-work taxi drivers will move on to next, given their skillset. Maybe deliveries, but robots are coming for this area as well.

10. Gig Workers

   Joblessness among US men in their prime working age, 25–55, who are not in employment or looking for work has risen from 2.5% in 1954 to 11% in 2024.[238] Many others have taken on non-traditional jobs, such as gig work or independent work. For example, Princeton economist Alan Kruger found that 94% of US jobs created in 2005–2015 were non-traditional jobs.[239]

McKinsey has estimated that 20–30% of workers in the US and Europe are involved in independent work.[240] Sometimes this is a preference, or because technology has enabled more people to connect to different types of work. Others are supplementing their income with extra jobs on the side. But others do so because they *have to*. Any job is better than no job. Given that these roles have far less job security, this trend creates less stability and more risk. And this impacts those workers' wellbeing. It is therefore possible that official employment rates do not reflect the scale of building tensions compared with previous periods, where traditional jobs were the norm.

MORE SAY IN DECISION-MAKING

This list of canaries is far from exhaustive, but it's a place to start as we try to understand and monitor how AI is impacting us. Given that AI's impact will be pervasive—touching white-collar and blue-collar jobs, those with high and low qualifications, every part of society and every country—many will be in the firing line or know people who will be, and it will become very personal very quickly.

Change will also become more visible as we see physical robots moving around us. As outlined in Chapter I, 4 billion moving robots by 2050 will change our environment dramatically. Walking in Heathrow airport recently, I passed a cleaning robot that asked me to "please move aside." I was just walking by, not obstructing it or deliberately annoying it. This trivial moment amused me, probably because it was novel, but it is unclear how willingly we will accept robots once they become pervasive. This cleaning robot has taken part of someone's job. Similar to the loss of shops on our high streets or self-checkouts replacing cashiers in stores, we will start to notice the absence of human cleaners, waiters clearing plates, and taxi drivers when autonomous vehicles roll out.

Our reactions to AI will depend on how positive its impact is. If growth, jobs, and wages are buoyant, AI robots that improve our lives will be welcomed. The opposite will happen if AI has a negative impact, threatening our livelihoods. Concern levels are already high; in a recent Gallup survey, 49% think AI is "very different from the technological advancements that came before and threatens to harm humans and society."[241]

Whichever path we take, even optimists acknowledge that a huge transition period will be needed as AI is rolled out. Transitions are usually hard, and it will be harder this time, given the pace, scope, and nature of the changes discussed in Chapter II – The AI Industrial Revolution. There will be losers, and the larger their number, the higher the probability of upset, protests, or public disorder. AI, the digital "foreigner taking our jobs," will be blamed, and there may be more blade runners and people seeking retribution wearing Guy Fawkes' masks.

Most will agree that policy changes tend to occur after an issue has caused problems rather than before it emerges, given how many urgent areas politicians have to firefight. If enough people are worried, vexed, or worse, politicians will be forced to react. Their inability to resolve what people are angry about breeds populism. Social unrest is an extreme version of this process, but AI outcomes could also be extreme.

So, if we acknowledge that AI will raise anxiety over jobs and this is likely to spill over into demands on leaders, what will workers ask for? The simple answer is "more say:" more agency in how AI impacts their work, rather than more AI agents and more say to shape AI rather than be shaped by AI.

It sounds simple, but it is worth looking to the past to see how this might play out.

DEMOCRACY HAPPENS SLOWLY

Historically, democracy has been the exception, not the rule, and a greater say in decision-making has often emerged because of the anger of the many, not the benevolence of the few. This can be seen in the protests and riots that erupted during the Engels' pause, as discussed earlier in the chapter, when working-class wages stagnated as profits soared after the Industrial Revolution.

Wealth and power have been intertwined throughout history. In 1831, when only 1% of the British population could vote, Parliament decided against giving industrial towns better representation. Outrage followed, bubbling into some of the most significant riots in British history. When the Bishop's Palace in Bristol was set alight, and 500 people died, the military got involved. Yet this rioting was a catalyst for three Reform Acts, in 1832, 1867, and 1884. Each broadened the criteria for citizens to vote, expanding the electorate and ushering in an era of greater democracy.

Votes for women, and men over 21 who did not own property, had to wait until 1918, in what is sometimes known as the Fourth Reform Act. Yet women did not gain the right to vote on the same terms as men until the Equal Franchise Act of 1928, meaning that fully equal democracy in the UK is less than a century old. Power is not usually surrendered lightly or quickly.

Passing the first Reform Act, Parliament also had one eye on unrest across the English Channel. The 1830 French Revolution led to the abdication of Charles X, sparking other uprisings in Belgium, Brunswick, Italy, and Poland. Remember the IMF paper that concluded that the most important determinant of unrest is "past turmoil"? Backlash can spread just like technology. The catalyst for the French Revolution was also the desperation of the many. Poor grain harvests in the 1820s had pushed up grain prices, and the people were asking for relief. An economic downturn from 1827 to 1830 had already pushed them to their limits. Yet Charles X didn't listen, bowing to pressure from landowners to keep tariffs on grain in place.

We can take some simple lessons from this period. When economic hardship, unemployment, and inequality become extreme, so too can reactions, even to the point of revolution. Yet if we take revolution out of the equation, it's clear that even if unrest forces governments to act, obtaining a greater democratic say can take a really long time.

While there is much to celebrate in the Industrial Revolution, we must not forget that while the spread of technology and the backlash against it happened relatively quickly, democracy followed slowly. Working-class demands for political change were ignored for years. Wealthy landowning elites influenced Parliament, and elections were often blighted by corruption and bribery. Eventually, job substitution, stagnating wages, and rising inequality from technological change grew until they forced reform. Yet this transition period was difficult for a significant portion of the population for a long period of time. The Luddite riots started in 1811, yet the first Reform Act only materialised in 1832 and the second in 1867.

Looking ahead to the age of AI, we are likely entering the biggest period of change in work that we've ever seen. We would be wise to learn from history and make work transitions as easy as possible for most of the population. Part 2, Chapters VII to XII, offers a variety of solutions towards this end, including those that governments can implement, in terms of social policy, and measures that businesses can take, or might have to.

PART 2

Work WITH Human Workers

VII

AI ABUNDANCE

"A future of abundance. A future where there is no poverty, where people can have whatever they want in terms of goods and services."

—Elon Musk[242]

"[AGI] could help us elevate humanity by increasing abundance, turbocharging the global economy, and aiding in the discovery of new scientific knowledge that changes the limits of possibility."

—OpenAI[243]

THE SOUND OF ABUNDANCE

AI advocates often paint a utopian picture of AI taking society into a period of "abundance." One of the best current examples of this abundance thesis is music.

If you were to travel back 150 years to 1875 and you wanted to listen to music, you would need to find someone to play for you, and they would need an instrument. At that time, a piano would cost the average worker the equivalent of 2,400 hours of work. So, let's make this easier by saying you are an aristocrat who can afford to assemble an orchestra. After the logistical challenge of getting 100 musicians[244] together to practice and then play, you listen to them bring Wagner and Beethoven to life. It turns out your partner fancies a bit of Irish folk music instead, but that is not on the music menu.

Thankfully, the record player was invented shortly afterwards, in 1877, by Thomas Edison, and this improves your and your spouse's options considerably—but only if you can afford it. The first phonograph retailed at $150 in 1891, the equivalent of over $5,000 in today's money. And you'd likely struggle to buy one, as they only started to be released to the masses in 1895. Even then, it would be difficult to get hold of some records to play. And at this point, they weren't even easy to hear, as music critic Herman Klein described an early demonstration, "It sounded to my ear like someone singing about half a mile away or talking at the other end of a big hall, but the effect was rather pleasant."[245]

Roll on to 1906, and music was broadcast on the radio for the first time ever: a Christmas Eve violin solo of "O Holy Night." But you didn't have much choice in what you listened to. For that, you had to wait another 15 years, when radio stations started multiplying in the 1920s. The first radios cost $200 in 1920, over $3,000 in today's money. The BBC was founded in 1922, but music lovers had to wait until 1967 for the UK's first music-dedicated radio station. At that time, a record cost about $4, or $40 today. Many of us saved our weekly pocket money just to be able to buy one record.

Another big breakthrough came in 2001, with Apple's iPod. Other MP3 players already existed, but Steve Jobs captured the zeitgeist with the iPod's slick design, ease of use, and the marketing catch phrase: "1,000 songs in your pocket."

Now fast-forward to today. Log on to Spotify, and you have access to over 100 million tracks, wherever you are in the world. Listen to your heart's content. Switch songs whenever you want. Discover new artists or play your old favourites, get personalised recommendations, and share music with friends. You can even have your own personalised, always-on AI DJ. Over 400 million users get the basic service for free.[246] Another 268 million pay a subscription, at $11.99 a month. Multiple competitors, like Amazon Music, Apple Music, Deezer, Pandora, SoundCloud, Tidal, and YouTube Music, offer similar competitive packages, which keep pricing low.

As you can see, technological progress in music over the last 150 years has allowed costs to decline towards zero, access to be instantaneous around the world, and choice to be multiplied to more songs than you can listen to in seven lifetimes. This *is* abundance.

Now extrapolate that concept of abundance into other areas. We already have an abundance of content—written, audio, and TV—and AI will help create even more, as well as translate content into every language. If you have a phone and an internet connection, many forms of education are already abundant. YouTube is arguably the largest free education resource in the world, allowing you to learn about almost anything at any time. For more specific educational content, the non-profit Khan Academy is a free provider to over 100 million people in 190 countries and in over 50 languages.[247] And they have already rolled out an AI teaching assistant, Khanmigo, that acts like a personal tutor. Unlike human tutors, Khanmigo is available 24/7/365, offering real-time feedback, and it remembers all your past learnings—all this for just $4 a month.

Parts of healthcare are also becoming more abundant, such as health content. We make hundreds of millions of health-related web searches globally every day. With over

5,000 new scientific papers published daily, AI will help patients and doctors keep on top of new developments far more easily.[248] AI is also helping us monitor and analyse our health data via wearable devices, like watches, that track our sleep, fitness, heart rate, and more, offering personalised predictions. It will help increase remote access to health services, reduce healthcare costs, and aid the discovery of new science and medicines to help billions of people live healthier lives. For example, Moderna's 2020 mRNA COVID-19 vaccine was designed in just two days with the help of AI.[249] As mentioned earlier, DeepMind's AlphaFold breakthroughs on folding proteins using AI are estimated to have saved over a billion research hours.[250] And Hippocratic AI can offer health services to patients that were simply not affordable before.

Demis Hassabis, co-founder of Google DeepMind, declared, "We are in the renaissance of scientific discovery... [and] AI has incredible potential to help with humanity's greatest challenges. It will be one of the most transformative and beneficial technologies we will ever invent."[251] Microsoft CEO Satya Nadella believes that AI could deliver more societal benefits than the Industrial Revolution.

In their book *Abundance: The Future Is Better Than You Think*, Peter Diamandis and Steven Kotler conclude that, "Growing technologies will enable us to make greater gains in the next two decades than we have in the previous 200 years. We will soon have the ability to meet and exceed the basic needs of every man, woman, and child on the planet. Abundance for all is within our grasp."[252] They suggest technological progress will allow us to solve many of the world's biggest problems and lead to an abundance of food (using solutions such as lab-grown meat), water (desalination), energy (solar), education, transportation, communication, and healthcare. Their positivist conclusions ask us to shift to a mindset of possibility when it comes to AI rather than the zero-sum thinking of a scarcity mindset.

Similarly, while the first part of this book focused on the risks of job substitution, AI robots and agents could also bring abundance to many, whether it's as chauffeurs and butlers, personal assistants or agents for tasks, coaches for work, life coaches for outside of work, personal tutors, healthcare assistants, music tutors, dating concierges, therapists, and even virtual friends. These are only available to the rich today, but in the next decade or two, they will be feasible for many.

As OpenAI CEO Sam Altman told the US Senate, "The next decade will be about abundant intelligence... [and a world] where people can do more—be more fulfilled, live a better life."[253] So not just abundance but the allure of a better life with more fulfilment—this is the big opportunity of AI. The outcomes of an abundance of intelligence, accessible on demand and at a cost that heads towards zero, are unknowable at this point, but as trends develop, some will always overreach when predicting the future. There is talk about "radical abundance," the "elimination of scarcity," and a Star-Trek-type world in which goods are freely available to all, money becomes obsolete, and poverty is eliminated. As Elon Musk has commented, in this world, jobs may also be obsolete because they are not needed.[254] A utopian abundance thesis extrapolates the billionaire lifestyle to the many, allowing them to choose how they spend their days. It's easy to see the appeal of this vision.

A WORLD TRANSFORMED

If this sounds like science fiction to you, consider what a person in 1875, even a king or queen, would have made of having access to limitless music or intelligence on demand for free in 2025. Abundance theorists rightly highlight the amazing technological changes we've experienced over the past few hundred years and the transformative impacts they've had: flushing toilets became widespread in the mid-1800s, and sewage began to flow away in pipes rather than down the street; running water in homes became common in the late-1800s; electricity became the norm in homes in the early 1900s, providing abundant light and heat and, later on, powering washing machines, fridges, cookers, TVs, and wi-fi. On a broader scale, developments in food production have allowed for an abundance that's enabled an eightfold increase in the world's population since 1800. And progress in science and healthcare has increased life expectancies by a remarkable four months each year since 1950.[255]

Abundance already exists in communication. No American had a telephone in 1870, and its inventor, Alexander Bell, only ventured to suggest that a telephone in each town was possible.[256] Now we can all use messaging apps and video calling to communicate with friends, family, or clients around the world instantly, from the palm of our hands, at a near-zero cost. While we cannot yet teleport, we do have an abundance of transport options, from bicycles (1790) and trains (1825) to cars (1886) and planes (1903), having previously been dependent on our feet or horses.

In the last 150 years, school education has gone from the preserve of the rich to free for all in most countries. As a result, we have gone from most people being illiterate to over half attending university in England.[257] Education opportunities helped increase the participation of women in the workforce in the US from 33% in 1948 to over 56% today.[258]

Improvements also extend to wealth. As Steven Landsburg notes, "Modern humans first emerged about 100,000 years ago. For the next 99,800 years or so, nothing happened... then—just a couple of hundred years ago—people started getting richer. And richer and richer still."[259] In 1950, almost half the world lived in extreme poverty. This has fallen to less than 10% today.[260]

In 1900, the average American started work at 14, spent much of their life in backbreaking work, and died aged 47.[261] Today, many work in comfortable, air-conditioned offices, live to over 80, and spend half their lives in education and retirement. Commenting on this progress in 2017, President Obama said, "If you had to choose any moment in history in which to be born, you would choose right now… The world has never been healthier or wealthier, or better educated, or in many ways more tolerant or less violent."[262] Surely, if Adam Smith, when he was penning his *Wealth of Nations* thesis in 1776—by candlelight, with a quill pen, in a house without running water, flushing toilets, electricity, or cold beer—found out what we would achieve by 2025, he would have been amazed at how quickly we reached abundance.

DYNAMIC CAPITALISM AND AI FOR THE MANY

As remarkable as this progress has been over the last few hundred years, the new hope is that AI will supercharge it, along with productivity and growth. AI could lead to an intelligence explosion—a new renaissance of science and creativity to help solve our greatest challenges. The *UN Activities on AI Report* highlights over 400 AI projects already taking place that support the UN Sustainable Development Goals.[263] This shows the possibility of AI "for good" and "for the many."

A primary reason why capital is flowing, or indeed flooding, into AI is that new transformer models appear to be game-changing for productivity. Initial studies point to productivity improvements of up to 50% in coding, 37% in writing, 45% for first-time drafts in law, 25% in consulting, and 14% in call centres. These could signal a step change after sagging productivity in advanced economies over the past two decades.

Many have tried to quantify the opportunity, and it has become a game of one-upmanship. Price Waterhouse Coopers (PwC) forecasts AI could contribute up to $15.7 trillion to the global economy by 2030.[264] McKinsey believes AI could add $17.1–$25.6 trillion by 2030.[265] Aghion and Bunel estimate that AI could increase productivity growth by 0.8% to 1.3% annually over the next decade,[266] while Erik Brynjolfsson thinks US productivity could be double the 1.4% forecast by the Congressional Budget Office.[267] AI investor and uber-bull Cathie Wood, CEO of ARK Invest, predicts that technology will cause global GDP growth to more than double, from 3% to 7–8% per year.[268] Top of the charts goes to Epoch AI's view that economic growth could exceed 20% per year.[269]

Techno-optimists see this AI engine room reviving economies, acting as a rising tide that will benefit most. Unlike zero-sum economics, which posits that one person is better off because someone else is worse off, this abundance would create many winners. Not surprisingly, this thesis has a strong appeal for politicians, many of whom are backing pro-AI innovation policies. For example, in 2024, Tony Blair argued that AI was our big hope, given rising debt levels and the fact that we've reached the upper limits of the traditional tax and spend approach. He said, "The only game-changer is the full embrace of technology, especially the new developments in artificial intelligence… [this] is the only answer to Britain's productivity challenge, and over time, it can turbocharge growth."[270]

For them, capitalism's profit motive will only aid this AI-driven growth, and indeed, it has proven successful over the past 200 years in encouraging entrepreneurship, innovation, and dynamism. "Creative destruction," first coined by Werner Sombart in 1913, in which capital, resources, and people are better deployed in a continuous cycle, is a natural part of this model. So, while some jobs are lost, new ones are created, and workers adapt. Entirely new markets are started, while cheaper goods and services increase demand, leading to higher overall employment, not lower. This crucial concept—how AI can create new jobs to offset the ones lost—is explored in more depth in the next chapter. Suffice to say, the abundance theorists are right to note that fears of technological unemployment over the past 200 years have proven incorrect.

THE THEORY OF ABUNDANCE VERSUS THE REALITY

There is a lot to like and aspire towards in this quest for abundance. Leaders can use it to inspire optimism and hope. However, before leaping towards unfettered AI adoption, driven by unfettered capitalism, there are several counterpoints that need some discussion.

1. It's Not How People Feel

    Explaining the abundance thesis can provoke strong reactions. One person told me, "Can the abundance peddlers just 'fuck off' or come and speak to people in the real world?" Telling people who might be struggling that they are lucky to have flushing toilets, electricity, and abundant internet content will make many feel frustrated and patronised, not inspired.

    Engagement levels at work are dreadfully low globally, as is trust in businesspeople and political leaders. A 2025 survey by Pew showed that just 26% of Americans and 19% of British people believe the next generation will be better off than they are.[271] Research also shows this is not a post-pandemic lull or a short-term blip. A 2015 YouGov survey asked, "All things considered, do you think the world is getting better or worse, or neither getting better nor worse?" The best score came in Sweden, with 10% feeling things were improving, but others believed it was worse, with the US at 6%, Britain at 4%, and France at 3%.[272] Most people feel they are going backwards, not progressing into abundance.

When people feel so gloomy about the present and future, you have to ask why. Some posit that it's because of unrealistic expectations, laziness, or the paradox of choice, in which an abundance of options can counter-intuitively lead to less satisfaction. Yet the reality is that we've had poor productivity in advanced economies for the last few decades, so these beliefs may not be far off the mark. Digitisation has been more mirage than miracle. Worse still for many, digitisation has brought increased competition, rather than increased progress. A popular term for this in China is "involution," with escalating effort required not to fall behind in education and work, altering the notion that increased effort leads to increased reward. And involution has spread. US economist Daron Acemoğlu notes, "Digital technologies severed the link between economic growth and shared prosperity."[273] As AI accelerates, leaders should not just assume that more digitisation is better; in a recent US Harris Poll, two-thirds of respondents said they would prefer to return to a time when they were not "plugged in."[274]

2. We've Had a Drop in Productivity

Productivity, the primary determinant of living standards, has slowed across the OECD, from an annual improvement of 2% in the 1990s to 0.8% in the last decade.[275] In the UK, the Office for National Statistics noted that total factor productivity in the market sector, which excludes government, fell 0.6% in 2024.[276] Despite the fact that the internet era gave workers access to abundant knowledge and the ability to connect and collaborate with people around the world, productivity regressed rather than soared.

There are many arguments for poor productivity, from mismeasurement to the low-hanging fruit having already been picked or a shift towards services, but we should acknowledge that productivity opportunities from digitisation have not materialised as hoped. This is partly because computers, and then the internet, have primarily focused on making existing services more efficient, driving prices down and increasing concentration and profits in superstar firms. This has created a bifurcation in productivity, with a rise for leading firms while the majority have lagged. Even if the abundance theory is appealing, it would be remiss of us to ignore this lesson. The same dynamics are very possible in the AI age.

3. Productivity Can Take (A Long) Time

   How long are you willing to wait for a rise in productivity—for the long-awaited reward? One of the arguments for the current "productivity paradox" is that it *will* come in time—that the digital economy is still in its early phases, and productivity improvements happen with a lag. Given that computing and the internet have been with us for decades, this *mañana* argument highlights a risk inherent in the AI abundance thesis.

   As fast as the pace of change is, it's true that, historically, productivity gains from general-purpose technologies have taken decades to emerge. For example, it took 61 years for steam engines to improve productivity, 32 for electricity, and 15 for the internet, according to J.P. Morgan.[277] While AI could be much quicker, its adoption still faces friction when it comes to business implementation, people's resistance, regulations, and the technology itself. And it's worth noting that we have had AI, in some form, since the 1950s, and there's not yet been a noticeable uplift to productivity.

We can talk about theories and trends, but the real world is often far more complicated. For example, since Diamandis and Kotler's book *Abundance* came out in 2012, educational technology tools have grown rapidly, as they suggested they would, yet college tuition fees have risen 37%, and school tuition prices are up 59% between January 2012 and 2025.[278] Despite the rapidly declining price of solar energy, driven by technological innovation, household energy costs are up 41% since January 2012. Similarly, despite the promise of new digital services reducing healthcare costs over the last few decades, medical care prices rose by 40% between January 2012 and 2025. Going back even further, during the last four decades of digitisation, healthcare prices have risen over 200% and education over 600% relative to US household income.[279] There are many factors that go into these supply chains, but the result, so far, has been the opposite of abundant education, energy, and healthcare.

There have been bottlenecks in AI supply chains that have slowed down our path to abundance, such as building data centres and new power plants, upgrading energy grids or legacy technology, organising data assets, finding top AI talent, and training staff. These physical asset upgrades cost trillions of dollars and therefore take time.

4. AI Might Not Have as Big an Impact as We Think

While it is possible that the productivity upsides of AI are better and faster than expected, this is not a given. Nobel Prize winner Daron Acemoğlu estimates AI will only have a very modest 0.05% annual impact on productivity going forward, to produce a GDP increase of 1.1–1.6%, in total, over the next 10 years.[280] Yes, total, not annual.

The latest estimate for labour productivity by the US Congressional Budget Office is 1.3% for the next 30 years, despite all the talk of how AI will supercharge it.[281] This is lower, not higher, than the 1.6% experienced over the *last* 30 years. Given the productivity disappointments of the last 20 years, seeing may be believing.

Even if AI productivity surprises us, demographics will likely drag real GDP growth the opposite way, as the working-age population (WAP) increasingly shrinks. In advanced economies, the WAP increased by 0.5% per year between 2000 and 2009, yet this fell to 0.0 in 2010–2020, and it is projected to decline by 0.3% per year, on average, between 2023 and 2040.[282] This makes AI gains even more important, but it means that a growth miracle may not be as buoyant as people hope.

5. The Rewards of Abundance Are Often Unequal

If the gains of abundance had been more widely distributed throughout history, there would probably be many more abundance optimists. Rising inequality is primarily a political economy issue rather than an AI one, but as Hicks noted in the 1930s, technology can be biased against labour. This was true in the First Industrial Revolution, and similarly, pay has not risen in line with productivity since the 1980s. As a result, income inequality has risen sharply since 1980 to levels last seen in the 1920s,[283] and there is little evidence of the political will for redistribution policies to change this situation within countries, let alone between countries.

Despite the declining poverty levels mentioned, many remain in a financially precarious position. Almost 40% of OECD households risk falling into poverty if they lose three months of income, and 21% of those in European OECD countries report difficulties in making ends meet.[284]

After five decades of US economic growth, real wages have declined for workers with less than a college degree.[285] Many others have been forced out of the workforce or have opted out. The proportion of economically inactive men of prime working age has grown in America from 2% in 1954 to 11% in 2024, and almost half of these cite obsolete skills as a barrier to employment.[286] And globally, a worrying one in four young people in 2025 are NEETs—not in employment, education, or training.[287]

Joblessness has knock-on implications for self-esteem, health, happiness, mortality, crime, and social unrest. Levels of depression have risen. So too have "deaths of despair," from suicide or drug or alcohol abuse, to levels three times higher than road deaths and six times higher than homicide.[288] For those continuing to struggle financially and worried about the security of their jobs, it is difficult to believe that abundance is just around the corner. And as we've discussed, the outlook for jobs, wages, and inequality *could* get much worse in the AI age.

6. AI May Increase Time Poverty

Finally, AI may steal rather than add to the thing we all want more of: time. We only have 24 hours in a day to juggle the multiple aspects of our lives, and for many of us, the best gift would be an abundance of time. However, digitisation has increased rather than decreased time pressure: more devices, more multitasking, and more always being "on." Research suggests workers feel more time-squeezed, rushed, and harried than ever. The promise of digital technology to free workers up has not materialised yet. Instead, like the Red Queen in *Alice in Wonderland*, many feel they have to run even faster to stand still. Will AI come to the rescue to create more time, or will the treadmill just spin faster? This is explored in more depth in Chapter IX – Better Jobs.

AN ABUNDANCE OF WORKERS

Abundance optimists will argue that AI can improve all the areas above. A productivity boost could increase economic growth and wealth at a faster pace than we have seen before. AI can free people up from mundane tasks to reduce time poverty. AI could make people feel better and more fulfilled. These seductive arguments may prove correct, but going full speed into AI is also likely to lead to a different form of abundance—an abundance of workers.

In contrast to the increase in price of education, energy, and healthcare since Diamandis and Kotler's book *Abundance* came out, the computer component of US inflation data has fallen 47% between January 2012 and 2025. While this benefits consumers, cheaper technology also competes with workers. This trend will continue ahead.

Digital formats also bring a paradigm shift in competition. Unlike physical products, digital products can be replicated at zero cost; be dematerialised to be distributed at near-zero cost; be non-rivalrous, so consumption by one person does not reduce the amount available to others; create instant feedback in the form of data, which can then be used to make products better, such as adding new functions or greater personalisation; and be updated or upgraded often to make products better rather than obsolete. Returning to the original example in this chapter, it was the digitisation of music that made it abundant.

Chances are, you access music today via a smartphone, but take a moment to think about other apps on your phone. Before smartphones existed, you probably physically owned an alarm clock, a torch, a calculator, a diary, a camera, a video camera, photo albums, an answering machine, computer games, a sat nav, and a wallet or purse containing cards, tickets, or keys. These, and other physical items we used to own, have often been replaced by free digital apps. This is good news for consumers and for abundance, but it was not good news for the companies that previously made these products. They got digitised and disrupted. Prices fell towards zero, and their profits disappeared or shifted.

A similar process could happen next for work and workers, moving from physical atoms to digital bits. AI and AI agents are made of bits. NVIDIA's point about aiming to have 50,000 employees and 100 million AI agents points to a new proliferation of AI workers. Physical AI robots are different, given they are made of atoms, but their brains and ability to do more via updates are largely down to bits—digital brains in a physical shell.

Previous chapters have detailed the potential explosion of AI tools, AI agents, and AI robots, as well as the decline in the price of intelligence towards zero, even as AI capabilities get better. AI will create more AI, and robots will make more robots. The result, an abundance of AI workers, would clearly have a big impact on human workers. By extension, given that labour is a critical factor in the cost of goods and services, lower labour costs could increase corporate profit margins and lead to an abundance of returns to investors. This is why investment is flooding in.

AN ABUNDANCE OF CHOICES AND DILEMMAS

Abundance is not a new idea. This compelling concept has resurfaced throughout the ages. In Greek mythology, Plutus, the god of wealth, is often depicted holding a cornucopia—a horn overflowing with produce. Romans prayed to Pomona, the goddess of fruitful abundance, and Copia, the goddess of abundance and plenty. Carlo Tapia's 1638 *Treatise on Abundance* offered governments practical tools to tackle famine and poverty, which had become a common problem. John Randolph Price's international bestseller on manifesting wealth, *The Abundance Book,* was published in 1987, and today, a search for books on abundance on Amazon offers 50,000 alternatives to choose from.

Yet those who write about abundance tend to focus on the positives of a post-scarcity society in which many goods are free to all. While it's true that jobs may not be needed in a world of abundance, this would be a big leap from where we are today, and there's a high risk of a long and dystopian transition on the path towards utopia. There may be more pain before gain. People, therefore, rightly want to *see* rather than *read* about abundance. And they want to understand *how* we will get there. The reality is that abundance won't be a linear process. It will take place for certain products, such as music, because it can be digitised, and certain people, such as the wealthy, first.

Given abundance is very unlikely to benefit all at the same time, it seems wise for society to discuss and agree on what to prioritise. Otherwise, in a capitalist society, AI will likely be pointed at the biggest profit opportunities rather than the areas that most benefit humanity. For example, do we want innovation in AI to focus on labour substitution to create higher profits or on abundant healthcare and education in the service of all? It *is* possible to incentivise which AI investments we want most. These choices are explored more in the final chapters of this book, focusing on how leaders can direct the future of AI with intention. Ultimately, it's about asking how we create the world we want our children to inherit.

In contrast, Ezra Klein and Derek Thompson, in their 2025 book *Abundance: How We Build a Better Future*, argue that putting too many checks and balances in place is precisely what will prevent abundance in the long run. They argue that rules, process, and bureaucracy are reducing the progressivism needed to reach it. Their key solution is to reduce political and regulatory barriers to unlock more innovation. This "go faster" approach could accelerate positive abundance outcomes, but it could also accelerate negative consequences, such as job substitution.

Regardless of which approach we take as a society, we must debate *where* we want to go and *how* we will get there. At this point, most politicians are taking a pro-innovation stance on AI, hoping for more growth and fearing being left behind. This extends to corporate leaders, worrying they will lose market share, or worse, become irrelevant, if they don't evolve quickly enough. In general, political and corporate leaders are not focusing on the more difficult and polarising political economy topic of how to distribute the gains from technological progress. We know that tackling difficult issues—high debt levels, climate change, energy independence, business concentration, or inequality—often requires sacrifices that are difficult to get agreement on. So, instead, we kick the can down the road and hope things don't break.

None of this is easy. How does one balance the utopian allure of abundance versus dystopian fears of existential risk to humanity or a job apocalypse? Is it different this time or not? If these decisions—and debates—were not complicated enough, the speed of change makes it difficult for anyone to stay on top of AI developments, and AI can be technically challenging to understand. Even experts don't agree on what path to take or what the risk levels are.

There is a lot to admire in the AI visionaries and doers who are creating the future. Having seen many CEOs and entrepreneurs sell their ideas to investors over the years, I have also learnt that strong convictions do not always translate to being right. The tunnel vision needed to sell their products convincingly and bring to life the future opportunity of their company is also what can lead to blind spots and a lack of objectivity. This is what plagued Wall Street before the financial crash in 2008 and distorted investments during the 1990s TMT boom. The reality is almost always more complicated than the idea.

Given the complexity of the AI picture, including the many conflicting upsides and downsides, there is a danger that overwhelm leads to decision paralysis. An abundance of choices and dilemmas can reduce our ability to make decisions or be satisfied with them when we do. But debate, choose, and enact we must. It would be a mistake to outsource these decisions to AI.

To end the chapter, I want to draw out some key thoughts on how abundance has evolved over time:

1. We can be inspired by the concept of abundance, yet we should be thoughtful about which areas we want abundance in, rather than leaving the choice to the invisible hand of the market.
2. Having seen and studied innovation for 30 years, I believe this time it's different, and I am very optimistic about AI innovation opportunities and a new renaissance of discovery ahead.
3. Mindful that digitisation has not delivered the productivity and growth that it promised, I am still somewhat optimistic that AI will improve both. However, bottlenecks will slow the path towards abundance.

4. I am very concerned that the abundance of non-human workers will happen before we reach points 1–3 and, by extension, that there will not be enough transition support for human workers.
5. Given the world's track record of dealing with challenging dilemmas, I am very pessimistic that the rewards of abundance will be widely or equitably shared for some time.

So, what options do workers have to help steer AI towards the upsides from abundance and away from the downsides—towards points 1–3 and away from 4 and 5? These are explored in the next chapters, starting with the need for a boom in intelligence and innovation, leading to a boom in new jobs.

VIII

NEW JOBS

"If men have the talent to invent new machines that put men out of work, they have the talent to put those men back to work."

—President John F. Kennedy, 1962[289]

"A new era of production has begun. Its principles of organization are as different from those of the industrial era as those of the industrial era were different from the agricultural. The cybernation revolution has been brought about by the combination of the computer and the automated self-regulating machine. This results in a system of almost unlimited productive capacity, which requires progressively less human labor."

—Open letter sent to President Lyndon B. Johnson in 1964, from a group of scientists and social theorists, including several Nobel Prize winners[290]

A WORLD OF POSSIBILITY

Did you have a favourite programme when you were a small child? One of mine was *Mr Benn*. Growing up in the UK in the 1970s, before satellite TV, videos, the internet, or gaming, our viewing choice was limited to four TV channels. The cartoon character Mr Benn was an ordinary man, living on an ordinary street, who used to walk to the local costume shop to try on outfits. He would then walk through another door in the fitting room into new worlds. In one episode, he was a knight; in others, he was a wizard, a clown, a hunter, a zookeeper, a spaceman, a diver, a chef, a gladiator, and a cowboy. In each episode, viewers were taken on a different adventure, where they could see him embodying a different role. Then, at the end, we'd return with Mr Benn to the comfort and stability of home. We saw a world of possibility, with layers of morality. There was a lot to admire in Mr Benn's kindness and his desire to do the right thing and make the world a little better.

In the real world of work, Seamus McSporran holds the record for the number of jobs held at the same time.[291] Living on the Isle of Gigha, off the west coast of Scotland, Seamus was the driver of the ambulance, school bus, bus, and taxi. He was the accountant, the boatman, the shopkeeper, the police officer, the insurance agent, and the undertaker. He did what was needed, carrying out an impressive 14 jobs simultaneously for the residents of this 10-mile-long island, until he retired in 2000, two years before the community buyout of the island.

If you think that's impressive, meet Jan Leighton, who holds the world record of 3,395 acting roles across TV, film, and commercials.[292] While not different jobs per se, I am guessing Mr Benn would have been impressed.

One of our great skills as humans is the ability to adapt. In the world of work, that includes moving to jobs that are in demand and away from those that are not. Research suggests workers will have 12 jobs and seven careers across their working lives, on average, so getting good at change is a life skill.[293] It helps to know which areas are growing and which are declining. Yet it also requires there to be enough new jobs to go to. As AI encroaches on many existing roles, it could interfere with our ability to adapt and thrive in the new world of work.

A RICH HISTORY OF NEW JOB GROWTH

The quote at the start of this chapter, from experts writing to President Johnson, echoes the fear that's surfaced many times over the last 200 years: that this time it's different and that technological unemployment is just around the corner. Writing at the dawn of the computer era, these experts were, in fact, wrong, and Kennedy was right: we *have* kept producing new jobs for workers. Despite waves of digitisation and automation, US unemployment reached a 53-year low of 3.6% in 2022.

And we're not just talking about more jobs but *billions* more jobs. This low unemployment is even more remarkable given that global population levels have risen from 2.5 billion in 1950 to 8.2 billion in 2024.[294] Coupled with more women entering the formal economy, the working-age population increased from 1.5 billion to 5.2 billion over this period.[295] This absorption of billions of workers happened because more jobs were created than were lost to automation. And as happened in previous industrial revolutions, workers adapted. In 1500, 74% of UK workers were in agriculture; now just 1.4% are.[296] In 1953, 32% of the workforce was in manufacturing; now only 7.9% are.[297]

Economists have proposed several theories to explain why jobs keep growing despite substitution by technology. The first started as an observation by William Jevons in 1865; he noticed that when steam engines became more efficient, requiring less coal per engine, it increased demand for engines, and overall coal consumption rose. This has become known as the Jevons paradox: as costs come down, consumption rises.

Shortly afterwards, in 1891, British economist David Frederick Schloss expanded on this concept. He said that if new innovations reduced wages, it would become cheaper to hire more workers. In addition, new innovations can create entirely new industries, requiring more workers. New workers increase consumption and economic growth. So, while roles change in a dynamic economy, the overall pie grows. This is known as the lump of labour fallacy. In other words, there is not a fixed amount of work to be done in an economy, and work is not zero-sum in that a machine substitutes for a person. Politicians from the left and the right often anchor their policies to this "grow the pie" concept, even if they differ in how to share the pie.

The automation paradox, also called the automation fallacy, builds on this further, with a specific focus on technology. In his book *The New Goliaths,* James Besson notes automation can lead to more employment if it *helps* workers rather than *replaces* them—in other words, if it is task-augmenting rather than task-replacing. Bessen uses the example of the introduction of the ATM in the 1970s, which freed bank tellers from handing out cash to do more complex, higher-value tasks for customers. Bank branches grew. Contrary to fears, three decades after the first ATM, there were more, not fewer, bank tellers. Yet the world can be complicated, and change is not linear. It's also true that bank deregulation took place, and now, bank branches are being shut at a rapid rate. But people like simple explanations.

And as discussed in the last chapter, the process of creative destruction, where innovation disrupts jobs and industries in the short term but leads to gains in the long term, is evident throughout our capitalist history. As an example, the pager died when the smartphone emerged, and since 2008, an entirely new $600 billion app economy has boomed.[298]

A final economic concept is elasticity of demand. When goods have high elasticity, people buy more of them when the price drops, and overall revenue rises. This was what Jevons and Schloss observed, but it is not the case with *all* goods. Tobacco is very inelastic, so when prices rise or fall, demand does not change much. The same is true for some other goods, such as basic foods, and for some jobs. AI can create more jobs when it is directed towards areas with high elasticity of demand. Adding to these elasticities, the significant rise in populations has created demand for more goods and services, and therefore jobs, while the rise of the middle classes has increased consumption of goods that were out of reach to previous generations: phones, cars, holidays, and so on. We will come back to this concept later as it is an important topic that does not get enough airtime.

Turning from theory to real-world data, an excellent paper by Autor and colleagues in 2021 calculated that 63% of US employment in 2018 was in job titles that did not exist in 1940.[299] Research by Acemoğlu and Restrepo also shows that job substitution from automation between 1947 and 1987 was offset by the growth in new jobs and that half of employment growth between 1980 and 2010 came from the creation of new jobs.[300]

We can take comfort from this rich history of new job growth throughout periods of technological innovation and in the economic stewardship of countries' central banks, especially during the 2008 Financial Crisis and the COVID-19 pandemic shocks. Looking forward, the WEF sees this trend continuing, predicting 170 million new jobs will be created between 2025 and 2030, which will more than offset the 92 million lost.[301] The authors conclude that rather than AI displacing lots of jobs, the jobs pie will grow 7% by 2030.

WHERE WILL NEW JOBS BE?

It is always easier to pick out existing jobs that are vulnerable to this creative destruction process than imagine new ones that have yet to be invented. However, it is possible. Helping investors see around these corners was part of my previous roles.[302] New economic themes and new jobs must start somewhere, and then they grow. Finding big, job-hungry megatrends is what we are after here—wide swim lanes that will carry lots of workers along and upwards. The good news is, three of these megatrends are already up and running, and a likely wild card is coming up behind them. Let's explore them in more detail.

1. Technology Jobs

   Even though AI's coding skills are threatening coders, and robots can manufacture more robots, AI will create plenty of new jobs in the technology sector. Here are some examples: AI engineers; prompt engineers; data annotators; AI content editors; AI talent managers; AI managers; AI psychotherapists, to better understand algo thinking; AI supply chain managers; AI ethicists; AI regulators; AI auditors; robot design, testing, sales, installation, and maintenance; installing and running the internet of things, from connected homes to connected factories; wearables experts; virtual world designers; quantum computing programmers; security analysts; blockchain and digital currency specialists; data centre and smart grid builders; digital death managers, assisting with the management of a deceased person's digital footprint; avatar builders; and even grief tech specialists, helping people talk to digital representations of deceased loved ones.

Combining transport and technology, a new industry will grow around autonomous vehicles, from designers and builders to managers and maintenance. The drone market will soar. A new electric aircraft and air taxi market is just starting to take off. With even higher ambitions, literally, the space economy will boom, from space tourism to space mining. Spurred by advances in technology and Trump's support, the defence tech industry is also growing fast.

Given AI has a part in most of these jobs, developing these skills is obviously crucial. A recent report from PwC, which analysed almost a billion job adverts around the world, found that workers with AI skills were being paid 56% more than workers without AI knowledge. PwC noted, "Contrary to fears about job losses, job numbers—and wages—are growing in virtually every AI-exposed occupation, including the most highly automatable jobs."[303] It has also been reported that some top AI professionals have been offered $100 million bonuses to move firms.[304] Yes, $100 million per professional. So, growth in jobs and in wages.

2. Green Jobs

Climate change requires an enormous reengineering of the way we power factories, homes, and transportation, which is why Al Gore has described sustainability as the biggest investment opportunity in history.[305] While political tailwinds have slowed recently in the US, the longer-term need for climate change mitigation will create new jobs, from the installation of renewables and building of electric vehicles to energy auditors. Although this trend also comes with a substitution of brown jobs, those in the fossil fuel industry, the IEA estimates that, by 2030, in the move to net zero, 30 million new jobs will be created and 13 million will be lost globally.[306] To put this 17 million net addition into context, 161 million people were employed in the US at the end of 2024.[307]

3. The Care Economy

The largest number of new job openings will come from the care sector. This includes both the traditional healthcare industry and eldercare, as the number of people in the world over 60 grows from 1.2 billion in 2024 to a predicted 2.1 billion by 2050.[308]

A second big need and growth opportunity in healthcare is improved prediction and prevention of medical issues. Digital healthcare will help, from wearables and remote monitoring to telehealth. This is an area in which lower prices *will* increase demand. It is illegal in many countries not to have an MOT on your car each year, but most people around the world do not have a yearly MOT on their body; this could change as it becomes cheaper and more accessible. And why stop at yearly? Can you ever be *too* well? The demand for wellness professionals will continue to rise.

AI will also power new scientific discoveries, as seen recently with DeepMind's AlphaFold or Moderna's mRNA COVID-19 vaccines. Innovations in biologics, immunology, genetics, and genomics could bring enormous benefits to billions of people.

As noted above, the wider care economy includes eldercare, as well as social care, childcare, mental healthcare, fitness coaches, and talent management. AI can help in some of these areas, such as robots helping people walk or AI offering therapy, but most humans will prefer intimate care of this type to be from another empathetic human that they know and trust.

Putting some numbers on this opportunity, the US Bureau of Labour Statistics forecasts the healthcare and social assistance sector will account for a quarter of new jobs in the US by 2030.[309] Globally, the World Health Organisation forecasts a shortage of 11 million health-care professionals by 2030.[310] Given rising demand, the projected shortage of workers, and relative protection from machine substitution, John Burn-Murdoch suggests that "learn to care could replace 'learn to code' as the go-to career advice for the next generation."[311]

4. An Innovation Boom

A wild card opportunity for job growth could come from an AI-induced innovation boom. As discussed, an intelligence explosion is probable as AI's exponential improvements continue, AI agents multiply and mate, and the price of intelligence drops dramatically.

Secondly, new tools could lead to a boom in creativity. It is said that LLMs are just "statistical parrots" that mimic existing content, unable to produce anything original, but there are signs of AI's growing creativity: image generation; hallucinations; an AI generated song, "Walk My Walk" by the virtual artist Breaking Rust, reaching number 1 in a Billboard chart list in 2025[312]; digital twins iterating ideas; or move 37 in AlphaGo's world-beating game, which had never been used before. Either way, new AI tools will help creative people produce more content, with more immersion and personalisation, such as stories that change depending on the reader, new virtual worlds for education, or multi-sensory, interactive experiences, like sitting in the front row of a concert or sports game. A Citi report on the creator economy estimated that although this market barely existed in 2018, by 2023, it already had 120 million creatives producing videos, podcasts, written content, and educational materials.[313] AI will supercharge this.

The changes taking place in the creator economy will be accelerated by the move to Web 3.0, with new tools, such as blockchain and NFTs, facilitating direct relationships with clients or fans. Web 1.0, the internet's initial phase, produced read-only interactions. Web 2.0 included the ability to share more widely and respond, known as read and write. Web 3.0 will allow creatives to monetise content directly with clients, without the need for intermediaries or gatekeepers.

New tools and reduced costs all intertwine to help entrepreneurship. It has never been easier to start and grow a company. Digitisation has made it far more economical to reach customers around the world, continue relationships with them, hire talent from anywhere, outsource parts of your company, and scale quickly. AI will speed up and expand this process.

As AI unleashes a wave of human creativity, innovation, and entrepreneurship, this will, in turn, create new jobs. This is not sector specific. The true potential of a general-purpose technology like AI is its ability to spread across the whole economy.

AN OPTIMISTIC VIEW ON NET NEW JOBS

When analysing the impact of these new job opportunities, we need to understand the net quantity of new jobs, meaning the jobs created minus jobs lost. Techno-optimists argue that technology is essential because we will run out of workers as our population ages. There is some truth behind this, but the demographics argument does get overplayed and is not entirely accurate.

It is correct that the working population has passed its peak. While the United Nations estimates the world's population will grow from 8.2 billion in 2024 to 10.3 billion in the mid-2080s, the biggest drivers of this growth are emerging markets and people living longer.[314] According to the United Nations, the working-age population (WAP) for industrial countries peaked in 2011 at 388 million. In contrast to the significant growth of 120 million between 1980 and 2011, the UN forecasts the WAP will be 30 million lower by 2030.[315] Japan's WAP peaked in 1995, Germany's in 1998, and China's in 2020; the US is projected to peak in 2026. The number of countries with a declining WAP is projected to reach 77 by 2040, up from two in 1980. A more recent report from the OECD estimates that the WAP for OECD countries peaked in 2025 and will decline by 8% by 2060.[316] Without human workers, we will need robots.

This sounds convincing, but it's not that simple. Citi's *Technology at Work 2.0* report examined this argument and concluded that demographic changes happen very slowly compared to technology trends.[317] The 8% WAP decline predicted by the OECD only equates to a 0.24% decline per year through to 2060. In comparison, the Citi report notes 47% of US jobs are susceptible to automation. Don't be fooled that declining WAPs will counteract the risk of technology substitution quickly enough, especially when AI is progressing at an exponential pace towards AGI.

Secondly, don't forget that our declining populations will also reduce growth by 0.3% annually between 2023 and 2040, compared to a positive 0.5% annual impact between 2000 and 2009.[318] On the way up, rising populations create more demand and more jobs. This equation also works in reverse.

There are several related considerations. Immigration policies have become more restrictive in many advanced economies, reducing the size of the workforce. On the other hand, high public debt levels and our increasing longevity mean that people are retiring later, increasing the labour force. The OECD estimates that the increasing retirement age and the shrinking gender employment gap could mitigate over half of the WAP issues.

These points are important as they highlight that outcomes can be shaped by policy decisions as much as developments in technology and AI. For example, it could be ruled that certain services, such as medicine, teaching, or law, have to be carried out by a person, even if AI tools are superior. Or as Jamie Dimon illustrated recently, if the US wanted to create 40 million new jobs, it could ban the use of tractors and fertilisers.[319] Dimon's example will not happen, but it demonstrates how governments also have the power to create entirely new jobs to counteract unemployment.

Indeed, as a solution to joblessness and economic depression in the 1930s, Keynes suggested "the government should pay people to dig holes in the ground and then fill them up."[320] Governments have recently started to do something akin to this in and around the defence sector, with rising levels of spending, and this could be extended by increasing levels of national service, or conscription, in order to employ millions. Or governments could pay more people to do non-profit work to help society. Clearly, this sort of induced employment would have to be financed somehow, so it's not a simple fix, but the point is that new jobs *can* be engineered.

A PESSIMISTIC VIEW ON NET NEW JOBS

So far in this chapter, we have seen that, throughout history, new job creation has offset jobs lost, that there are several job-hungry megatrends ahead, and that both demographics and government policy can help create net new jobs. It's clear that the optimists have a number of strong tailwinds supporting their arguments. However, there are also several currents going in the opposite direction.

1. This Time It's Different

In earlier chapters, we argued that this time it's different—and this extends to new jobs.

The data already shows that leading growth companies require fewer workers than they used to. As discussed in Chapter V – Data Over People, AI will only extend this trend. Responding to questions on AI and job cuts at the 2025 Milken conference, the CEO of Ernst & Young, Janet Truncale, said, "I like to think we can double in size with the workforce we have today."[321] Marianne Lake, CEO of J.P. Morgan's consumer bank, recently said, "[We are] at the tip of the spear on using and leveraging new AI tools and capabilities... We expect headcount will trend down by about 10% over the next five years or so, even as the business grows by another more than 25%."[322]

It is also probable that a significant portion of new jobs will go to non-human workers. This means that while the lump of labour fallacy, that the amount of work and jobs in a society is fixed and cannot increase, is still a misconception, there will be a reduction in the share of work that's allocated to human workers. This would be an important change from the past that policy makers need to consider.

This new abundance of non-human workers was explored more fully in the last chapter, so there is no need to repeat it here, but note the following prediction from the World Economic Forum: work tasks performed by humans alone will fall from almost half in 2025 to a third by 2030, whereas tasks performed by technology alone are forecast to rise from 22% to 34%, with the balance a combination of man and machine.[323] The year 2030 is not far away.

Let's imagine what this might look like in practice. If an advert is made by AI rather than a human team, not only are the actors not needed, but neither are the makeup artist, stylist, videographer, or sound technician. And this isn't just about the loss of human jobs: those people cannot then spend money in the economy on flights, hotels, food, and taxis to get to the location. AI may be a good worker, but it's a terrible consumer.

We have been used to growth, having what economists call a "multiplier effect." When a new company starts and grows, new people are hired across multiple roles, from design and sales to finance and HR. These new workers then spend their income across the economy, whether it's travel, food, or going out, creating further new jobs. Quantifying these effects, the economist Enrico Moretti estimates that each new technology job creates demand for five new service jobs in a city.[324] However, the same is not true for non-human workers, and the multiplier effect does not just work upwards when jobs are created but downwards when jobs are lost.

Let us also return to another key concept that has historically supported the lump of labour fallacy. If demand is elastic, a reduction in a product's price often leads to people buying more of it, driving an increase in jobs. Humans like buying more, but not more of everything, and some industries won't see new jobs created as prices fall. You only need a certain amount of toothpaste, bikes, or wills. Digitisation adds a new dimension to this concept. Prices falling is one thing, but if digitisation means that prices fall towards zero, making money becomes increasingly difficult, even if it does lead to abundance; we can see this in the music example we explored earlier. Market share will be eaten up by just a few companies with scale, or those who can monetize in different ways, or those who have deep pockets to loss lead. While these companies may grow, the total number of jobs in that area can decline. This has been happening in several content and marketing areas for two decades now, and it could expand to other job areas. In other words, what might be appealing to consumers could be bad for jobs. Indeed, in a recent survey of UK CEOs by PwC, almost a quarter doubted their business would be economically viable in a decade's time unless things change significantly.[325]

2. Timing Matters

The timing of AI adoption matters and will impact the net new jobs created. We know that adoption will not happen overnight, given that implementation into existing IT platforms, business processes, and regulatory frameworks takes time. However, compared to previous technology cycles, AI adoption will be much faster, partly because exponential growth is dramatic and partly because every company is racing to implement solutions. To quote H. G. Wells, "Adapt or perish." This increased speed versus previous cycles creates two problems.

If transitions are slower, as happened in agriculture and manufacturing, workers have time to adapt and reskill more easily. Rapid change is much more challenging, especially if new roles are technical in nature, such as switching from building a combustion engine to electric vehicles or a taxi driver becoming a quantum computing expert.

Secondly, the big productivity and economic growth opportunities usually come when entirely new industries are born. The car industry, for example, was not just about building and servicing cars. It had knock-on effects as it required roads, petrol stations, and petrol, and it facilitated the growth of the travel industry. AI will create entirely new jobs, such as AI auditors or robot maintenance, but big derivative new industries will take time. The first phase of AI is more about making existing jobs more efficient, and it is likely that this period will come with a decline in jobs before substantial new industries take off. A timing mismatch could be painful.

Could AI adoption be paused to allow for more reskilling and for other industries to start? This could be engineered via greater regulation, such as insisting every AI professional is licenced, but this is highly unlikely to happen. Most governments are taking the pro-innovation, growth, and abundance path. However, even if a slowdown was possible, there is a big looming problem that trumps all others: each year, we get ever closer to AGI.

3. The AGI Game-Changer

There are different definitions of and timelines for AGI, but if we accept that AI will exceed humans across many economic tasks at some point, the logical conclusion is that it will substitute more workers. We have come to expect computers to win in data processing, but now AI is competing with human traits, such as seeing, hearing, communicating, moving in crowded environments, passing exams, and making decisions. As AI continues to surpass humans across a range of fields and gets cheaper, more tasks will migrate to non-human workers. In the race between humans adapting and AI improving, there will only be one winner.

What lies on the other side of AGI is unknown; we've already explored the prospect of an economic singularity in Chapter IV – Falling Wages, but it could be a game-changer that upends the historic trend of net new job creation. No one has answers to this problem yet, but we need them, and quickly.

4. Human-to-Human Jobs

   At this point, it is fair to assume that human workers will increasingly huddle into the jobs that computers cannot do. These could be roles where we prefer the empathy or relationships of humans, such as eldercare, childcare, or experiences. While there is already a robot "Olympics," we will likely continue to prefer to watch sportspeople play against other people.

   There are plenty of examples of the growth of human-to-human (H2H) roles over the last 50 years, such as in the experience economy, the pay-for-care economy, or the creator economy. The last two decades have also seen the rise of the gig economy, with platforms like TaskRabbit facilitating jobs between humans, such as personal tutors helping students pass exams and coaches or therapists helping people live happier, more successful lives. Nail bars have multiplied, and new sports activities, such as padel and Hyrox, have boomed. All of these create jobs.

   These examples show we are not yet done dreaming up new ways in which humans can help or entertain each other. However, it would also be rational to assume that H2H roles will not grow fast enough to absorb all the workers displaced by machines. We have had several thousand years to invent new H2H jobs, so most are already in place by now. Also, these roles are not historically well paid, and there's no evidence that this will change, especially if more people crowd into them and supply outstrips demand. Coders becoming carers, or lawyers becoming manicurists, would not be pay enhancing.

Also, these roles are by no means safe from AI. Jobs that we may have assumed were guaranteed to be in the H2H domain are going in the opposite direction. Customer service is one of the big areas AI is moving into. Even parts of human resources are being automated, from talent acquisition and queries to training. IBM, for example, has reduced its spending on HR by 40% in the last four years alone.[326] So, even if H2H roles help, they are unlikely to produce a new jobs boom.

INVENTING THE FUTURE

So, will we create enough new jobs to offset jobs lost?

The answer you hear will probably depend on who you ask and what their agenda is. While these are generalisations, here are a few versions of the answer to this question from different angles, before you hear mine.

Economists can help us understand the arguments we looked at in this chapter, but as President Harry Truman famously said, "Give me a one-handed economist. All my economists say 'on one hand…' then 'but on the other…'"[327] Experts do not agree, and given that many economic thought leaders who have been concerned over the years about the risk of technological unemployment, from Keynes to Ricardo to Gordon, have not been correct, most economic decisions will be led by data rather than theory. If unemployment rises, so will their calls for action.

Many of the warnings of job losses are coming from technology leaders. They are closest to understanding the capabilities of AI, but they could also be biased, as they are selling AI-driven products. Given the trillions being invested, one of the easiest ways to argue that AI will produce a return on investment is by improving the efficiency of existing roles, and that comes with job substitution. However, it seems they may be right as they've been cutting jobs overall and not adding them, as we would expect during a boom period for AI growth.

Business leaders are well placed to know whether AI is driving new jobs and net employment, given they are the ones investing in the technology across their businesses, but they may also feel they need to present a more positive picture to their employees to keep morale high. Indeed, leaders often cite the history of technology innovation driving new job creation, and I'm sure they hope this happens again, but they may be playing down their true fears. Given surveys conducted by the investment bank Citi have consistently shown that companies are financing AI investment by reducing headcount,[328] actions may speak louder than words.

Understanding what investors think is relatively easy, as the wisdom of the crowd is captured in the stock market. The market's focus on AI opportunities is clear from the wave of capital being allocated and high valuations. Given the low levels of revenue generated by AI companies currently, much of this has to come from improved productivity and efficiency, which includes reducing headcount. This is important because investors are the owners of businesses, so they influence business leaders.

Politicians will be influenced by leading business and technology experts and the drive for economic growth. As economist Paul Collier noted, "Growth is not a cure-all, but lack of growth is a kill-all."[329] Currently, politicians appear to be going full speed on AI adoption, and they are trying to reassure us that things will be OK, knowing that economic outcomes are heavily influenced by confidence. If unemployment rises, they will become more influenced by voters. Their answer to the question could then change.

But what if we take a different path? Niels Bohr once quipped, "Prediction is very difficult, especially if it's about the future," and given that the future is unknowable, this allows strong voices to give their diverse opinions.[330] Instead, we should move from *predicting* the future to *inventing* it. If we put in place measures to mitigate the downside and encourage job growth, we can shape the answer to this question. This is too important an issue to leave to opinion or fate, crossing our fingers and hoping it will work out. We can do much better than that.

In practice, the easiest way to do this is by pointing AI investment towards task-augmentation rather than task-substitution. This is key for the continuation of the automation paradox—the idea that as automation grows, we become more, not less, important, taking on more complex, higher-level tasks where human judgment is crucial. How we influence this is discussed more fully in the following chapters, but employees, one of the most important stakeholders, should have a say in how we steer this process. We cannot just rely on history to repeat itself and the invisible hand of the market to create enough new jobs for humans. Nor should we rely on other companies to create new jobs while our companies cut them, known as the fallacy of composition: what may be rational for one firm, such as cutting jobs, becomes harmful if everyone does it as demand falls and the economy shrinks.

Secondly, we need transparency. A simple solution is for each company to report on how many people it employs. US public companies have done this since a 1977 SEC ruling, but greater transparency across all sizable companies globally, both public and private, would help us understand if companies are adding more jobs than they are removing. If this is easily discoverable by employees and society, it could push leaders to acknowledge the problem and drive new job creation. In turn, we should encourage the celebration of leaders who have a net positive employment ratio over their tenure. Currently, we often celebrate the reverse, as shareholder primacy usually means leaders are judged by stock prices, and one way of getting stock prices up is by cutting costs. If media outlets and politicians put companies that create jobs on a pedestal, customers may choose to vote with their dollars by buying from them, and employees may choose to vote with their feet by working for them.

Next, we must make sure there is a better understanding of where new job opportunities are or will be. This is needed by employees, future employees, educational institutions, and governments. Leaders can tell their stakeholders. AI-based talent intelligence platforms, such as Eightfold or retrain.ai, can provide these details within companies and within countries, if asked to do so. These platforms can also help guide reskilling or upskilling efforts that are needed to create a bridge between old and new jobs, as discussed in Chapter X.

Governments can shape new job growth through their industrial strategies, providing confidence in the direction of travel to businesses, educational institutions, and workers. They must also invest in homegrown AI solutions, known as sovereign AI, rather than relying wholly on those based in the US. If not, they'll see the transfer of new jobs from their country to US companies.

Let's return to Kennedy's words at the start of this chapter: "If men have the talent to invent new machines that put men out of work, they have the talent to put those men back to work."[331] It's clear we can invent amazing new AI innovations, so let us also invent ways to make new jobs for people and to make work work.

IX

BETTER JOBS

"There is more to life than increasing its speed."

—Mahatma Gandhi[332]

"Action speaks louder than words but not nearly as often."

—Mark Twain[333]

THE WORST JOB YOU CAN IMAGINE

What is the worst job you have ever had? What is the worst job you could have—something that you would really hate doing? Now ask someone you know well, a good friend or family member, for their views on the worst job for you. And do the same for them. It might be illuminating, funny, or just make you appreciate your current role more.

For example, not many would choose to work in an abattoir or as a restroom attendant. Few would want to be on a submarine for 201 days, as those working on HMS Vanguard were in 2024. Remember that famous picture of 11 construction workers sitting on a beam of the half-built Rockefeller

Centre in New York, having lunch 850 feet in the sky? For those who struggle with heights, there are better places to work—and to have lunch.

Go back further in time and there were many tough jobs: a bone grubber would collect rotting bones to make toothbrush handles or soap; plague bearers would collect rotting corpses at night and isolate in the day to stop the spread; leech collectors would wade through marshes, allowing leeches to latch onto them, to be used in bloodletting to cure illness; vomit collectors at Roman feasts would make the rounds, allowing people to consume more food; and gong farmers would remove human excrement from privies or by wading into Tudor cesspits. No thanks. It is worth celebrating how much better most people's jobs have become. We've progressed from backbreaking farm work in 1900 and factory work in 1950 to many of us being employed in air-conditioned shops or offices.

LESS DANGEROUS, DIRTY, AND DULL

While we have come a long way, there is still more to be done to make work better. A stark example is given by the UN, which notes there are still 139 million children involved in child labour around the world, with 54 million of these involved with hazardous work; its Sustainable Development Goal 8 states there should be "decent work for all." [334] AI can help with this in multiple ways, and arguably, it will have failed workers if this does not happen. A good place to start is in jobs that are dangerous, dirty, and dull.

As discussed in Chapter I, AI robots are increasingly taking on dangerous tasks, whether it's bomb disposal, firefighting, security, unmanned submarines used in combat, or cleaning nuclear facilities and skyscrapers. Few would argue against AI taking on more dirty tasks, such as autonomous trucks going into mines or the use of robot cleaners. There are already robots that can scrub toilets.

Most people would also vote for AI that liberates them from mundane tasks, freeing up their time for more valuable and meaningful work. Take doctors, for example. Thirty-six percent of doctors in the US spend over 50% of their time on admin.[335] AI can record conversations with patients and transcribe these notes so doctors can spend more time with patients. In one survey, 56% of doctors did not think they had enough time to show patients compassion.[336] AI can save costs, improve outcomes for patients, and improve job quality for doctors.

AUGMENTED AND EMPOWERED

For many, and certainly for now, the A in AI will mean augmented rather than artificial intelligence. AI agents will not just help with admin; they will enhance people's intelligence. Returning to doctors, AI will help them diagnose issues and cross-check the applicability of medicine options for each person to reduce medical errors. LLMs have already outperformed humans in medical exams,[337] and Microsoft's AI Diagnostic Orchestrator has claimed it is four times more successful than human doctors at diagnosing complex medical issues.[338] Humans will act as supervisors and retain ultimate decision-making power, known as humans-in-the-loop, but their skills will be amplified by AI. They will have a supersmart assistant that's always with them, reading all the latest science developments or regulatory guidelines to support them.

One of the don't-worry-isms offered for AI is that it will empower more workers in this way. This is true in terms of the increased productivity it will offer you, but what most workers mean by and want from empowerment is greater autonomy and decision-making in their jobs. This does not mean following a guided script. Despite talk of greater empowerment, the computer age has seen task discretion decrease since the 1990s. This measure of how much influence people have in their work fell from 62% in 1992 to 34% in 2024, according to the UK Skills and Employment Survey.[339] And this reduced empowerment has spread from lower paid to higher paid jobs.

One argument is that digital technologies have increased measurement and metrics, empowering managers more than workers. AI could extend this. Continuing our example above, AI can support doctors to investigate potential options and make the best decisions, or it can be used as an oversight tool to mark every decision they make. If we want better jobs, we must find the right balance between using AI for workers or for managers. Data from the European Working Conditions Survey suggests this is very possible.[340] Professors Zhou and Galie show that trends in task discretion vary substantially across countries in Europe and that they are driven by national policies and employer strategies rather than technology.

Now expand this healthcare example and multiply it across all jobs. Taking drudgery to zero, focusing on augmentation, and increasing empowerment should be an aim that workers endorse. Employers must work with employees to identify these areas and prioritise AI investments that cut bureaucracy rather than jobs. If pointed at the right areas, AI can improve not just productivity but engagement at work.

Positive engagement at work is a central theme of this book and a core pillar of and for better jobs. Better jobs can increase satisfaction, motivation, and engagement, as suggested by self-determination theory. And going the other way, better engagement can make jobs feel better, creating a self-reinforcing cycle of improvement, which psychologists call the gain spiral. Chapter XIII – The Pro-Human Leader goes into detail on why this is needed and how to create this positive spiral.

It breaks engagement down into nine separate areas that can be measured and improved today. Chapter XIV – Pro-Human Capitalism envisions the society and workplaces we want to aim for: a better place with better jobs. And the final chapter, The BESST™ Framework: A Hopeful Path, brings together all the solutions in this book, with "better jobs" at the start, offering the most ideas for how we can take action. Indeed, better jobs are the core of Part 3 of this book on pro-human leadership.

Better jobs and better engagement are where we should be heading in the AI age. For all the talk of how AI supercharges productivity, we must not forget that the productivity opportunity of a more positively engaged workforce is currently estimated to be double that of GenAI.[341] The good news is that these productivity opportunities are not mutually exclusive; we can have both. A study by Pew highlights that workers whose jobs are aided by AI are more optimistic about AI and more likely to support its implementation.[342] A win-win.

AI-POWERED WORK-LIFE BALANCE

In addition to making jobs better, another huge potential upside from AI could be improving people's work-life balance. This will likely be more contentious among employers, but it's not only possible; it could be probable post AGI.

We are still a long way from Keynes' prediction, in his 1930 essay "Economic Possibilities for our Grandchildren," that technological advances would enable people to work a 15-hour week, but it is worth noting how far we have come.[343] In 1800, the average working week in the UK was 66 hours, with the typical labourer working six days a week.[344] By 1900, average working hours had fallen to 56. In 1926, Henry Ford introduced a standard five-day workweek, and the weekend was born. By 1940, work schedules had normalised at eight hours a day, five days a week.

Hours worked have continued to fall in most countries. OECD data shows that between 1970 and 2022, hours fell 28% in Japan, 26% in Denmark, 24% in France, 14% in the UK, 13% in Canada, and 5% in the US. On average, across the OECD, hours fell 11% to 1751 per year.[345] Using different estimates from the ILO, the average working week has fallen to 31.2 hours in the Netherlands, 35.1 in the UK, 37.6 in the US, and 45.7 in India.[346] There are obviously economic and cultural reasons for the variations across countries, but given that AI could be a game-changer here, it may be sensible for employees in countries with longer working days to ask why this is the case and if there is a different path.

As well as reducing hours worked, technology has allowed many to work more flexibly, helping make work fit into people's lives rather than the other way around. This allows more people to drop their children off at school or watch them in plays or in sports games, improves their commutes, and gives them the space to build community. This has even started to impact the rhythm of working lives, with some people deciding to work less intensely during the year and instead work more years. For example, the Netherlands has low average working weeks, but retirement ages have increased. As a sidenote, the Netherlands also has the happiest children in the OECD.[347] Around the world, the rise of the gig economy, which has partly been enabled by technology, is allowing some workers to take more time out of work earlier, when they are healthier, rather than waiting until retirement; in extending their working lives, it also helps them maintain purpose and relationships when they are older. Indeed, a combination of lower working weeks, longer lives, and more time spent in retirement means cumulative lifetime leisure time has increased 50% from 1890.[348]

While there is much to celebrate in the use of technology for many workers, this is, of course, only part of the story. Many feel busier than ever as technology and mobile computing reduce the boundary between life and work; people are "always on," even during weekends and holidays. Digital tools provide flexibility, but they also demand constant availability. This simultaneous increase and loss of freedom is known as the autonomy paradox. Also, new digital tools often push people towards self-service rather than getting help from a person. We see this in self-service checkouts in shops, but in offices, there has also been a trend of secretaries or HR personnel getting downsized and AI tools taking over. Employees must get to grips with these tools without a human guide, spending more time doing things they are not good at. Research shows employees feel overstretched across the economic ladder, and time poverty, as a 2022 study by Zheng and colleagues shows, is shown to negatively impact wellbeing and work engagement.[349]

Moreover, for many, greater work efficiency just means more work and more work intensity, not less. This is captured in Parkinson's law, penned in 1955 by Northcote Parkinson in his essay for *The Economist:* "Work expands so as to fill the time for its completion."[350] Oliver Burkeman echoed this sentiment in 2021, in his bestselling book *Four Thousand Weeks*: "Almost all new technology from steam engine to mobile broadband has permitted us to get things done more quickly than before, yet people in our modern era of acceleration have been responding not with satisfaction of time saved but increasing agitation at not getting things done faster still."[351] This is not just a theory. Data shows our lives *are* speeding up. Tracking changes in public spaces between 1980 and 2010 in New York, Boston, and Philadelphia, research shows walking speeds have increased 15% and people linger a lot less.[352] Indeed, if you look around, you'll likely notice that many people walk with their heads down, staring at their mobile phones.

And this problem matters to people. In 2025, a survey from Randstad of 26,000 workers around the world found work-life balance had become, for the first time in 22 years, the leading motivator for workers,[353] and for digitally native Gen Z employees in particular.

If we acknowledge that working hours have gone down, yet true work-life balance still seems like a dream for many, it's possible that AI could be a positive game-changer. Some of the time saved from AI taking on mundane tasks and improving productivity could be given to employees. Leaders have a choice to make. A&O Shearman's David Wakeling recently told the *Financial Times* that AI will "not lead to job losses as senior lawyers with freed-up time would be redeployed elsewhere."[354] What does redeployed mean in this context? It could be more work, more time for employees, or a bit of both.

SHORTER WORKING WEEKS

An alternative scenario needs to be thought through. If AI leads to an enduring increase in unemployment and underemployment, shorter working weeks could become a preferred option for policymakers. There are clearly many considerations here, such as how to ensure that clients are serviced, business continuity, and total staff costs. However, it could potentially reduce inequality of work, taking it away from those who are working too much and giving jobs to those who are underemployed or unemployed. Giving work to those who need it brings multiple benefits, such as social attachment and personal worth, and these workers vote. Practically speaking, there are different paths to shorter weeks, from optional to mandated, but one way is initially cutting back to a 4.5-day week, which is not a big leap, and then decreasing by half-day increments if unemployment levels require more.

History shows that reducing standard working hours is not a new idea, but also that change usually takes a long time. Henry Ford gets credited with introducing the 40-hour workweek in 1926 without reducing pay, but trade unions had started demanding shorter workweeks in the late 1800s and early 1900s, using the slogan, "Eight hours for work, eight hours for rest, eight hours for what we will."[355] Ford showed that fewer working hours came with increased productivity and morale, creating a win-win for the employer and employee. Then, when unemployment soared during the Great Depression, shorter working weeks became a solution to the problem. The 1938 US Fair Labor Standards Act followed, promoting the 40-hour workweek and the two-day weekend.

Jump ahead another three decades, and in 1956, President Richard Nixon suggested Americans would have more family time by working four days a week.[356] "Short Fridays" started in the 1960s among advertising agencies in New York and then continued to spread. By 2019, Gartner found 55% of North American organisations offered "Summer Fridays," allowing employees to leave early on Fridays between Memorial Day and Labour Day.[357] Many companies in Australia offer a similar version between June and August.

More recently, France introduced a 35-hour workweek in 1998. In 2017, Japan started "Premium Fridays," allowing workers to leave at 3:00 p.m. on the last Friday of the month, to reduce the risks of overworking, called *"karoshi"* or "death from overwork."[358] In 2021, China's Supreme People's Court declared "996" work—working 9:00 a.m. to 9:00 p.m. six days a week—illegal, which had become increasingly common.[359] The negative impact on employee health sparked a public outcry, and the court ruled it was a violation of worker rights. In 1983, Spain voted to shorten weekly working hours from 48 to 40 hours, and then to 37.5 hours in 2025. Spain's minister of labour and social economy, Yolanda Díaz Pérez, said, "We are modernising the world of labour and helping people to be a little happier."[360]

The pandemic in 2020 was a catalyst to offer more flexible working and experiment with four-day working weeks. "Work-from-home Fridays" and "no meeting Fridays" have become more common. In 2021, the UAE expanded its weekend to 2.5 days,[361] while Belgium gave workers the right to condense their hours into four days in 2022.[362] Several countries have been testing the idea of four-day working weeks, including Iceland and New Zealand. The world's largest four-day working week trial took place in the UK in 2022. The results included improved productivity, wellbeing, retention, and recruitment; 92% of companies continued this new way of working after the trial.[363] One UK poll found most British people expect a four-day working week to be the norm by 2030, with no loss of pay.[364]

The momentum towards a four-day workweek was building before GenAI burst onto the scene. If we just extend the falling trajectory of hours worked in the OECD since 1970, a four-day workweek would, on average, be reached by 2045. AI could accelerate this if employers share its productivity gains or if policymakers force them to as unemployment rises. There are, of course, several caveats, and there will, no doubt, be loud objections. There is no magic money tree, so unless productivity is extraordinary, fewer hours likely come with less pay, a trade-off many will not want to accept. Working less must not be an excuse not to work hard, otherwise the reduction in revenue would lead to less employment. Another argument against shorter working weeks will be maintaining international competitiveness, but given that AI will impact companies everywhere, shorter weeks could be a cascading policy across many countries.

If we all agree that a core long-term outcome of AI should be the improvement of jobs for most in society and that that includes work-life balance, this topic is worthy of more debate. Let's hope that as the wheel of change spins faster, we are not too busy to do so.

NEW WORKERS' RIGHTS

In addition to better jobs and fewer working hours, workers can take much comfort from the raft of rights that democracies have voted for in the last century, including sickness pay, maternity and paternity leave, unemployment insurance, free education, and state pensions. Since the 1950s, civil rights have also improved for women, children, and those in the LGBTQ+ community. The drive towards better awareness and enforcement of ESG (environmental, social, and governance standards that impact society) has extended the debate further into areas as diverse as sweatshops, pollution, and fairness, while a focus on DEI has increased awareness of and action to improve diversity, equity, and inclusion in the workplace.

What worker rights could come next in the age of AI to make jobs better? Given the discussion on how workers are always on, debates over the right to disconnect and the right to flexibility have increased since the pandemic. Better jobs aren't just about reducing the number of hours someone works; it's also about the control they have over those hours. This extends to their start and finish times, their ability to take breaks when they want or need to, and asks to them to work non-standard and unpredictable hours.

In Chapter V – Data Over People, we discussed the risk that AI brings more surveillance into the office and a move into an algoracy in which workers are managed by algorithms. This has already started with hiring, and Rule 144 in New

York followed, preventing employers from using automated employment decision tools (AEDTs) without disclosure and an independent auditor.[365] AI will be used in performance reviews, which feed into promotions and exits. Bossware can already monitor keystrokes or watch workers. In an article titled "Superfluous People" in the *Financial Times*, a venture capitalist warned that "there will be only two types of jobs in the future: those that tell machines what to do and those that are told by machines what to do."[366] Eventually, this will no doubt come to a head; we will need to debate worker rights in the algoracy.

With a growing trend towards self-employment, there has been more debate about the rights of contingent workers. While there are, of course, upsides to being self-employed, on average, it comes with fewer rights, less stability, and an earnings gap. While some do earn considerably more than paid employees, on average, the National Bureau of Economic Research found 57% of US self-employed people earn less than paid employees.[367] Data from the US Bureau of Labor Statistics provides similar conclusions for independent contractors. In the UK, the Resolution Foundation and ONS found the self-employed earned 40% less, on average, than employees in 2019.[368] If workers are being forced into the gig economy, forming a new precariat, this will become an issue in need of solutions.

The UN highlights the scale of this issue: "By 2024, 57.8 per cent of the global workforce was informally employed, meaning they were not adequately covered by social security arrangements, legal protection, or workplace safety measures."[369] The UN also measures companies' compliance with labour rights around the world; the average level of compliance is just 4.86 out of 10, and scores have dropped 7% since 2015. Clearly, this should be higher, and it certainly shouldn't be getting worse.

It is possible that AI can help measure and call out problem areas. Given that it is also certain that AI will bring enormous change, if the disruptive business philosophy of "move fast and break things" morphs into "move fast and break workers," we can be sure that calls for worker rights will rise.

TURNING WORDS INTO ACTIONS

Even if you don't think AI will cause job losses, few would disagree that improving jobs should be a core aim in the AI era. But we face three problems with this premise. Firstly, this is not what has happened during the digital era. The number of workers who are currently positively engaged with their work is shockingly low—just 21%; 62% are not engaged, and 17% are actively disengaged.[370] In his book *Demanding Work: The Paradox of Job Quality in the Affluent Economy*, Francis Green shows that important aspects of job quality have been deteriorating, such as job intensity, discretion, and stress.[371] If digitisation has not yet improved jobs or engagement, we should not assume that AI will do so. How we use AI to create better engagement and jobs depends on leadership, as explored in more detail in Chapter XIII.

Secondly, jobs may get worse in the AI age, not better, because the balance of power in the employer-employee relationship will likely shift towards the employer. An abundance of workers, human and non-human, will cause supply to rise much faster than demand. Workers will therefore become price takers, with employers dictating their terms: more self-serve automation, more work intensity, more real-time metrics, and so on. We are seeing this happen now as many firms mandate workers return to the office rather than work from home, and graduates navigate AI-based interviews with companies.

This will only be exacerbated by higher demands from human workers. By asking for more—whether that's rights, pay, flexibility, or time off—workers make themselves less attractive compared to AI agents and robots, which have no rights, will cost less and less, and will turn up 24/7/365. This could accelerate the adoption of non-demanding, non-human workers. Every day we get a little closer to AGI, the power of human workers declines. Without policy intervention, the delicate dance between better jobs for workers and better margins for companies may feel more like a sumo wrestle. At the crux of this debate is whether AI investment is pointed at job augmentation or job substitution. You cannot have a better job if there is no job to have.

If we want AI to create better jobs, we need a conversation between employers and employees on what better looks like. Top-down policy could help, but it is really the millions of bottom-up work decisions that count. This starts with an honest, two-way discussion about the issues, and then it allows workers to have agency in shaping the direction of AI. These conversations should acknowledge that business disruption *is* coming and that worker anxiety over job security is understandably high. In a recent poll, 49% of Americans said they believed AI could improve lives, while 49% believed it was different from previous technologies and could harm humans and society.[372] More believe it will reduce the need for humans to perform tasks than believe it will free people up from mundane tasks to do higher impact work. Fears about AI are already here and will only multiply as AI capabilities continue to grow.

This brings us to the third point: trust. A huge 68% of people do not trust business leaders, and the same percentage believe leaders deliberately mislead them, according to the latest Edelman survey.[373] AI is likely to erode trust further. There are many wonderful companies and leaders who will navigate this period of change well, creating new and better jobs and improving engagement at work for employees while delivering strong returns for shareholders. Yet there are others who will find this period very challenging. With so many conflicting demands to balance, leadership can be really hard, and some will reassure employees that AI will augment and improve jobs while also trying to cut costs and drive the business ahead at full speed. This could sow seeds of suspicion in employees. To navigate this period of uncertainty and mistrust, leaders need to deliver on their promises.

The importance of turning words into actions is, of course, as old as the hills. "Let us not love with words or speech but with actions and in truth," said John in the Bible (1 John 3:18). Mark Twain's take, in the quote at the start of this chapter, "Action speaks louder than words but not nearly as often," is a reminder that it is easy to say you'll do something but harder to follow through. Leaping forward to today, Simon Sinek has cynically suggested, "All companies say they care, right? But few actually exercise that care."[374] Yet we *can* change that dynamic as work enters a new epoch, making better jobs a central goal, discussing what better looks like, and making a plan of action. Reversing the question posed at the start of this chapter, let's aim for "the best job you can imagine."

X

UPSKILLING AND RESKILLING

"Education is the passport to the future, for tomorrow belongs to those who prepare for it today."

—Malcolm X[375]

"When you're finished changing, you're finished."

—Benjamin Franklin[376]

THE FROG WHO DID NOT BOIL

Once, in a quiet pond, at the edge of a meadow, lived a frog named Fern. Fern was curious but often distracted, content to float wherever the ripples carried him.

One afternoon, Fern hopped into a pot of cool water that some villagers had left by the fire. The water was pleasant, so he stayed. But slowly, as the fire crackled below, the water began to warm. Fern barely noticed. *It's just a little warmer than before,* he thought. *I'll get used to it.*

On the bank nearby, his friend Lira, a watchful and sharp-eyed frog, saw the pot steaming. She croaked loudly, "Fern! The water is changing. You must get out!"

Fern blinked, surprised. "But it doesn't feel so bad," he said. "Maybe I'll just adapt."

Lira didn't give up. She leapt to the rim of the pot and shouted again, "Fern, the danger is not in how it feels now. It's in where it's going. Come, take my hand!"

Fern hesitated, but as the water grew hotter, he realized she was right. With one last effort, and with Lira tugging at him, Fern leapt out of the pot. Together they hopped back to the meadow.

There, they found a shady pond with cool, fresh water. Fern gasped in relief and croaked,

"I nearly stayed until it was too late. I thought I could simply get used to the change."

Lira smiled. "Adaptation is a strength, Fern—but so is awareness. We must know when to stay and when to leap."

From then on, Fern and Lira made a pact: they would watch out for each other, warning of dangers that the other might miss. Doing so, they not only survived but also thrived, carrying with them the wisdom that true resilience comes from both adapting and knowing when to change course. The End.

The story above was generated by ChatGPT using a prompt asking it to bring to life the boiling frog metaphor: that a frog dropped in boiling water will immediately try to jump out, whereas a frog dropped in cold water that is gradually heated will stay until it boils to death. It warns of the dangers of complacency and not reacting early enough to warning signs when we experience gradual change. Right now, in the AI era, there is a danger that we are like the frog floating in a slowly heating pot of water. As industries and jobs change, we need to notice and act. As AI makes some of our existing knowledge and capabilities redundant, we must take action, and upskilling and reskilling are necessary survival steps.

While the boiling frog parable has been told for years, it is actually incorrect. But facts can get in the way of a good story. The original experiment, carried out in 1869 by Friedrich Goltz, found that frogs with their brains removed would not jump, while in 1872, Albert Heinzmann found that frogs do jump out once the water reaches around 25–35 °C. Scientific nuance was clearly lost over time. But let's get back to how we can better understand and tackle this era of change with facts and solutions.

EDUCATION IS THE ANTIDOTE TO AUTOMATION

The second most valuable skill in 1950 was "strong hands, arms, backs." Times change. The machines moved in to do the heavy lifting, people shifted into the knowledge economy, and critical thinking became a core skill. Now, machines are moving in to take on the cognitive heavy lifting. It's clear that change is heating up, so how should we adapt?

As we've seen in earlier chapters, both techno-optimists and techno-pessimists agree that AI will bring enormous disruption to millions of workers. And experts' predictions suggest this disruption will range from very big to enormous. McKinsey believes 30% of hours worked could be automated by 2030 and over 45% by 2035.[377] Combining the effects of AI, automation, and digital labour, Citi estimates two-thirds of US jobs will be disrupted.[378]

Almost everyone agrees that upskilling or reskilling is a big part of the solution. The World Economic Forum estimates 59% of global workers will need new skills or training by 2030.[379] In his book *The Skill Code*, Matt Beane estimates 2.7 billion workers will need to relearn and reskill due to AI.[380] There are three reasons this aligns well with the AI revolution.

Firstly, there is a healthy symbiotic relationship between the advancement of AI tools and the need to train workers to use them effectively. Companies are investing a great deal in these new tools, and to maximise their returns, they will invest in workers who can use them. Secondly, data shows it is cheaper to upskill existing workers than hire new ones. Thirdly, investment in learning and development (L&D) helps attract and retain talent. Research has found 92% of job candidates use L&D offerings as a deciding factor when comparing employers, while 86% of employees say frequent L&D opportunities would make them stay in their firms for longer.[381] So, in theory, we have the stars aligning behind a wave of upskilling and reskilling ahead. This will build an essential bridge between old and new jobs.

WE HAVE AN INVESTMENT PROBLEM

So far, so good. However, despite almost universal agreement on this need for upskilling and reskilling, we have a big problem: currently, this solution is more rhetoric than reality. Corporate spending on L&D has been falling for over two decades. UK employers' investment in skills per employee has fallen 29% in real terms since 2011.[382] It is true that UK investment has been poor across many areas, but a similar L&D trend has also been taking place in the US, with a 35% fall in real terms between 2009 and 2023.[383]

But why? Unfortunately, there is no one simple answer. Part of it could be that skill mismatches may be too wide to bridge. While those optimistic about AI creating net new jobs often quote the World Economic Forum Future of Jobs report, they don't often dig into the details. As we explored in Chapter II, the WEF predicts the largest growth in jobs to be farmworkers, delivery drivers, construction workers, and food processing workers. In reality, out-of-luck marketers, lawyers, or financiers are unlikely to reskill for these careers.

Within companies, an unspoken reason is that tax systems currently favour investing in capital over people, a topic discussed more in the next chapter. Companies might argue that they are providing an abundance of learning opportunities to their employees with access to online digital courses. While these can save money, it is debatable how effective they are, and it can appear to employees to be more of a box-ticking exercise.

Moreover, some traditional training dollars and time have probably been diverted to compliance courses. In the 2008 Financial Crisis and then in the 2020 pandemic, more funding was cut as belts were tightened, with training often viewed as a discretionary expense. Companies may also be less willing to invest in people as employee tenure has declined; if a worker moves on quickly, paying for training no longer provides a return. US labour data highlights job tenure has fallen from an average of 4.6 years in 2014 to 3.9 years in 2024, and down to 2.7 years for those aged 25–34.[384] Like it or not, as the employer-employee relationship has become more transactional, a willingness to make both economic and psychological investments has declined.

Whatever the reasons, there is a mismatch, and we're not seeing implementation of upskilling and reskilling at the level required. In a 2020 national survey of American workers by MIT researcher Paul Osterman, only half had received any training in the prior year.[385] The picture has worsened since then. In a 2025 survey by Gallup, 45% of employees received training in 2024.[386] More discussions on what is needed, followed by more investment from both employers and employees, would help build this needed bridge.

AND A TIMING PROBLEM

As discussed, the pace of change is much faster than any other technological revolution in history. This means workers have less time to adapt. The move from foraging to agriculture took 10,000 years, and the move away from agriculture took 200 years; change is happening 36 times faster today than in the Industrial Revolution. It is not surprising that almost 80% of people around the world believe change is happening too quickly and that this creates anxiety about adapting.[387]

However, could these fears be worse than reality? Possibly. While AI's technological improvements have been exponential, business implementation does take time. We should remember Amara's law: we tend to overestimate impacts in the short term. Take, for example, one of the poster children for AI job obsolescence: radiologists. In 2016, AI Nobel Prize winner Geoff Hinton said, "I think if you work as a radiologist, you are like the Wilie E Coyote in the cartoon. You are already over the edge of the cliff, but you have not looked down yet. There is no ground underneath. People should stop training as radiologists now. It's just completely obvious that in five years, deep learning is going to do better than radiologists."[388] A decade on, and radiologist employment has grown, not shrunk, as the volume of work has increased and radiologists have focused on more complex and higher-value work. However, don't forget the other half of Amara's law: that we tend to underestimate impacts in the longer term. Hinton may well just be early in his predictions rather than wrong.

For most learners, speed is a problem for several reasons. The greater the pace of disruption, or worse, unemployment, the greater the need. New courses take time to set up, and new learning can quickly become outdated. We have already seen the half-life of knowledge fall rapidly, meaning how long it takes for half the knowledge in a domain to be superseded.

For example, it has been estimated that the half-life of an engineering degree in the 1920s was 35 years; this fell to a decade by 1960, and it can be just 12–18 months today for a software engineer.[389] Combine this rate of knowledge obsolescence with a tidal wave of new information being created daily, and it is understandable that workers feel overwhelmed, unable to keep up, and perhaps even like they're moving backwards rather than forwards.

This issue is compounded further by education systems that have been slow to adapt. For example, it is challenging for college degree programs to disrupt themselves by adding more adaptable, stackable, short courses. It is also challenging for colleges to reduce costs to aid affordability for learners. This issue has become more pressing, but it is not new. The phrase "a race between education and technology" was coined in 1974 by Nobel Prize-winning economist Jan Tinbergen. Tinbergen noted that technological advances outpaced the education system's ability to produce skilled workers, leading to widening inequality between skilled and unskilled workers. The big danger now is that this will lead to widening inequality between AI workers and human workers.

The need for urgent and regular upskilling and reskilling across people's lifetimes presents an opportunity for universities. They could become multi-versities by offering courses and credentials to workers at every age. Of course, making sure these are highly relevant to businesses is essential in the era of AI. With 75% of companies saying graduates are not as skilled as they need to be, the traditional school-college-work pathway is being contested when we need it most.[390] The good news is everyone recognises that AI could be a game-changer; this may be the catalyst we need to make the necessary changes to education.

This leads us to an important takeaway. In an interview I conducted with one of the UK's leading educationalists, Sir

Anthony Selden, he emphasised that schools are so busy teaching the existing curriculum that they are not creating the room to teach the skills of the future.[391] This extends to colleges and company workdays. Lack of investment is not just about dollars but carving out enough time to reskill and upskill workers. If AI does boost productivity and saves time, some of this could be allocated to skilling.

UPSKILL TO WHAT?

Even if we manage to invest in learning, in both dollars and time, at the pace needed, many rightly ask: What skills do we need?

While this seems a simple and important question, research by the Edge Foundation shows that less than half of young people understand the skills employers are looking for,[392] and fewer than half of workers say they know what skills will be needed in the AI age.[393] This issue became more challenging and urgent with the arrival of LLMs, such as ChatGPT. As Sir Anthony noted in the interview, schools are still educating children for twentieth-century cognitive skills that AI can now perform in a fraction of the time and cost to PhD level. A rethink is needed.

Understanding what the skills of the future will be in the AI age was a topic I researched in a 2024 Citi GPS paper titled "What Machines Can't Master."[394] We first looked at a long list of areas machines *could* master, including superhuman powers of data usage, vision, and language; speed; endurance; access to information; knowledge sharing and being upgraded; self-learning; and cost. While machines have been making inroads in many fields, historically, humans have exceeded computers by having a wide range of capabilities: we can walk, talk, think, and carry at the same time, for example. Yet now, multi-modal AI is fast encroaching on this area of human advantage.

One obvious area to upskill in is digital literacy, including AI, so we can race *with* the machines rather than *against* them—and this is the essence of AI augmentation. There is a skill shortage and wage premium for AI talent, but it's about harnessing it, not emulating it. Don't rush out and learn to code—AI can now code for you—but understanding and using AI tools will become necessary for many jobs. AI literacy and an understanding of human-to-machine collaboration are arguably already as important as the three Rs were 50 years ago.

A second area is "hand skills," such as hairdressing and plumbing, that are currently beyond the capability, or relative cost, of robots. However, as discussed in Chapter I – The Rise of AI Robots, don't be deluded that hand skills will be immune to AI automation. Greater robot dexterity, mobility, and intelligence are coming.

And how about "head skills"? Given this is where AI's cognitive industrial revolution is heading, you could argue that humans have already reached "peak head skills," but critical thinking, problem-solving, self-awareness, and ethics will remain very important. So too will change skills, such as perspection (forward-minded thinking), adaptability, creativity, and entrepreneurship.

Humans' main area of competitive advantage will be in "heart skills," such as empathy, compassion, communication, collaboration, and leadership. Anne-Marie Slaughter captured this idea well in her 2016 University of Utah commencement address, saying, "In the industrial economy, we hired hands. In the knowledge economy, we hired heads. In the human economy, we will hire hearts."[395] As discussed in Chapter VIII – New Jobs, the obvious growth category for humans is the caring economy, whether that's healthcare, eldercare, social care, mental healthcare, fitness, or a coming wave of transhumanism—the physical merging of man and machine. AI will move into areas such as therapy, coaching, and eldercare, but it will not provide the same human-to-human connection.

In the Oscar-winning film *Good Will Hunting*, the psychologist, played by Robin Williams, says to the maths genius, played by Matt Damon, that he "knows everything and nothing." In other words, he has vast amounts of knowledge from all the material he has absorbed and processed, much like LLMs today, but being so young, he has little personal experience. Williams notes that Damon has not yet seen amazing places with his own eyes, been touched by music, or fallen in love. These real, felt experiences, genuine connections, and the heart skills that they slowly build will be superior to artificial intelligence's facsimile. This will be our enduring area of competitive advantage compared to machines.

How much humans value these heart roles is a different matter. Despite their importance, many meaningful care roles often don't pay very well. And if more workers move from head to heart roles, the extra supply of labour will reduce wages even further. However, creating jobs to move to is important if millions of knowledge workers need to be reskilled as AI moves in and up. Better valuing these heart skills would help this transition.

From our vantage point today, is there another big new category of jobs that will come to the rescue to replace knowledge work? An intelligence explosion is very possible, bringing a new age of discovery and ideas. How many jobs this will generate is unknown, but a core meta-skill will be learnability—learning to learn. As futurologist Alvin Toffler suggests, "The illiterate of the C21 will not be those who cannot read and write, but those who cannot learn, unlearn, and relearn."[396] Learning will no longer be a one-off, early-life phase, but a lifelong skill that is worth getting great at.

This brings us to another change that's coming. Having identified what new skills we need, how do we prove to employers that we have them? In the knowledge economy, we marched children and workers through courses and exams, such as A-levels, to prove they had the necessary head skills. Given AI can already pass more exams than any human can, if our competitive advantage lies in softer skills, we need to get much better at credentialling these. For example, most interview candidates will say they are good team players or have empathy, yet most interviewers have to guess at the truth; in the future, we will need to find ways to quantify and measure these skills. Somewhat ironically, the use of AI and psychometric tests is part of the answer. Do you know what they say about you?

Once we have found a way to credential soft skills, they should be placed into verified and interoperable skills wallets, so employers don't have to reevaluate them each time someone is hired or promoted. AI can help with this, too, so humans don't have to. This will improve transparency about skills, yet we must be able to better understand and compare credentials. This is currently a problem, as there are over 700,000 unique credentials in the US alone. AI can help recruiters with credential complexity. This process is starting to happen in forward-thinking countries, like Singapore and Australia, with EuroPass or the use of CTDL (Credential Transparency Descriptive Language), but we have a long way to go. Rather than wait, students and working learners alike should both create the room to skill themselves and make it easy for employers to know they have the right skills.

ARE HUMANS GETTING DUMBER?

While the pace of change and the need to keep up can feel overwhelming, it is best not to stick our heads in the sand

and hope magic solutions will arrive. Although we need more L&D investment from companies and countries, most workers will have to proactively own their reskilling. The risk of not doing so is too high. As General Electric's CEO Jack Welch once warned, "If the rate of change on the outside exceeds the rate of change on the inside, the end is near."[397]

The good news is that technology tools can help us make time for learning by freeing us up from some tasks. The downside is that those same tools can also enfeeble us. How many phone numbers or passwords can you remember by heart? We have outsourced this, just as we have offloaded map reading to AI. Autocomplete means you don't even need to finish sentences. AI finds potential partners for you, and then AI "dating concierges" help you communicate with them. If building a relationship with a real person is too much work, you can now meet virtual companions instead.

This process of "cognitive offloading" to free up more capacity for higher-order tasks could be a sensible trade-off, but as we know, it does come with risks. As we outsource skills, like memory or critical thinking, they atrophy. We become over-reliant, dependent, or even enslaved by digital tools. When algos feed us material to interact with, we spend more time in automatic mode, the System 1 thinking described by Daniel Kahneman.[398] This makes us more predictable, enabling AI to understand us, but our deep thinking suffers. More unthinking, less thinking. We get dumber while AI gets smarter.

This is not just a theory. The results of a significant recent OECD study of 160,000 adults in 31 countries showed literacy trends have declined significantly over the last decade.[399] Attention spans and deep-thinking time have also declined. There is even a lawsuit against TikTok that claims using it has resulted in the "loss of analytical skills, memory formation, contextual thinking, conversational depth, empathy, and increased anxiety."[400] Capturing this deterioration, the Oxford

University Press word of 2024 was "brain rot."[401] And there is a danger we surrender further. After losing to the chess computer Deep Blue, world champion Gary Kasparov said, "I lost my fighting spirit."[402] Enfeebled *and* dejected.

Amazing new time-saving AI tools could enfeeble us more, and faster. Google gives you multiple choices of sources to click on, yet LLMs just package up the answers for you so you don't even need to choose. This outsourcing to AI can create the illusion that we are gaining knowledge and understanding, but it will impact our expertise and wisdom. For example, research shows novice programmers become more complacent when coding using GenAI.[403] Other research found doctors were 20% less likely to find abnormalities on their own when they had been using AI.[404] Research by Hank Lee from Carnegie Mellon University and Microsoft found that although GenAI can reduce effort across a range of critical thinking skills and improve worker efficiency, it can also lead to an over-reliance on AI and a reduction in our critical thinking skills.[405]

In addition to our skills atrophying and delusions about our competency when using AI, there is an increasing risk that we trust the output of machines too much. We may laugh at the well-known phrase "computer says no," used in the sketch show *Little Britain*, but the real dangers of computer errors were highlighted by the UK's Post Office scandal, vividly depicted in the TV series *Mr Bates vs The Post Office*.[406] The black-box nature of most LLMs—their complexity means it's difficult to know how they reached a conclusion—will make this "automation complacency" even harder to avoid. What is more likely is that we will outsource the checking or policing of AI systems to AI. Will we trade convenience today for enfeeblement later?

This is a difficult process to halt, as businesses are always seeking to improve productivity, reduce errors, and cut costs, and technological innovation aims to make things easier.

History tells us that this trend isn't new. David Hounshell, in his book *From the American System to Mass Production, 1800–1932*, shows that technological change during the Industrial Revolution was largely deskilling.[407] Roll forward to our current era, and Matt Beane, in his book *The Skill Code*, warns that the proliferation of tech tools is "weakening challenge, complexity, and connection. This will send our ability to build new skills down the drain if we let it run its course."[408] Beane goes on to state, "We have started a war between technological productivity and human skill, and skill is losing." This is a key area that workers must find a way to win to remain valuable.

There are millions of opinions on this subject, but given that we are after solutions, here is one: be proactive. But what does this mean?

1. Be aware of the risk of algos making us dumber.
2. Use perspection—thinking forward—to work out what you need to learn.
3. Create the room to learn.
4. Capture new learning in a skills wallet so others can understand and compare your qualifications.
5. Get good at asking questions, as this will help with the other points.

In 2019, I did an interview with Larry Summers, previously the president of Harvard University and US Treasury Secretary. I was struck by his sage advice that "success will be about asking the right questions rather than knowing the right answers."[409] This was three years before the magic ChatGPT genie arrived to serve us answers on demand. Asking good questions is one way to ensure you do not get dumber in the age of AI.

THE YOUNG VERSUS AI INTERNS

A key problem that we need to solve is the skilling of younger workers. The young tend to be enthusiastic learners, both highly adaptable and digitally native, but they face tough competition from new AI interns. As we discussed in Chapter VI, AI is often pointed at the easiest tasks, but these are also the first rungs on the career ladder for new hires. If that means some of those rungs are knocked out, and there are fewer ladders to climb, this will create problems down the line.

Back to Matt Beane. His research into 31 occupations showed that, "In our quest for productivity, we are using new technology in ways that make using novices more and more optional in expert work."[410] If AI interns do more and human interns do less, the traditional apprentice-to-expert formula breaks, as most learning takes place on the job, and mastery comes from doing. At least it breaks for humans—AI, on the other hand, steps in to do more.

As AI improves, the impact on youth hiring could worsen. The CEO of Anthropic has warned that technology could wipe out half of all entry-level office jobs in the next five years.[411] New recruits at technology firms are already down 25% from 2023 and 50% from pre-pandemic levels.[412] This is particularly worrying as the tech sector should be booming on the back of AI, and these firms are early adopters of AI, so they may signal what lies ahead. As we've learned, rising growth with declining jobs is very possible in the AI age.

So, what do we do? Clearly, more apprenticeships have to be part of the answer. Another solution is ensuring more roles are augmented rather than substituted; otherwise, we are removing the ladder entirely for many. Next, we must acknowledge that cuts to save money—short-term thinking—will enfeeble us down the road, as we won't be training enough humans to oversee AI in the future; longer-term thinking will help us preserve the expert skill pathway. At the same time, we have to accept that AI will take on more junior tasks, so more training and accreditation of young workers must take place to increase their capabilities more quickly. And guess what? AI can help with this, too.

HOW AI CAN HELP WITH SKILLING

There is a lot to do as we build this skill bridge between the old and new world. One area that would help is better information on skill gaps and guides on educational paths—not just for current workers but for children and parents. The good news is that AI can be part of the solution. Digital platforms are doing a better job of matching workers to work, and now talent intelligence platforms (TIPs), driven by AI, can revolutionise the mapping of people's skills to job opportunities.

The founders of one of the leading TIP providers, Eightfold, came from Google around the time the transformer technology that underpins LLMs was invented. Instead of pointing their model at content discovery, as ChatGPT or Gemini largely did, they pointed it towards skills discovery. Eightfold was trained on over two billion CVs, extracting several hundred features from each profile. It ingests enormous quantities of information about your skills, from educational qualifications, training, social media posts, LinkedIn data, and so on. This allows it to infer your capabilities based on your past, your relationships, and professionals who are adjacent to you. The AI extracts all this without you having to input information, then it uses pattern recognition and prediction to give you suggestions. The level of data used by TIPs is unimaginable for humans.

So, how do they help? For organisations, they provide transparency, measurement, and suggestions on skills inventories, skill gaps, pay gaps, upskilling paths, and mobility opportunities. They can operate across an organisation or be customised down to teams or individuals. They help with hiring candidates and resurfacing previous candidates who are suitable for other roles, known in hiring as the "black hole" problem. Leading TIP provider retrain.ai suggests they can improve upskilling by 27%, increase internal mobility by 57%, reduce hiring time by 55%, and boost engagement by 62%.[413]

How about for individuals? TIPs can illuminate new opportunities, suggest upskilling opportunities, and even provide personalised career path guides. It is often easier to find new jobs in other companies than it is within your company, and TIPs can help redress this imbalance. They can also provide some support if managers are too busy, or worse, if they are talent-hoarding their best team members. Asking an AI system how to get promoted or move jobs could be easier than asking your manager.

A final thought: Most TIP providers are focused on providing services for commercial customers, but this AI solution should be made available for free to everyone, by governments, to increase transparency and understanding of future jobs, skills needed, and potential pathways. The information is there, as TIPs can already monitor labour market data, job adverts, pay data, and skills in real time on a national level. Society as a whole needs help in making this transition.

DO WE NEED POLICY NUDGES?

In an ideal world, capitalism would efficiently reallocate talent from old industries, jobs, or tasks to new ones. Companies, given that they need talent, would be incentivised to build this skilling bridge themselves. However, it is not quite as simple as that. The decline in L&D budgets discussed at the start of this chapter highlights that something is broken. In addition, companies are now allocating budget to train non-humans, reducing the pot allocated to people. As we've seen, the young are particularly vulnerable to this competition from AI interns, but there will be *many other losers* from AI disruption who will find reskilling into new jobs difficult. Government policies will be needed to help workers transition; otherwise, skill inequality will have a long-term impact on career opportunities, family incomes, and the quality of life.

Governments already have policies in place to do this, of course, but as the UK prime minister recently said, the UK skills system is a "mess" and "fragmented and broken."[414] In a comprehensive 2024 UK Skills and Employment survey, the majority of workers were not satisfied with the training they received.[415] Given the quantity and pace of change coming, significant improvements are needed.

So, what can governments do to encourage more upskilling and reskilling to bridge the divide?

Firstly, the trend of investing too little in L&D has to reverse. If companies do not do this themselves, governments may need to use carrots, such as tax credits, and sticks, such as targets and reporting, to do so.

Secondly, given the importance of large employers to making progress in this area, they could be mandated to disclose information about what they are doing to this end, such as L&D budgets, apprenticeships, or the training of older workers. Given an unequal power dynamic, it is often hard for new employees to probe interviewers too deeply on the efficacy of their training. Being more informed will help talent choose more supportive companies that invest in skilling their workers.

Given that skilling matters to employees, more use and awareness of websites like Glassdoor and Fishbowl would help workers compare companies. This involves more workers taking the time to disclose their experiences and rate employers. If companies know that talent looks at these sites before accepting jobs, they would be incentivised to improve their ratings.

Given the importance of apprenticeships and graduate hiring, more understanding and implementation of best practices from around the world would help. For example, apprenticeship schemes in Switzerland and Germany have had good success rates. In the UK, the TUC is pushing for a funded "youth guarantee" scheme to ensure all 19–21-year-olds can access job support, training, or education. In China, which has high youth unemployment, companies have been encouraged to hire young workers as part of their social responsibility. One way to encourage companies to take on NEETs would be via tax incentives.

However, all the above require that there are enough jobs to go around. For example, if jobs are scarce, forcing firms to hire graduates may just bump other workers out. This is why more augmentation and less substitution of jobs must be part of the answer. This may require tax changes, as discussed in the next chapter.

Helping those who find themselves out of work must also be part of the solution. Governments need to improve lifelong learning to ensure the unemployed aren't left behind. Lessons can be learnt from forward-thinking countries, like Singapore, which have already implemented lifelong learning voucher schemes. Clearly, education is expensive, and these schemes have to be paid for, so a cost-benefit analysis is needed. But AI could be part of the solution to reduce costs, increase access, and improve outcomes. As discussed in Chapter VII, AI can create abundance in education. Just as the First Industrial Revolution led to free schooling for all children, the AI industrial revolution should lead to better lifelong learning for everyone.

Lifelong learning is about time, not just financial investment, as we explored earlier. In Sweden, workers can take time away from their jobs to train and still get paid up to 80% of their salaries for one year.[416] This scheme started in 2022 as a collaboration between employers, unions, and the government to "protect people, not jobs." Other countries could look at versions of the same, perhaps funded from AI savings or as an incremental payment for job redundancies.

Learning how to use AI has to be a focus of these initiatives. There is some truth to the often-used line, "You're not going to lose your job to an AI, but you're going to lose your job to someone who uses AI." To promote AI literacy in children and students, the US government has put initiatives in place, with material support from leading AI companies, including some free tools and accreditation. Other countries should follow their lead.

However, it's worth saying that while employers and governments are vital in helping build skill bridges, most employees know they have to take charge of this for themselves. Hoping others will deliver solutions to them on a plate when needed is not realistic. No one wants to be a boiling frog. Given that the average American worker today holds 13 different jobs before the age of 58, getting good at transitions, including learning how to adapt, is an important life skill.[417] And taking personal responsibility extends to understanding how AI may impact work and then voting for the solutions you think are best, as discussed in the next chapters. Indeed, your vote will impact future livelihoods and future lives.

XI

SOCIETY VOTES

"An economic system should work for people, not vice versa."

—Sargent Shriver[418]

"A man without a vote is a man without protection."

—President Lyndon B. Johnson[419]

DON'T BE A HORSE

As amazing as the play *War Horse* is, it's a hard watch, highlighting some of the extreme conditions horses had to endure. Eight million horses and donkeys died during World War I.[420] Thankfully, in most countries, horses now live a life of leisure for 25–30 years. This was not the case for most of history. During Victorian times, the average life expectancy for a working cart horse was three to five years. Heavy loads, long hours, pressure ulcers from friction, and beatings meant many dropped down dead on the streets from exhaustion.

The RSPCA, the world's oldest animal welfare charity, was founded in 1824 to try to reduce abuse like this. It followed the first law protecting animals—the Cruel Treatment of Cattle Act of 1822, or Martin's Act, after Richard Martin, the MP for Galway known as Humanity Dick, who brought a donkey into court. Despite the passing of this law and the work of the RSPCA, horses and donkeys were still primarily valued for their work for many years, with the unproductive taken to the knacker's yard to be slaughtered. Money mattered, and Victorians took the view that "sentiment pays no dividend."

New technology, in the form of the car and the tractor, dramatically changed the outlook for horses. The lucky ones got a life of leisure, but this was not the fate of the unemployed majority. They quickly went from being a useful economic tool to a financial burden, and the horse population fell from 25 million in 1900 to just 3 million by 1960, an 88% decline.[421]

What is the connection with AI? Similarly, in this era of technological innovation, a minority of us could have better jobs, lives, or upskilling opportunities, but the majority may not. However, unlike horses, who had no say in what happened to them, humans mostly live in democracies and can vote for the future they want. This chapter looks at what they could vote for.

In 1947, Winston Churchill stated, "Democracy is the worst form of government except all those other forms that have been tried." This morphed, over time, into the phrase: "Capitalism is the worst economic system, except for all the others," and was misattributed to Churchill, but there's truth behind both versions; neither democracies nor capitalist systems are perfect, but at least people can vote to change course. The outcomes are dynamic. For example, over time, safety nets have been added to reduce the downsides of capitalism, such as unemployment benefits, sick pay, and maternity leave—evidence that we do not just have to leave our fate to market forces.

And this is important when talking about AI. In democracies, people, not technology, determine what will happen next, even if it might not always seem that way. While the Tuatara sports car can drive at 295 mph, we voted to impose speed limits on public roads; we also voted that drivers must pass a driving test, be insured, not be drunk, be a certain age, and wear a seat belt. Similarly, we put rules around the economy, partly because politicians need to create positive economic conditions, in which there are more winners than losers, to get voted back in. As we head into the AI age, we should remember that the economy needs to work *for the people* and not the people *for the economy*. In practice, this means ensuring enough good jobs and income. It also means technology needs to serve humanity and not the other way around.

There are, of course, a couple of roadblocks. One is the time lag between problems surfacing and implementing solutions to course correct, and that may require voting in new people who promise to enact them. The second is the influence wealth has on political power and the storytelling around solutions. Marx and Engels warned in 1845 that "the ruling ideas of every epoch are the ideas of the ruling class."[422] We are seeing this storytelling now, with many governments going full speed ahead on AI in search of productivity, growth, new science, military protection, and so on. AI will not just supercharge intelligence but also profits and wealth—and that will benefit those at the top. And one way that profits will increase is by reducing labour costs—hurting those at the bottom. In a dynamic democracy, if the benefits of AI accrue for the few rather than the majority, the majority will vote for change.

If we vote for change, what could we vote for? This chapter looks at options for society in relation to policy, while the next chapter focuses on options within companies. The sole aim is to look for solutions in an objective and politically impartial way. The good news is that we have plenty of options that can be dialled up or down if needed. While all involve trade-offs and complications, remember the Kennedy quote: if we have the capability to invent superintelligence, we have the capability to design policies that benefit the majority.

WHAT WILL YOU VOTE FOR?

Several potential options are explored below, impacting individuals, companies, and robots, and ranging from encouraging outcomes to penalising bad behaviours. These fall into several categories, including social security support, taxation changes, new regulations, and economic policies. While choices will vary by countries and cultures, AI's impacts will be global. Personal circumstances and politics will, of course, influence which options below you will prioritise and vote for, but as you read, it is also worth considering which are more likely to become consensus thinking over time.

1. Encouraging Entrepreneurship

   The current hope is for AI to lead to a productivity and innovation boom, lifting growth, expanding the economic pie for all, and creating more new jobs than are lost. To support this, policies could encourage entrepreneurship, such as reductions in red tape, research tax credits, or new business funding. Entrepreneurship could also be stimulated when paired with other policies mentioned below, such as UBI.

2. Changing Education and Boosting Training

   As discussed in the last chapter, there is almost universal agreement that education is one of the needed antidotes to automation, from school to lifelong learning, training, and reskilling and upskilling.

The last chapter proposed a series of solutions, so there is no need to go over these again in any detail. However, in summary, these include pinpointing the right skills, making the room to learn them, use of edtech and AI to reduce costs and improve outcomes, multi-versities offering lifelong learning, apprenticeships, higher L&D budgets, and transparency about what's offered to employees, skill vouchers, certification, skills wallets, and TIPs. Given that AI developments will move so much quicker than education's ability to adapt, longer-term thinking is needed. As Glenn Hubbard notes in his book *The Wall and the Bridge*, "Bridges are forward looking, offering skill acquisition and support, not backward-looking attempts to prop up jobs, industries, or the economy that was."[423]

3. Implementing ALMPs

   Given that it is almost universally agreed that AI will bring significant disruption to work, governments need to provide safety nets for people during transitions. Active labour market policies (ALMPs) is an umbrella term used for policies that help people find jobs, whether that's training, job placement services, incentives to support self-employment, Earned Income Tax Credits (EITCs), or the lowering of tax wedges. EITCs in the US incentivise workers to find paid work because they receive a tax credit, or refund, if they have a low income. In Europe, several countries use low tax wedges, a wedge being the difference between gross income and net income after tax is taken off, to boost take-home pay and raise employment.

4. Adding Flexicurity

   In the Nordic countries, flexible security, called flexicurity, is provided if workers become unemployed, guaranteeing access to education, training, healthcare, and housing. This is really an extension of ALMPs, balancing paternalism with market forces. It reduces the fear of losing a job and helps support people switching into new jobs or industries.

Unemployment insurance is an important part of this process in Denmark, in which employees voluntarily pay monthly into a scheme, known as an A-kasse, which then provides up to 90% of income for up to 2 years when unemployed.[424] The scheme is financed both by the insurance funds and the state. Forms of unemployment insurance seem sensible in other countries as we head into the AI age.

5. Supporting Geographical Mobility

Policies encouraging geographical mobility are often needed if new and emerging jobs are not in the same locations as old jobs. As economic activity has concentrated in certain locations over the years, housing has become less affordable in high demand cities, creating barriers to mobility. The number of Americans moving each year has fallen by over half since the 1950s.[425] Governments can take several measures to help counter this, from paying people lump sums to move and improving transparency on where good jobs are to restricting companies from using non-competes. As research by the OECD notes, "The balance of evidence suggests that non-compete clauses suppress job mobility, firm entry, innovation, wages, and productivity."[426]

Going the other way, instead of people moving to jobs, jobs can move to people in the form of more remote work. Giving people the right to flexible work would help this, as would offering incentives; however, governments may fear that work will move to other countries rather than other regions within their country.

6. Taxing Capital

The most controversial policy debates will be around taxation. Taking a positive view, AI will lead to higher growth, profits, and wealth; then it will just be a matter of making decisions about how to redistribute those gains.

However, even in this best-case scenario, if AI causes the economy to become less labour intensive, taxes will need to shift from labour to capital. Income taxes are the biggest source of revenue in most economies. In the US, 51% of all federal tax revenues come from income tax.[427] Income tax in the UK accounts for 27% of all public receipts.[428] So, if unemployment were to rise and income tax falls, governments will have less money to spend on everything; they will either need to borrow more or find money from other sources, and one of the main other sources will be taxing capital.

For individuals, taxing capital would mean wealth taxes, especially if AI widens inequality further. Given that many forms of wealth are mobile, unless a global wealth tax is agreed upon, which is highly unlikely, the wealthy could just move their capital to low-tax jurisdictions. To fix this problem, wealth taxes could be raised on property or land, which cannot move, on financial transactions, such as shares or capital gains, or on wealth transfers, such as inheritance tax. For example, UBS estimates that over $80 trillion of wealth will be handed down in the next 25 years,[429] or the capital gain tax rates in Denmark are almost double those in the UK.[430]

7. Taxing Companies

    An alternative to taxing individuals is taxing companies. This could happen naturally if AI creates enough growth to increase profits available to tax, but it may also require higher tax rates. This is the opposite of what has been happening. Since 1980, global corporate tax rates have declined from an average of 40% to 23%, and in Europe, they've dropped even further, from 45% to 20%.[431] This race to the bottom is partly driven by a fear that companies will relocate to lower tax jurisdictions. Yet there are alternatives that can be considered. One plan for a global floor on corporate tax has been shelved by the US, but another approach is to tax profits according to where they're made rather than in the country where they are incorporated. Alternatively, revenues could be taxed, similar to VAT collection in the UK or sales taxes in the US. The proposed EU digital services tax is one version of this.

8. The Use of Tax Incentives

    Rather than taxing corporate profits or revenues, tax incentives can be implemented that encourage companies to support workers. For example, it may shock workers to realise that companies are actually incentivised to invest in labour-replacing technology rather than workers. The tax rates on capital, such as technology, in the US have fallen to 5%, while the effective tax on labour is over 28%.[432] These can be changed, equalised, or even reversed to tax labour less than capital.

    In theory, these lower taxes on capital are designed to promote employment as they incentivise businesses to invest and grow. However, if we get profit growth *without* employment because of AI, incentives will need to be retilted. For example, technology that substitutes jobs could be taxed much more than technology that augments jobs, similar to how low taxes are put on healthy foods while high taxes are placed on sin goods. Alternatively, subsidies could be used instead of taxes, offering companies financial support for retaining human workers. The exact opposite of this took place in the UK in 2025 when the government raised National Insurance, which made the cost of employing staff more expensive, leading more businesses to prioritise investment in AI over people.

Of course, tax incentives could be used to nudge many of the voting issues listed in this chapter, such as apprenticeships, L&D, or mobility. However, as mentioned earlier, many of our existing taxes are based on people—income tax, national insurance, apprenticeship levies—so if the number of people employed goes down, we need to shift to other methodologies.

Alternatively, we could go the other way and raise the cost to companies of laying off workers by paying higher redundancy payments, as seen in Germany. Classifying redundancy payments as normal charges in company accounts could also discourage layoffs. These are usually made as one-off charges, labelled as "exceptional" or "non-underlying," even though they have become commonplace for many companies. While increasing redundancy charges could reduce mobility within economies, it would increase mobility *within companies*, as firms would be incentivised to retrain existing workers into growth areas.

9. Taxing Robots

Bill Gates raised the idea of taxing robots in 2017.[433] As the number of physical robots moving around us increases, it would be possible to add a tax per robot, just as we have a tax per employee. For example, if we wanted to reduce taxi driver unemployment, we could tax driverless cars more. Consumers would have to pay a higher price, but the point is that it's possible to slow down the adoption of robots and human job substitution. Taxing individual physical robots is, of course, far easier than taxing virtual AI agents who are invisible and can move anywhere, but it is also possible to charge higher taxes on the installation of job-substituting technologies, or on data centres that have become AI factories. Alternatively, given that AI usage will likely inflate electricity prices, higher electricity prices could be charged on AI data centres to reduce negative price impacts on households.

10. Incentivising AI for Good

    Building on Chapter VII – AI Abundance, societies may decide to incentivise the use of AI in areas that benefit people the most, rather than leave this to the invisible hand of the market. For example, if profit were the only concern, AI would likely be used in areas such as marketing, content, or shopping; yet it's possible to use taxes, subsidies, or regulations to direct AI towards improving healthcare or education outcomes first. Healthcare may have one of the highest needs for AI support, but it has seen the lowest influx of AI talent.

11. Using Tax Tilt Signals

    Normally, tax collection follows economic cycles, with budgets replenished in growth periods. As we discussed above, if AI leads to GDP growth without labour growth, or worse still, unemployment rises, and income taxes fall, tax loads will need to shift away from labour onto other areas, such as corporate profits, wealth, or robots. This tax tilt or tax seesaw concept—as one side goes down, the other goes up—has been used before.

In 1979, Margaret Thatcher slashed UK income taxes, including the 83% top rate, and doubled VAT spending, so tax moved from labour to consumption.[434] Or in 1987, Denmark phased out employer contributions to unemployment insurance and raised VAT.[435]

Given that AI could upend traditional economic cycles, creating an enduring structural trend towards labour substitution, governments could signal that policy will shift from taxing labour to taxing capital. This signal may cause corporates to alter their investment behaviour, as tax rates impact return on investment calculations. If companies understand they will be taxed more as unemployment rises, they may decide to augment rather than substitute labour. When the same rules apply across industries in a country, the competitive playing field will be level. And as most countries are facing the same dilemmas, as AI sweeps around the world and impacts tax revenues, it would not necessarily impact international competition.

12. Changing Individual Tax Redistribution

Taxation is a politically polarising subject, but if changes can keep overall taxation high enough to support spending and public debt repayments, the next area to solve will be the tax burden for different groups and redistribution. Without policy intervention, AI is highly likely to lead to an even greater concentration of wealth and higher inequality. If AI does lead to an abundance of wealth for some and the loss of jobs or wages for others, there will be calls for the gainers to compensate the losers.

This likely means higher marginal tax rates for the wealthiest and lower tax rates, or even payments, to the least wealthy. This would be a reversal of the trend over the last 45 years. The OECD shows the average top statutory personal income tax rate fell from 66% in 1981 to 42% in 2010.[436] This 42% level remained the average in 2025 in European OECD countries and in the US.[437] Average income tax rates have also fallen over time, but far less, from 36% to 35% across the OECD from 2000 to 2023.[438]

Lower top tax rates are not always the answer. As Simon Kuper notes in the *Financial Times*, "There's a common belief in corporate America that what is good for the rich is also good for business, the economy, and the US in general. Exhibits A and B are tax cuts and deregulation. However, low-tax Mexico and Turkey are, bafflingly, poorer than high-tax Nordic countries."[439]

There are, of course, several arguments not to increase top tax rates: people move, incentivising entrepreneurship is needed to grow the economy and jobs, and if the overall economic pie grows, all will be better off. However, the vast majority of the gains from the computer revolution and digitisation since the 1970s have gone to capitalists and high-income earners, with many more people left behind. If AI grows the pie without benefiting the majority in a similar way, people may vote for redistribution and higher top-rate taxes.

13. Universal Basic Income

One of the most extreme forms of redistribution is the provision of a universal basic income (UBI) for all citizens. This is usually called universal basic income, but sometimes unconditional basic income, guaranteed income, citizens' income, survival income, or perhaps to make it sound better, universal high income. The idea is that either AI will create so much growth, wealth, and abundance that payments can be made to all to cover their basic needs, or alternatively, that mass unemployment will require this payment to ensure the security and survival of society.

The idea is not new—leading economist Milton Friedman and President Richard Nixon were supporters of UBI—but, as AI has advanced, calls for this approach have been growing. Small-scale UBI experiments and pilots have taken place around the world, including in California, Canada, Finland, India, Kenya, and Wales.[440] The longest continuous UBI programme has been running since 1976 in Alaska, in which a portion of the state's oil and gas revenues is sent to each citizen annually. These programmes have produced multiple benefits, including reduced poverty and food distress; improved wellbeing, stress, and anxiety; reduced inequality; and better financial stability, helping people move to new jobs or become entrepreneurs.[441]

Proponents also argue that UBI is easier to administer and less prone to gaming than other benefits. By some, it is deemed the fairest approach, given it is available to all, but critics see it as a blunt instrument, providing money to many who don't need it and disincentivising the unemployed to seek work or contribute to society. These issues could be somewhat mitigated by the level of UBI, if it were low enough to still require people to work, the use of ALMPs, or the more nuanced approach of conditional basic income described below.

14. Universal Basic Capital

A derivative of UBI is universal basic capital (UBC). This would give every citizen a one-time grant of capital, typically when they reach adulthood, rather than the regular payments made under UBI. The idea is that it reduces wealth inequality and provides a financial foundation for individuals, allowing them to pay for education or put down a deposit for a house. In America, the proposed Trump Account is an example of UBC. Originally called MAGA, Money Accounts for Growth and Advancement, the tax-advantaged savings plan for US children born between 2025 and 2028 would start with a deposit from the government.[442]

15. Conditional Basic Income and Civic Contribution

    A variant of UBI or UBC is conditional basic income (CBI), in which people earn benefits for their participation in civic society, such as volunteering or charity work. A wide variety of work can create societal value rather than economic value, allowing people to give back and make social connections. This may appeal to many, from the young starting out in life to people wanting a career pivot, to the unemployed or older generations wanting to use their skills to benefit others. Given the importance of employment to identity, dignity, and hope, CBI can help destigmatise unemployment and be an energising and meaningful bridge to new opportunities, enabling people to build skills.

    Again, CBI is not a new idea. Keynes predicted people would have far more leisure time as automation advanced, believing many would choose to use this surplus time to engage in civic service. In the 1930s, many *had* to choose this path. President Franklin D. Roosevelt's Works Progress Administration, which was set up in 1935 to reduce unemployment during the Great Depression by placing people in jobs, from infrastructure to the arts, could be seen as a form of CBI.[443] The scheme ran until 1943, giving jobs to 8.5 million Americans.

Today, many choose to volunteer or work in charities, known as the third sector, or in organisations with a social purpose, known as the social economy. Non-profits account for over 13% of the workforce in Europe and over 10% in the US.[444] In 2022, non-profits were the third largest sector in the US workforce, so CBI could layer onto these strong foundations.[445] A related idea is to provide citizens with a guaranteed job after a period of unemployment, to help them get back on the paid job ladder; work in the third sector alongside CBI payments could make this possible.

If AI does lead to joblessness, CBI and civic programmes are likely part of the answer. They are also areas that are more immune to machines taking over. If we encourage youth citizenship by extending social modules in school curricula, this can help build skills in these areas and be a gateway into the world of work. For older workers, this could be a bridge between full-time work and retirement. For those in work, employers could be required to allow employees to serve society via volunteering days. In this sense, CBI, driven by the rise in AI, could have a positive impact on society and citizens by better recognising and valuing human-to-human contributions.

Formal recognition of people's contributions would help give the scheme credibility. In his excellent 2019 speech titled "The Third Sector and the Fourth Industrial Revolution," the former chief economist of the Bank of England, Andy Haldane, notes that earning CBI would reduce concerns about UBI offering a free ride.[446] He then suggests that citizenship qualifications could be achieved that would reward people for their contributions and help future employability. These

C-levels would be similar to A-levels for cognitive skills and T-levels for technical skills. Haldane suggests the Chartered Institute of Personnel and Development could oversee this process and embed them as part of apprenticeship schemes.

A variation of this is already in place with the use of time credits from volunteering, which can be used to get discounts on goods and services. Since 2008, over 1,300 charities and community groups have signed up to the Tempo Time Credit scheme.[447] Alternatively, in Scotland, the Young Scot National Entitlement Card was introduced in 2006 to record points earned when people take part in charitable and volunteering activities. Over 850,000 young people now hold a card and can use their points to get benefits.[448] AI could help administer and record these types of CBI schemes.

This may be more controversial, but it is possible to extend the idea of civic contribution and skill-building to military service. According to the World Population Review, 66 countries currently have some form of military conscription.[449] Often this is aimed at younger people, but it can extend to periods as reservists for people of all ages or most-of-life commitments. Versions of national service may begin to appear across the world in response to rising defence budgets and the need to give young people a start in life if AI reduces their opportunities.

An obvious question, given high public debt levels, is whether welfare systems will be able to afford UBI, UBC, or CBI. If AGI leads to very high levels of unemployment, we may be forced to find a way. In the meantime, this is a redistribution question that societies can vote on. One idea is to pay for these schemes using profits made by sovereign wealth funds, as in the Alaska example above. Citizens in Norway and Kuwait also enjoy welfare benefits and subsidised services from their oil revenues. If data is the new oil, perhaps technology revenues will be used to support UBI or CBI models in the future.

16. Raising Minimum Wages

    Minimum wages were first introduced in the UK in 1909 and nationally in the US in 1938 to protect workers not covered by collective agreements.[450] They aimed to reduce poverty and limit employers' ability to get away with paying low wages when labour's bargaining power was poor. By creating a floor for all companies, they level the playing field rather than allowing a race to the bottom. For employees, minimum wages can be the difference between having one job rather than two, improving care of families and health outcomes, such as getting enough sleep.

    Critics have long worried that a minimum wage would incentivise companies to look for cheaper labour elsewhere, leading to automation or offshore hiring, which would reduce jobs. So far, this fear has not materialised, but it could. In the AI age, if most jobs are automated and our only choice is to go into a human-centric job that cannot be replaced, minimum wage policies could accelerate the transition into these roles and provide long-term support for workers making the leap.

17. Shorter Working Weeks

    The concept of shorter working weeks was discussed in detail in Chapter IX – Better Jobs. There's no need to go over old ground, but the simple idea is that if AI did cause a decline in the number of people working, we could shorten working weeks and spread work across more people, preventing the few working all hours and others working none. While companies may resist these changes, it is possible for society to vote for this outcome at the ballot box.

18. Increasing Job Sharing

    Job sharing is one way to implement shorter working weeks. It could mean more people doing so on a permanent or temporary basis. Fifteen percent of people work part-time across the OECD, but in the Netherlands, 34% already do, with 52% of those being women and 18% men.[451] In Germany, during economic downturns, job sharing is used as a solution, with the government providing incentives to cut work for all rather than allowing some to be laid off.[452]

    Job sharing may appeal to working parents or older people in their pre-retirement phase who want to work less but still contribute. Digital technologies have made it easier to work part-time, picking up where another person has left off, but in many firms, accounting systems can make it more difficult. Cost allocations are often made per employee, so they'd need to become agile enough to attribute part of a desk or facility cost and part of healthcare and pension benefits; otherwise, job sharing could cost the firm more. This is entirely possible, though, and it shouldn't be an excuse not to utilise job sharing.

19. Increasing Worker Rights

    There are numerous new rights that could be given to workers in the AI age, but for simplicity, let's group them into three buckets: rights in work, rights for contingent work, and AI-related rights.

Rights in work were discussed in Chapter IX – Better Jobs, including debates on the right to flexibility or the right to disconnect. In time, these could extend to four-day workweeks or job sharing. These legal rights can support workers as power shifts towards employers in the AI age and level the competitive playing field so companies are not disadvantaged within countries.

Rights related to contingent work, by freelancers and contractors, are more challenging. Many workers choose to freelance rather than be employed by one company. Companies choose to hire them because this provides extra flexibility and lowers costs, in relation to pensions, healthcare, or central facility allocations. There is already debate over the extent to which this is taking advantage of workers and how much responsibility employers have to support irregular workers. The AI age could accelerate these trends, firstly by making it easier to link work and workers, and secondly, if layoffs mean more are forced into the contingent workforce.

This leads us to the third rights category: AI's impact on work. The most comprehensive legislation to date is the EU AI Act. Agreed on in December 2023, for implementation at the end of 2025, the act identifies levels of AI risk and can implement fines of up to 7% of turnover. For example, there are rules around the use of workplace surveillance and the use of AI to make decisions, such as in hiring. Similarly, California recently considered a No Robot Bosses Act that would ban companies from using AI systems to promote or punish workers without human oversight, but this was later vetoed by California's governor.[453]

An additional area that may be worth thinking about here is the right not to be forced to train AI to replace your job. AI will go from being a co-pilot, helping workers, to learning from them, and over time, to taking over as the pilot. Similar to current debates over safeguarding artists' royalties, as AI trains itself using their work, could workers be compensated for training AI?

20. Increasing Data Rights

A looming battleground in the workplace is data collection, ownership, and privacy. The data that trains AI systems will increasingly be generated by human labour. AI tools will also increase the surveillance powers of employers, and this data can be used in promotions, disciplinary measures, or terminations. As mentioned previously, AI will allow companies to track workers in multiple ways, from clicks on your computer and being constantly watched at work to monitoring the time taken for bathroom breaks. As UNI General Secretary Philip Jennings notes, "Data collection and artificial intelligence are the next frontier for the labour movement. Just as unions established wage, hour, and safety standards during the Industrial Revolution, it is urgent that we set new benchmarks for the Digital Revolution."[454]

The UNI Global Union has developed 10 principles for workers' data privacy and protection that can be used to guide debate around issues such as access, transparency, and explainability.[455] They also suggest intercompany data governance bodies should be established. Some existing privacy rules apply and can be extended. For example, under the EU's GDPR, humans have a right to an explanation of a decision made by an algorithm and can challenge this decision in a human-led hearing. In the US, the Stop Spying Bosses Act proposes that employers disclose what surveillance is conducted.[456] Given the power dynamics within firms, it may also be necessary to protect employees if they inquire about AI data usage by using anonymous ethics hotlines.

21. Requiring Licences for More Jobs

Many professions enforce licensing to maintain high standards, such as airline pilots, healthcare practitioners, or finance professionals. Entry standards must be reached and maintained, with ethical conduct requirements enforced and bans or fines for those who breach them.

In an AI age, licencing could be extended to protect jobs or even slow AI adoption, allowing society to compel employers to support people. In many industries, human oversight should be required and enforced. For example, even if autopilot is responsible for 95% of an airplane's flying time, we still insist on a human pilot being in charge.[457] This could be extended across many jobs to prevent full automation, so even if AI is doing most of the diagnoses in healthcare, for example, or the analysis in finance, society requires a human to approve the interactions and outcomes. Taking this one step further, senior leaders, such as AI officers or CEOs, could also be held individually liable if material things go wrong. The UK's Senior Managers Regime already does this in finance.

In 2023, the Future of Life Institute published a letter signed by over 30,000 people, including many concerned experts, calling for a pause in the development of high-risk AI models.[458] Despite that, since then, AI development has accelerated, and many argue it is impossible to pause its advance. *It is* difficult, but *it's not* impossible. If governments chose to licence all AI developers, or even all in the technology industry, as happens in finance or healthcare, this would force a pause. If not, it's likely that when AI mistakes occur, some form of licencing will result.

22. Bans on Using Certain Technologies

    Throughout history, we've seen backlashes against technology leading to bans. In 1590, Queen Elizabeth I refused a patent to William Lee for a mechanical knitting machine as it would deprive her subjects of employment. Roll forward to 2025, and J.P. Morgan's CEO Jamie Dimon noted that we could create 40 million more jobs by banning the use of tractors and fertiliser—technologies that replaced what was human work.[459] This won't happen, but it highlights that policy can engineer the outcome here rather than technology.

    Indeed, in 2024, courts in Germany banned automated shops from opening on Sundays, given that humans were not allowed to work in shops on Sundays.[460] Similarly, if we did not want to see taxi drivers lose their jobs, we could prevent driverless cars from rolling out or ban cheaper foreign driverless cars from flooding the market. The idea of bans is not hypothetical; it seems highly unlikely that Chinese AVs, or Russian humanoids, will be allowed to roam freely on American streets.

23. Concentration Limits

    There are several issues around market share concentration as we head into the AI age. The idea of banning cheap Chinese humanoids on US streets may be easy to understand, but how about cheap American AI systems that foreign societies grow to depend on? Arguably, this is already happening. Technology underpins so many areas of our lives today, and much of this technology comes from US providers. As we substitute technology for jobs, we also substitute control and profits from domestic to US companies. For example, our cloud infrastructure comes from an oligopoly of US providers, and the classified content of the UK's three spy agencies—GCHQ, M15, and M16—is now hosted by Amazon's cloud arm, Amazon Web Services (AWS).[461] In October 2025, an outage in AWS caused widespread international disruption, giving us a taste of the problems that underlie this setup. The Bank of England has also noted that the UK's financial sector has significant concentration risk, and arguably systemic risk, on a couple of US cloud platforms.[462]

We are creating technological dependencies that are difficult to break. Just as TikTok has been called "digital crack cocaine" for consumers, it is also difficult for non-US companies to go cold turkey and stop using US AI providers, especially when an AI arms race is underway.[463] However, this only perpetuates dependency because digitisation—when these technology companies offer "free" services, you are the product, and your data is being harvested and monetised—leads to winner-takes-most economics in which the big get bigger. They undercut smaller companies because of economies of scale and data network effects, in which the growth in users helps create better products. AI will accelerate digitisation and concentration into the largest businesses. This is not just an issue with technology companies. Data is important for most sectors, and market share concentrations have increased across many US and European sectors over the last two decades.

There are several issues with this dependency. One is that political leaders, their policies, and international relations change, as seen recently with trade tariffs. Secondly, AI is not just about more efficiency, but jobs, wealth, power, and control. So, who owns it can shape policy, influencing what happens with AI safety or digital taxes, for example. Thirdly, this risk around who controls it could get worse as AI expands. In an excellent paper titled "Situational Awareness," published in June 2024, Leopold Aschenbrenner, an ex-OpenAI employee, warns that we are headed towards AGI quicker than most believe and "whoever controls superintelligence has power to seize control from those who don't."[464] He believes the US government must take control of the largest AI systems at some point, saying, "I find it an insane proposition that the US government will let a random SF start-up develop superintelligence. Imagine if we had developed atomic bombs by letting Uber just improvise."

And this concentration risk rises when the biggest companies can buy start-ups or poach talent using lucrative offers. This includes a new trend of "acqui-hires"—buying other companies primarily to hire their talent—with several seniors from Inflection AI joining Microsoft, Meta investing $15 billion into Scale AI,[465] and Meta reportedly offering $100 million individual signing bonuses to lure AI talent to its lab.[466]

Another way the biggest companies preserve market share is via lobbying. Lobbying in the US has risen 300% since 1999, reaching $4.4 billion in 2024.[467] Other analyses found that six big US tech companies employed almost 300 lobbyists in 2024, one for every two members of Congress.[468] In Europe, the number of registered lobbyists has doubled since 2012.[469] Remember Marx's warning in 1845, "The ruling ideas of every epoch are the ideas of the ruling class." Or as the *Financial Times* and economist Thomas Philippon noted in 2025, "Big corporations have captured the political system and regulators, blocking new entrants and establishing monopolies and oligopolies."[470] The rise of lobbyists is a sign and proxy of this political capture, as they push vested interests while delaying or ameliorating the interests of others.

Given we are after solutions in this book, and voting options in this chapter, potential ideas include imposing market share limits; limits on new investments that extend concentration, such as acqui-hires; the promotion of national champions who will "advance the interests of the nation;" building sovereign public sector AI models, or at least partnering on them, as the Swiss are doing with publicai.co; forced interoperability of technology systems to reduce the risk of being locked into one company's products; increased data rights and regulations to keep data within countries; increased limits on lobbying to separate financial power from political power; and legislation preventing AI from being used in political campaigns to influence voters.

24. Monetary and Fiscal Policy

Most politicians have a strong survival incentive to grow employment, but given political views can be polarising, short-termist, or just wrong, the majority of advanced economies have appointed independent central banks to help as guardians of the economy. However, you may be surprised to find out that, with the exception of the US and Australia, full employment is not the primary goal of central banks. However, things can change.

After the Great Depression, Congress passed the US Employment Act of 1946, meaning federal government policy was "to promote maximum employment, production, and purchasing power."[471] Thirty years later, during a period of high inflation and unemployment, the Federal Reserve Reform Act of 1977 gave them a dual mandate to maintain stable prices and promote maximum employment.[472] Australia has had the same dual mandate since 1959.[473] Other central banks consider employment, but this is not their primary objective, which is price stability. However, if AI does lead to high and enduring unemployment, there will no doubt be calls for more dual mandates.

Central banks are well-practiced in using monetary policy to manage economic cycles, but fundamental structural changes are more challenging. Demand could become an issue as machines take on more jobs, given that robots and AI agents make terrible consumers. Lower consumer spending would impact tax revenues and thus the ability of governments to spend on services or provide fiscal support. Even worse, reaching AGI and entering an economic singularity could completely change economics and force a rethink of traditional macroeconomic policies to shape spending and create stability.

There is also a link here to the primary mandate for most central banks: price stability. As seen in the 2008 Financial Crisis, the financial system is highly interconnected and leveraged. Problems in one area can create problems elsewhere. If aggregate demand becomes a problem, this could impact asset prices. For example, one way of replacing lost income is by liquidating assets. These issues need serious consideration, and scenarios must be modelled to generate potential solutions. Central banks need the resources and mandates to deal with the economic challenges the AI age may throw up.

25. Changing How Companies Make Decisions

    If central banks have their hand on the economic tiller, it is companies that are the engine rooms for growth and employment. They are so critical that it's possible societies will vote that companies must direct their decision-making more towards shared prosperity. This is discussed in detail in the next chapter.

LAMBORGHINIS AND SNAILS

The good news is that there are plenty of options, 25 in this chapter alone, for policymakers to consider and for citizens to vote for. While many are complicated and include trade-offs, we should remember Kennedy's proactive optimism that we have the ingenuity to create solutions.

History suggests this long-term optimism must be tempered by the fact that policy change moves at a snail's pace, unless an extreme meltdown occurs, such as in the 2008 Financial Crisis or the pandemic. For example, while the first successful nuclear bomb test took place on July 16, 1945, the first legally binding international agreement to prohibit nuclear weapons, the Treaty on the Prohibition of Nuclear Weapons, was only signed by the United Nations in 2017.[474] Similarly, scientists knew in the 1950s that smoking killed people, yet the UK only banned children under 16 from buying cigarettes in 1986. Finally, despite the overwhelming scientific evidence for and long-term existential risks of climate change, we can hardly be encouraged by how slowly climate change mitigation strategies are being implemented.

Nor can we take encouragement from inaction around social media risks, cloud computing concentrations, or AI safety. As Kevin Roose noted at a recent AI safety summit, it is like looking at "policy makers on horseback trying to put seatbelts on a moving Lamborghini."[475] Adding seatbelts to AI development will take time. Even in the pro-regulation EU, the AI Act was only enforced 4.5 years after it was proposed.

And the reality is that, instead of focusing on AI risks, most governments are leaning into the AI gold rush to try to increase economic growth, so asking for seatbelts may fall on deaf ears. As Jeremy Hunt, former Chancellor of the Exchequer, said at Davos 2024, people shouldn't "kill the golden goose before it has a chance to grow."[476] Golden geese don't come around very often, so politicians are excited to reap the benefits. Because of this, AI will likely influence politics in several ways. Given that business leaders, investors, and technologists all stand to benefit from greater profits, they tend to be pro-innovation and will influence politicians accordingly. It was symbolic that the CEOs of the leading AI companies were by President Trump's side at his 2025 inauguration. And politicians could also benefit from using AI to retain power; research has shown that AI can influence people's political views, offering new persuasion tools for politicians and to politicians.[477]

So, given that most agree that AI poses risks to employment and that policy solutions will move much more slowly than technology, what can be done?

We need data, forecasts, and insight from think tanks, researchers, and academic institutions around the world. AI's impact on work is a global issue, and good solutions need to start somewhere. We also need more scenario analysis from economists on the risks, including that of an economic singularity, and robust solutions. Maybe we should revisit computer scientist Stewart Russell's metaphorical suggestion that we lock a bunch of economists in a room and not let them out until they come up with a plan on how to respond to technological unemployment.[478]

It is also important that diverse viewpoints are considered and not just those who stand to benefit most from AI. One way of allowing the public to hear and vote on policy debates is by using citizen assemblies. Their conclusions can help inform large numbers of people who have not had the time to do a deep dive on the issues. Outcomes may be that we need incremental steps—such as expanding social safety nets, tax changes, or trials on UBI and CBI—that can be scaled up if required. Again, this experimentation may not match the pace of AI, but it's better to make a start and see what sticks.

Governments should also be role modelling AI implementation. They are big employers; one in seven workers in the US economy works for the government,[479] and AI is already being pushed across government departments to improve efficiency. This will include job substitution to reduce costs and the tax burden on society, but it is also possible for governments to use AI to improve services, improve jobs, and retrain workers. As we will discuss in Part 3 of this book, governments should also be role modelling pro-human leadership.

The most important takeaways from this chapter are that we, as voters, must protect our democratic agency and be proactive in shaping outcomes by voting for the measures we would like to see. This means we cannot just hope everything will be OK. We can't use the excuse of being too busy or outsource the answers to these questions to ChatGPT. Being proactive includes being aware of the issues and debates. This book is designed to help people in this process, but each voter should form their own opinions and preferences. These can also influence who they buy from. Lastly, given election cycles are long, a quicker proactive measure workers can take is to make their opinions heard within their companies and by choosing which company to work for—voting with their feet. We explore how this might work in the next chapter.

XII

EMPLOYEES VOTE

First, they automated manufacturing,
and I did not speak out because I was not a factory worker.
Then they automated distribution,
and I did not speak out because I did not do logistics.
Then they came for the operations roles,
and I did not speak out because I was not in operations.
Then they came for the coders,
and I did not speak out because I was not a coder.
Then they came for my work,
and there was no one left to speak for me.

—*Adapted from* **Martin Niemöller**'s *1946* poem
"First They Came"[480]

SHARING BREAD

Although the context of **Niemöller**'s original poem was very different, his warnings may be applicable in the AI age: of apathy and complacency, of silence and inaction, of a trickle becoming a flow, and of individual and collective responsibility. If the number of human workers in companies is at its highest point today, the ability to speak up and be heard may never be better than it is now. This chapter asks if and how employees can use their voices to influence AI's progress within companies.

Companies have grown to have dominant roles in society. They are the vehicles of economic growth and employment. They are the channel through which governments try to deliver policy, but they also influence policy and laws. As corporate power grows, the danger, according to Madoc Batcup, in his book *Companionism,* is that, "Gradually the governance of society moves in practice away from a democracy, government by the people, to a 'corpocracy' government by corporates."[481] At this point, it seems highly likely that AI will only increase the power of employers over employees and society, but if this goes too far, employee frustration could boil over, and the action they take could alter the way corporations are controlled, paralleling the move towards more democratic societies over the last 200 years. We shall explore this more later.

The word company comes from the Latin *"com,"* meaning "with or together," and *"panis,"* meaning "bread." The idea of a group of people who share bread together is rooted in companionship, hospitality, and trust. For most of history, companies were owned by founders, and there are good examples of founders who promoted the welfare of employees and communities, such as William Lever, George Cadbury, or Frances Cabot Lowe. The Industrial Revolution increased the need for investment to scale businesses and the use of more external capital, moving ownership from founders to investors. The bigger move towards the managerial capitalism we are familiar with today came less than a hundred years ago. You can see these ideas emerging in the 1932 book *The Modern Corporation and Private Property* by Berle and Means, who argued for the separation of ownership and control within companies, the former going to shareholders and the latter to managers.

Another big turning point came after 1970, with Milton Friedman's seminal essay "The Social Responsibility of Business Is to Increase Its Profits." Friedman argued the purpose of business was to make profits, not employ people or have social objectives. He accepted that these may be sub-goals if they drove greater long-term profits for shareholders, but he underlined that a manager's fiduciary duty was to shareholders. Management incentive structures using share performance as a metric have become supersized under this model of shareholder primacy, creating increasing wage inequality and psychological separation between leaders and workers; average CEO-to-employee pay ratios for S&P 500 companies rose from 42:1 in 1980 to a whopping 261:1 by 2024.[482] Incentives influence behaviours.

Unfortunately, these trends have coincided with shorter investor time horizons and manager tenures.[483] Both have encouraged a more short-term, transactional approach to business, which only makes the situation worse for workers. For example, share buybacks can increase shareholder returns more quickly than investments. And there are plenty of examples of share prices increasing when layoffs are announced, and rather than sharing the pain with employees, boards then reward CEOs with large bonuses that year.

This short-termism has been exacerbated by three significant trends in finance since Friedman's essay was published. Money invested by machines, such as index trackers, ETFs, and quantitative funds, has reduced the influence of long-term active shareholders. Amazingly, and worryingly, passive (digital) investment managers now hold a larger share of the US stock market than active investors.[484] AI will only increase the proportion of money run by machines. Secondly, the growth of shorter-term hedge-fund investors has also been substantial. Neither offers much support for the longer-term interests of employees. While this could be corrected by restricting voting to human-led investments and giving greater voting rights to long-term shareholders, there is little sign that this will happen.

Finally, private equity has ballooned, which is highly focused on maximising shareholder return, with private equity assets under management (AUM) growing from $700 billion in 2005 to $6 trillion in 2025.[485] In the UK, more of the top 500 companies were owned by private equity than by public markets by 2022.[486] As Pete Stavros, co-head of private equity at KKR, noted, "The underlying narrative that surrounds private equity is unflattering. The stereotype is that private equity firms use excessive amounts of leverage, strip down groups, fire workers, and sell off the pieces."[487] Private equity groups can have a big influence, as highlighted by Vista Equity Partners' aim to use AI to reduce its workforce by a third and save costs across its portfolio companies, which collectively employ over 10,000 people.[488]

These points come together to paint an unsettling picture for employees: most companies are run by leaders whose job it is to maximise shareholder returns, and an increasing portion of investments is made on a short-term basis, not for the benefit of long-term stakeholders.

Add this trend to the increasing importance and wealth of technology companies and the way that has changed their purpose and influence. Jony Ive, former chief design officer at Apple, recently noted about Silicon Valley, the epicentre of the technology industry, "When I first moved here [in 1992], I came because it was characterised by people who genuinely saw that their purpose was in service to humanity, to inspire people and help people create. I don't feel that way about this place right now."[489]

What does this all mean? We are moving into a new technological revolution and a new work revolution without strong long-term incentives to support workers. In fact, arguably, the quickest way to sell new AI products, grow profits for investors, and share incentive schemes for managers is by replacing human workers with AI. Given that election cycles and new policies take time, the rest of this chapter looks at options employees may consider to influence AI outcomes *within* companies.

VOTING WITH YOUR FEET

The starting point here is honest, inclusive conversations between team members and leaders about how AI can improve outcomes for clients, employers, and employees. Giving employees agency in the direction of AI is crucial. However, what happens if employers are more attracted by investments in technology than people?

The next easiest way for employees to express their views is to leave companies that treat employees poorly and join companies that treat employees well. It can be quicker to look after oneself by upping sticks and moving firms than by changing your current employer's mind about their approach to AI. However, this only adds more fuel to the fire when it comes to the short-termism and transactional work relationships that have been growing for several decades.

In her 1990 book *The Death of the Organization Man*, Amanda Bennett argued that the era of lifetime employment was coming to an end. A wave of mergers and acquisitions and layoffs in the 1980s changed the employer-employee relationship, with workers believing employers would happily drop them like a hot potato when needed. Loyalty fell. Tenure fell. Investment fell. Engagement fell.

There are ways out of this downcycle, as discussed more fully in the next chapter, but AI could create several crosscurrents. Pointing AI towards job substitution will further reduce loyalty, trust, and engagement. Secondly, AI is making it easier for workers to find work, giving them new tools to leave companies quickly. Lastly, technology can help workers better understand which companies allow talent to flourish rather than flounder. Sites like Glassdoor crowdsource ratings and reviews to help workers move to the best companies. Better transparency here can lead to better outcomes for all, given EX (employee experience) drives CX (customer experience), which drives revenues. And better alignment on values could eventually encourage longer-term relationships between employers and employees.

VOTING WITH YOUR SHARES

Many companies argue that employees, employers, and shareholders can be aligned towards the same goals, of share maximisation, via Employee Stock Ownership Plans (ESOPs). ESOPs started in the US in 1956, and almost 15 million employees are now part of these schemes.[490] They can be cashed out after a few years, or on leaving your job or retirement. There are lots of positives of share ownership schemes, including employees benefiting when leaders make layoffs and share prices rise; however, their importance is often over-egged.

The way ESOPs and similar schemes work is that the shares are held in a trust, so employees do not have direct legal ownership or control over a company's operations. In many ESOPs, employees aren't even given direct voting rights. They have limited pass-through voting on significant events, such as mergers, but for most decisions, the ESOP trustees vote in line with the board's recommendations. In addition to little say in a company's direction, share schemes are of little benefit to the employees who lose their jobs.

The truth is that, as currently used, share schemes can be a control mechanism. Part of an employee's compensation, such as a bonus, goes into the ESOP, and this can be taken away from the employee for all sorts of reasons: for wrongdoing, as part of a bonus clawback if future targets are not met, or when you leave. Therefore, instead of giving employees greater voice, share schemes can have the opposite effect, as compensation can disappear.

As AI rolls out, what employees want is more control over the decisions about how it is used, not to be more controlled. In his recent TED Talk, "The Secret of Business Success," KKR's Pete Stavros made it clear that a winning formula in employee ownership schemes is the inclusion of employees in decision-making. If share schemes don't provide this, other methods below could.

VOTING VIA HR

Is HR (Human Resources) the answer to giving employees more representation? They are clearly part of the solution as they help both employees and managers by upholding policies and ensuring people's welfare. In my experience, people who go into HR do so because they want to help humans and make a difference—and most really do. However, HR must straddle the needs of bosses and workers, and it is the bosses who pay them, allocate their resources, and set their KPIs. As Laszlo Bock, former head of people operations at Google, asked, are HR "the secret police of corporations [or], as they claim to be, champions of employees."[491]

As we head into the AI age, it would be helpful if HR were independent champions for workers, but how they are valued and positioned within organisations will determine their influence in decision-making. For example, while many companies will say that people "are our most important asset," less than 5% of CEOs globally come from an HR background. In contrast, almost 20% of CEOs come from a CFO role.[492] Given that CFOs mind the tills for shareholders, this may tell us something about the current prioritisation of profits over people in most companies. Indeed, HR leaders sometimes report to the CFO. Another indication of the relative (un)importance of HR leaders, according to a remuneration survey by CEG, is that they appear to be the lowest paid in the C-suite.[493] If workers are to be prioritised, we may need to better value HR leaders and aim to hire more CEOs with HR experience.

How about HR representation at the other decision-making table—company boards? Most are mandated by regulatory bodies to have three committees: an audit committee, looking after finances; a nominating and governance committee; and a compensation committee. If you think the latter is looking after the interests of employees, think again. The compensation committee ensures executive compensation aligns with the company's performance and shareholder interests. Some boards added an environmental, social, and governance committee when ESG rose in prominence. Could mandating the addition of an employee committee offer the same consideration to workers' welfare in the AI age? Data from the Chartered Institute of Personnel and Development in 2023 suggests that only 2% of boards have an HR leader on the board, so this would redress a current imbalance.[494] In contrast, 99% have a CFO on them.

Or perhaps regulatory bodies should mandate the addition of an independent representative of employees on boards to highlight talent-related issues and give workers a greater voice. They would need to be armed with lots of data to surface these issues and potential solutions, answering questions like, "What is the expected ratio of job substitution versus augmentation from AI in the next three years?" or, "How are external ratings from companies like Glassdoor on what it is like to work at the company?" Given that AI can help collect more data, there is also an opportunity for important data to flow down from leaders, not just up from workers, improving transparency around people-related metrics. Employees would then be better informed about new job categories the company is investing in or mobility and L&D opportunities, enabling them to grow and adapt.

Data could help HR better support employees, but employees may need to support HR as well. HR is one of the areas already impacted by digitisation, and this will only increase under AI. Automated self-service systems divest previous HR tasks to managers and employees; this means HR gets downsized, and employees have less in-person contact with the HR team that remains. In many cases, HR has also been relocated to a lower-cost location, meaning HR personnel who are needed by employees can only meet them online, even when workers are being let go. If people and work culture are important, shouldn't we be rehumanising, rather than dehumanising, Human Resources?

HR software provider Personio notes that three out of five business leaders think AI will take over HR in the future.[495] Indeed, AI can already do 90% of the hiring selection process, sifting of applications, marking of psychometric tests, and judging of one-way AI video interviews. The best of the best *are* interviewed in person, but at that point, AI has already had an outsized influence on the choosing of human candidates.

HR is an important test case for AI being used for job augmentation rather than substitution. While it *could* free up HR from mundane work to focus on higher-value tasks that support employees, such as in-person training, welfare, and engagement, the trend is unfortunately towards more automated self-serve learning systems. Moreover, as AI agents and robots become the norm, what time they do have left could be diverted to looking after this growing non-human workforce, giving human employees even less attention.

Companies should also rethink the label "human resources," first used in 1893 by the economist John Commons in his book *The Distribution of Wealth*. Classifying humans as resources makes them feel interchangeable with other forms of capital equipment, emphasising a more transactional approach to people management. Over time, some companies have adopted more humanising labels for HR and HR leaders, such as head of people, head of people and culture, human experience management (HXM), and talent management (TM). My personal recommendation is a symbolic upgrade to the term human talent management (HTM). This phrase is in line with the message of Part 3 of this book and its aim to lift human talent up, rather than allowing AI to push it down or out.

VOTING VIA UNIONS

Trade unions grew out of discontent over exploitation, poor wages, and poor working conditions during the Industrial Revolution in the UK. Their unions were legalised in 1824, after the Luddite movement in 1811 and the 1820 Rising in Scotland. It may not surprise you to hear that union activity rose again in the late nineteenth and early twentieth centuries with Taylorism, as his "process management" techniques reduced worker independence and increased layoffs to improve efficiency and productivity. Workers feared being turned into "automatons." Indeed, a 1912 US House of Representatives report noted Taylorism gave managers a "high level of power." Strikes and collective action became commonplace in the US and Europe as workers pushed back against these "dehumanising time-and-motion methods."

Union membership continued to grow in the US and UK until the late 1970s, but it declined thereafter as manufacturing was offshored and Friedman's shareholder primacy doctrine rose. Unions were viewed as raiding corporate profits, so offshoring silenced workers, reduced costs, and increased returns. Union membership in the US fell from 20.1% of workers in 1983 to 9.9% in 2024, according to the Bureau of Labor Statistics.[496] However, there are signs this trend may be changing. Union approval bottomed out in 2009, and Gallup data suggests 71% of Americans now approve of labour unions, the highest since 1965.[497] A 2023 US Treasury report showed that unions have raised wages for union members versus the wages of similar workers in non-union jobs, with Secretary of the Treasury Janet Yellen noting that unionising "could contribute to reversing the stark increase in inequality we've seen in recent decades, promoting economywide growth."[498]

Concern for workers in the pandemic increased not only union approval but also union coordination. This coordination is now being supercharged by collective fears over AI. US unions representing grocery store cashiers, delivery drivers, workers in casinos and hotels, and those in the film industry in Hollywood have been seeking to limit the negative effects of AI, automation, and robots. As discussed in Chapter VI – AI Anarchy, the demands from longshoremen in 2024 led to a pay increase of 62% over six years.[499] Sixty-two percent and a say on the use of automation and AI will galvanise others. Unless AI abundance appears quickly, it seems highly likely that membership and activity of unions will rise around the world. Indeed, although union membership in the UK hit rock bottom in 2016, the country saw more strikes in 2023 than at any time since the 1980s.[500] And the China Labour Bulletin noted that protests in the Chinese manufacturing sector in 2024 reached the highest level in a decade.[501]

There are several other issues around unions that will shape whether they can provide workers with influence in the AI era. Many of the sectors most exposed to AI do not have strong unions. For example, unions only represent 1% of finance workers in the US.[502] This will probably change, but it will take time. Many employees don't even know if they have a union and who to contact to learn more. There are also concerns around victimisation or blacklisting of those who join unions. Under the 1935 National Labor Relations Act, union membership in the US is a "protected characteristic," but this is not the case in all countries, such as the UK. Rules around union-busting tactics may also need to be looked at. In 2024, workers at Amazon in Coventry, England, tried to collectively improve working conditions, pay, and hours. They needed a majority vote and reached 49.5%, but Amazon reportedly brought in temporary workers specifically to dilute the vote.[503] Similarly, TikTok made redundancies in London one week before employees were holding a ballot on unionisation.[504]

There are tools out there that can help workers. As discussed in Chapter VI, social media can help amplify the concerns of groups that do not have formal power or influence, and new technologies are providing ways for workers to join together. Worker rights platform Organise offers advice and provides free and open technology for workers to run polls, start campaigns, create petitions, or even write letters to CEOs. Over a million people are part of Organise's network.[505] Alternatively, the UNI Global Union, which now represents 20 million workers across 150 countries, provides advice on best practices, educational resources, and databases on union-negotiated agreements.[506] Technology can also help companies work with employees on the issues they care about most. Despite survey fatigue, it has never been easier to use surveys to poll for preferred outcomes, track results, and communicate improvements.

The best way to avoid growing union action and worker demands in response to the rise of AI is for pro-human leadership to smooth the path ahead, as discussed in the next chapter. If this does not happen quickly, leaders may have to face more extreme pushback or even a change in the structure of company leadership, as discussed next.

VOTING VIA WORK COUNCILS

Understandably, leaders may fear that unions will increase company costs and make them less competitive. In Germany, this risk is reduced as unions are organised on an industry-wide basis. Seventeen large unions negotiate collectively with management to improve the outcomes for all workers in that industry. Of course, this could mean German companies are less competitive than companies in other countries, but within the country, the playing field is level. Also, unions in Germany are not affiliated to any particular party, reducing the polarising politics around unionisation.

If AI does negatively impact employment, other countries may vote for this kind of industry collectivism or go even further. In Germany, a system of codetermination, called *"Mitbestimmung,"* gives workers representation in worker councils and on supervisory boards, which oversee and appoint the executive boards that run companies. The level of representation depends on the size of companies, with employees having a third of the supervisory board in companies with 500 or more employees and a 50% share in companies with more than 2,000 employees. Formally allowing workers to have a say in decision-making changes the balance of power and thus the board's priorities, allowing issues such as worker welfare to be balanced with corporate profits.

The 1976 Codetermination Act, which brought this into force, was designed not only to balance economics with social responsibility but also to promote long-termism, supporting stable jobs, rather than a focus on short-term shareholder gains. Building on Germany's 1952 Works Constitution Act and a post-World War II desire to reduce economic instability, prevent authoritarianism, and improve worker rights, it aimed to solve the misalignment between the goals of shareholders and workers. Balancing economics and society, this disconnect between the needs of investors and workers and the conflict between short-term and long-term views are likely to become even trickier and more relevant issues in the age of AI.

As with unions, the need for work councils likely depends on how corporate and political leaders manage job transitions in the age of AI, but it's an option to consider. Codetermination systems also exist in Denmark, Norway, and Sweden, but each mandates different levels of worker representation. Forms of worker representation on boards also exist in Austria, the Czech Republic, France, Hungary, Luxembourg, the Netherlands, Poland, and Slovakia.[507] If AI disruption is significant, codetermination may spread to other countries.

VOTING VIA WORKER COOPERATIVES

Codetermination is an example of increased democracy at work, offering employees a say in how a company is run. But if shareholders and leaders worry about ceding this level of control, they should consider the fact that an even more drastic change is possible.

Democracy has been the exception and not the norm in advanced economies. The ability for citizens to vote for outcomes is still relatively new compared to the long history of control by monarchs, the wealthy, or by arms. However, democracy still doesn't extend to companies. The overwhelming majority today are plutocracies; they are governed by the wealthy: the more money you have, the more shares you have, leading to more voting rights and more control. And given there is an increasing concentration of wealth, that is a lot of control in the hands of the few. A 2023 Institute for Policy Studies analysis found the wealthiest 1% in the US owned 54% of the public equity market.[508] And Oxfam found that the richest 1% across the world have more wealth than the bottom 95%.[509]

As Madoc Batcup says in his book *Companionism*, "It is perhaps ironic that, partly as a result of the Cold War, corporate capitalism has also enjoyed the advantage of often being linked with democracy, to heighten its distinction from communism. And yet for all this, the vehicle through which capitalism is most powerfully expressed today—the corporate structure—is wholly undemocratic."[510] Batcup goes on to say, "It is difficult to imagine the population of any democracy choosing a system where the electorate votes in accordance to wealth, where there is no legal system, and where the executive and the legislative is rolled into one."

One of the big changes in how companies were run came in the nineteenth century, with limited liability legislation. Previously, owners of companies had unlimited liability. As they were personally responsible if things went wrong, they needed more control. The rise of limited liability companies (LLCs) broke this need for control by shareholders, and this could be extended further today, given that investments have become more short-term and transactional. As John Kay notes in his recent book *The Corporation in the 21st Century*, "The development of capital as a service renders ownership of capital largely irrelevant for management authority."[511] Kay warns that, "Intrinsic motivation and professional ethics were replaced by targets and bonuses. The purpose of business, MBA students were told, was not to meet the needs of customers and society but to create shareholder value for anonymous stockholders… Today, the twenty-first century corporation faces a crisis of legitimacy."

The data supports Kay's concern about a "crisis of legitimacy." In the US, the global heartland of capitalism, 62% of Americans have a negative view of big business, with just 37% positive, down from 58% in 2012.[512] And just 54% of Americans are positive about capitalism, down from 61% in 2012. In other surveys, Americans under 30 felt more positively about socialism than capitalism.[513] If AI does lead to higher unemployment, this may get worse. And as discussed at the start of this chapter, the changing nature of investors and investment—towards short-term funds, machines, and private equity—suggests they will not be the ones looking to change course.

Is there an alternative? Just as the Industrial Revolution led to political democracy, in which votes were no longer based on property ownership, it is possible that corporate democracy breaks the link between share ownership and control of companies. This model of worker cooperatives would involve the transfer of voting rights from shareholders to employees. It would be one person, one vote, as in political democracy, and employees would have the ability to appoint and dismiss the executives and the board. Management would be responsible to, not just for, employees. Of course, leaders would still need to drive innovation and growth and help the company adapt to market conditions, but under this system, the long-term growth of employees could become as important to them as the short-term growth of profits. It would transform incentives and outcomes.

While worker primacy rather than shareholder primacy would be a dramatic change for most, and would likely be abhorrent to many leaders and investors, this model of worker cooperatives does exist. Examples, such as John Lewis in the UK or Mondragon in Spain, have higher employee engagement levels. Mondragon has over 70,000 employees and maintains a 6:1 pay ratio between the highest and lowest earners.[514]

According to the International Cooperative Alliance, there are over 3 million cooperatives globally, providing jobs to 10% of the employed population.[515] This idea is not fringe, and policy could encourage more companies to use it. For example, recent inheritance tax changes in the UK allow business owners to avoid tax if they sell at least 50% of their company to an employee ownership trust (EQT). EQTs are managed by a trustee, but they give workers more say in decision-making.

If voters wanted even more say, it would be possible to change the tax code and tax companies at a higher rate if they did not ensure greater employee representation. Or, going one step further, if AI were to increase wealth but reduce jobs, it may be possible to move to an ownership model in which everyone owns a piece of the production system. Indeed, in *Stellar: A World Beyond Limits and How to Get There*, James Arbib and Tony Seba lay out this vision. They believe we are on the edge of a revolutionary change in technology and society and see us moving from an extraction and scarcity economy to an abundance and post-scarcity society. They suggest moving to community ownership in this new context, so the benefits are widely shared, helping protect people rather than jobs.

THE ROOM WHERE IT HAPPENS

The award-winning musical *Hamilton*, which looks at the early political history of the United States, features the song "The Room Where It Happens." It tells the story of the Compromise of 1790, a deal made between Hamilton, Jefferson, and Madison, demonstrating that the real decisions were made behind closed doors. The song captures the tensions and trade-offs that are part of reaching a compromise and the hope that leaders achieve the right outcomes without sacrificing too much. Given that motivations vary and side-deals inevitably happen, the song title underscores how important it is to be "in the room where it happens." [516]

This brilliantly captures the anxieties employees often feel that they are not allowed into the metaphorical decision-making room, and unfortunately, even for those *in* the room, it's not always as scientific and measured as workers would hope. Leaders have to guess at the future, which is complicated, and there are pressures, politics, and incentives to balance. Given that workers are central actors, not spectators, in the workplace, it is important that they have a say. They need someone fighting their corner in the room where decisions about AI get made.

There are many amazing leaders who *will make sure* workers have agency in the direction of AI, but we must also recognise that the current incentive structure for many leaders will be towards greater efficiency and profitability rather than protecting their workers. Everyone has a boss, and even CEOs are accountable to the board, which is accountable to shareholders. Yet it would be wrong if employees became like the frog in the boiling water metaphor—uncomfortable but unable or unwilling to act, their fate determined by others turning the dial. It could even be argued that workers invest more in a company than investors do. Many investors are driven to make short-term returns, buying and selling a diversified portfolio of shares using other people's money. Employees, on the other hand, often invest a much longer chunk of their lives and attention in their company.

One action towards change took place in 2019 when the Business Roundtable, an association of CEOs from America's leading companies, redefined the purpose of a corporation as serving *all* stakeholders, including employees, rather than just shareholders.[517] This was a departure from their 1997 statement that the principal objective was delivering economic returns to a company's owners. This is significant as Business

Roundtable member companies account for almost a quarter of US GDP and one in four American jobs, and 181 CEOs from major US companies signed the statement. While this felt consequential, five years on, *Harvard Business Review* research suggests not much has actually changed. In fact, workers may worry that things have gone backwards. Climate change concerns had been a big driver in the 2019 pledge, yet the biggest recent trend has been companies backtracking on their ESG or DEI pledges after President Trump's 2025 inauguration.

Workers enter this AI age, and the work revolution it's bringing, with dreadful engagement, low investment in their reskilling, low collective representation, low influence in boardrooms, and a less paternalistic shareholder base. That is a tough combination, and it could be about to get much worse. The traditional symbiotic relationship between capital and labour is in the process of changing, with less dependence on labour as AI grows. Given the trends outlined in the first part of this book, towards more robots, AI agents, and digital labour, as well as the rising value of data, it is possible to argue that employee bargaining power will only fall from this point onwards.

The issues and options discussed in this chapter could impact employees, employers, investors, and politicians. The mention of separation of ownership and control, of worker cooperations, codetermination, and trade unions could elevate the blood pressure of some readers. Whether we need to take any of the more extreme paths outlined will likely depend on how extreme the impacts of AI on workers are. The traditional paths of employees asserting their power by voting with their feet or via equity ownership plans will continue if we have positive outcomes. However, if the AI transition fails to provide inclusive growth for most, a more acute worker backlash is possible; indeed, we must learn our lesson from the first Engels' pause.

Change is usually incremental, and this gives people time to adapt, but AI does not appear to be giving us that luxury. When change accelerates quickly, as it did in the 2008 Financial Crisis or the pandemic, overreactions are more likely. To steer society away from dramatic change and potential damage, there is another possible path that can lead to positive outcomes for all: pro-human leadership. This is leadership that can protect us from the negative possibilities, including anarchy, raised in the first part of this book. Leadership that plants solutions and grows hope. We'll explore this win-win scenario in the final section – Part 3.

PART 3

Pro-Human Leadership

XIII

THE PRO-HUMAN LEADER

"The best way to predict your future is to create it."

—Abraham Lincoln[518]

"The ultimate determinant of the shape of tomorrow's world will be the quality of leadership."

—Anthony Howard[519]

REMEMBER YOUR HUMANITY

$E = mc^2$ is arguably the world's most famous equation. Behind its simple brevity lies some of the most profound concepts in physics. They laid the foundations for nuclear physics and, in turn, led to the invention of nuclear bombs that threaten us and nuclear plants that power us. Albert Einstein gave birth to this equation in a paper on mass-energy equivalence in 1905, aged 26, while working as an assistant at the Swiss Patent Office. He went on to be named *Time's* Person of the Century in 1999.[520]

What I want to focus on here is Einstein's last public act before his death in 1955, aged 76. At this point, he was a genius with a lifetime of wisdom. With Bertrand Russell, he produced a manifesto to contain nuclear weapons, known as the Russell-Einstein Manifesto, in which they plead, "We appeal as human beings, to human beings, remember your humanity and forget the rest."[521] Brilliantly simple. Brilliantly impactful. It was signed by eleven Nobel laureates.

Observing that the world was at a tipping point, driven by an arms race that could cause mutual destruction, they offered this politically neutral declaration to remind people what was most important. Russell noted, "We have found that the men who know most are the most gloomy." Several years later, when asked what wisdom he wished to pass to future generations, Russell said, "Love is wise."[522]

The world is at another tipping point with another technology that will both power us and threaten us. For the first time in human history, a new technology is in the process of becoming more intelligent than us. An AI arms race is underway, with experts warning of existential risks, autonomous weapons, and a potential economic singularity.

While we don't know what wisdom Einstein would have offered about AI, when considering the multitude of complicated options, the profound simplicity of his 1955 statement seems fitting: "We appeal as human beings, to human beings, remember your humanity and forget the rest."

So, what does this mean? If we prioritise our humanity, we become pro-human, directing AI towards benefitting the greatest number of human beings. To do so, we need pro-human leaders—people who can build a bridge between the risks outlined in Part 1 of this book and the solutions and societal changes outlined in Part 2. If leaders can use these ideas to manage AI transitions to benefit the many, connecting everyone in a shared mission, the more extreme changes discussed in the last two chapters may not be needed at all.

Of course, leadership takes many forms, including leaders in society, of organised labour, of technology, or even leadership of the self. However, given our focus is on work, let us first look at business leadership. These are the leaders who are investing for the future, implementing AI, deciding how many workers are needed, and managing talent. Holding Einstein's suggestions in one hand—to remember our humanity—this chapter digs deeper into how we can apply pro-human leadership in practice.

THRIVING AT WORK

Even if you are a techno-optimist and believe that AI will lead to abundance, not anxiety or anarchy, you need to know that we still have a major problem in the workplace: just 33% of workers are thriving at work, versus 58% who say they are struggling, according to data from Gallup.[523] Those not thriving at work have a lower probability of thriving in life.

Gallup's dataset of 64 million employees started in 1998 and has grown to 183,806 businesses across 160 countries. Their 2025 workplace survey concludes that just 21% of employees worldwide are positively engaged at work. This is marginally better than the 17% who are actively disengaged, but a dreadfully large 62% are not engaged. The US has leading positive engagement metrics at 31%, compared to Europe at 13% and the UK at 10%, but all these numbers are poor, and the figures have been trending down, not up. Given that engagement is more important to most employees than pay, it is not surprising that 50% of respondents in the Gallup survey are looking at job adverts or actively seeking a new job. We may be heading into a period of AI anxiety, but something is already seriously wrong.

Most employers would want their employees to be engaged for the sake of their own happiness, but also because it's a key driver of business health. A meta-analysis of 263 research studies found organisations with the most engaged employees outperformed those with the least engaged across a series of metrics: 22% greater profitability, 21% better productivity, 65% lower turnover, and 10% better customer ratings.[524] Engagement pays.

The most successful organisations reach 70% positive engagement, up from 52% in 2006, so some firms are getting it right. Gallup estimates that if the world's workplace were fully engaged, $9.6 trillion in extra productivity could be added to the global economy—the equivalent of an additional 9% in global GDP. This approach could beat AI in terms of upside, but it does not need to be an either-or situation. It is possible to have both.

If we agree that positive engagement is far too low and the upsides of prioritising it could be significant, we need to ask if AI can help improve it or whether it will make it worse? All agree that more disruption is coming, and this will increase anxiety. A poll by Pew found that most Americans believe that generative AI will impact jobs, and mainly negatively.[525] In an Ipsos survey, only 37% of respondents felt that AI would improve their jobs.[526] Already exhausted by constant change, workers know the pace of change continues to accelerate. Many fear there is a sword of Damocles hanging over their job, but they also fear that surviving requires doing more, and more.

As Jon Clifton, the CEO of Gallup, notes, "We are witnessing a pivotal moment in the global workplace—one where engagement is faltering at the exact time artificial intelligence is transforming every industry in its path… The question, then, is how to master AI in ways that spark growth… If mishandled, AI could diminish engagement by severing the vital human bonds—friendships at work, a sense of being heard, and genuine care from colleagues—that keep teams thriving. We stand at the edge of a new era of work."[527]

LEADING CHANGE AND CHANGING LEADERSHIP

Clearly, we need leaders to navigate the implementation of AI so more people thrive, but we must also recognise that leaders have steered us to where we are now. They not only need to lead change, but they also need to change the way they lead if more people are to thrive. Changing the way they lead will include a new phase of leading AI agents and robots and managing hybrid teams of human and non-human workers. The danger is that this new set of responsibilities and the skills they will need to develop to handle them could distract them further from the goal of positively leading people.

We also have to recognise that there is only so much we can ask of leaders. One cause of the recent drop in engagement, according to Gallup's data, was a nosedive in positive engagement from managers to just 27%. If managers are not positively engaged, it is difficult for them to lead others well. The demands on managers have been rising, and they have a tough job balancing competing priorities. Managers need support, not more outsourcing of people's roles to AI.

Turning the glass from half empty to half full, this is the moment to ask how we can do better. We all know that major change is coming, so this can act as a catalyst to debate what good looks like. By envisioning a better tomorrow, leaders can offer workers more agency in the direction of travel and help create the conditions to turn hope into reality. As Abraham Lincoln noted, "The best way to predict your future is to create it."[528] Leaders do have the power to build bridges towards the solutions discussed in Part 2 of this book: abundance, better jobs, enough new human jobs, upskilling and reskilling, the right worker rights, and agency for employees in deciding how AI is used.

Leaders must commit to being part of the solution to create flourishing work environments. Most are paid based on profits, and the combination of shareholder primacy and business-centred leadership has resulted in a focus on financial growth. In contrast, human-centred leadership puts the growth of people at the heart of decision-making. However, leadership does not have to choose between profit maximisation and being people-first. Pro-human leadership holds both people and profits as equally important. It aims for financial growth *and* human growth—a win-win.

So, how can leaders lift both people and profits? One simple way is by asking at each meeting, "How can we be more pro-human?" It is a simple question, but it explicitly brings intent and the possibility of solutions into the room. Secondly, there are many core tenets of human-centred cultures that we know work to improve positive engagement and outcomes. The rest of this chapter breaks these down and then recombines them into a holistic solution.

GROWING PEOPLE

Without question, machines deal with numbers better than humans, and humans deal with people better than machines. Extending this, machines will work to grow profits, and we need leaders to work to grow people. Most leaders have every intention of doing this, but they are often so busy getting the job done and growing profits that they don't have enough time to grow their people. Time freed up by using AI should be rechannelled into growing people as well as profits.

Helping people grow is both a mindset and a process. The mindset includes making their development a priority, while the process includes having collaborative coaching conversations on how to make this happen in practice. It sounds simple, but unfortunately, research has found that most employees do not feel confident about their current role or how to progress.[529] This can be changed.

Given leadership aims to get the best out of people, a good place to start is by identifying strengths. Most successful people anchor on and build from their strengths. One of the founders of positive psychology, Abraham Maslow, noted that the highest form of human flourishing, self-actualisation, includes fulfilling one's potential by doing what one is best at. Psychometric tests can now help place employees in roles that fit their innate talents, but managers are the ones who will then align strengths and goals. It is worth the effort. Gallup's meta-analysis of 103 studies and 20,201 teams shows that strengths-based organisations, those that specifically leverage the talents of their employees, significantly increase employee and customer engagement.[530]

Layering on top of intentionality and strengths, we next need to add communication. In his book *The 27 Challenges Managers Face,* Bruce Tulgan asked tens of thousands of non-managers, "What is the one improvement you'd like to make in your relationship with your manager that would help you do your job better?"[531] The number one answer was better communication. This means more direction, more feedback, and more coaching on how to improve. Research studies show that frequent check-ins work best to improve engagement, wellbeing, retention, and performance. And data from 11 million check-ins at Cisco highlighted that live, in-person check-ins are most effective.[532]

Another ingredient is investment in the upskilling or reskilling of employees, as well as the room for them to learn, as discussed in Chapter X. This doesn't just allow companies to attract and retain talent; it is critical if employees are going to surf the AI disruption wave and for many of the other factors mentioned below, such as trust. Leaders need to build this bridge, and while we must not outsource growing humans to machines, the use of AI, such as talent intelligence platforms and coaching bots, can help improve transparency on opportunities and paths.

A key factor in all the areas discussed above is leaders carving out the time to create cultures of growth. People need attention. Indeed, it can produce better results than assessment, but consistently engaging every direct report is time-consuming, and few leaders feel they have enough space in their schedule to do so. One of the reasons coaching helps people is that it provides the gift of time and space, away from the hustle, to help people think deeply and develop. We will have failed if some of the time saved by AI is not recycled into helping leaders and their teams grow.

GROWING PURPOSE

If AI can be used to make work more meaningful, it would be a win-win for employers and employees. This is not a new concept. The ancient Greek philosophy of *eudaimonia,* or flourishing, involves living a life with meaning and purpose. More recently, Viktor Frankl's highly influential book *Man's Search for Meaning* stresses the importance of purpose,[533] while Simon Sinek's book *Start with Why* highlights how purpose can attract and inspire employees.[534]

Work occupies a significant portion of one's life, so finding meaning and purpose in it is important. In contrast to previous generations, who had to work to guarantee their survival, today we want to do meaningful work as well as earn a living.

Surveys show that COVID-19 accelerated this desire to work with a company because you want to and not because you have to.[535]

This is not just an altruistic strategy for employers. The ability to tap into people's intrinsic motivation, their internal drive, leads to better results. People are not coin operated. The Work Human Index found "meaningful work" to be the largest contributor to a positive employee experience,[536] and research shows that connecting with purpose in the workplace improves productivity by 22%, engagement threefold, fulfilment by 64%, and retention by 40%, leading to more growth for companies and individuals.[537]

However, there is much room for improvement. McKinsey found that although 70% think work defines their sense of purpose, only 18% of employees feel they get enough purpose at work.[538] This purpose gap is significantly higher for employees than for upper management. Other data from Gallup suggests that less than half of employees understand their company's purpose, just 27% believe in their company's values,[539] and only 30% connect to their company's purpose.[540] Many workers see mission statements as generic, bland, or even worse, as "purpose-washing" facades. We can do better. Without a shared purpose, employees see their roles as transactional or as some sort of joke: "They pretend to pay us and we pretend to work."[541]

Given that digitisation has not helped so far, will a future where we work with AI agents and AI robots make things better or worse? It is worth heeding the results of a 2024 study of 20 European countries by the University of Groningen that found that workers in industries with high levels of robot penetration reported significantly less purpose and meaningfulness in their jobs.[542]

So, if we know there is a big opportunity to improve, and a risk that things will get worse, what are the solutions?

Mission statements need to be meaningful, communicated frequently, lived constantly, and celebrated often. Employees should not just be able to understand and feel what their organisation stands for; they should be able to articulate how their role makes a difference towards this purpose. Better still, they should be able to say what makes them proud to do the work they do. This process needs to start early. One of the most important criteria for new hires should be fit, encouraging employer-employee alignment behind a shared purpose. However, all of this is easy to say and really hard to do. It takes effort and time.

AI can help in three ways. The most obvious is using AI to reduce mundane tasks, as discussed in Chapter IX – Better Jobs. The second is directing some of the time and effort freed up by AI towards meaningful work and a shared purpose other than profits. The data suggests companies need to work harder on this and that the investment will pay off. Thirdly, job substitution by AI will push more workers into meaningful jobs that AI cannot do well, such as caring, but we must not let exploitation take place here, allowing people to give up financial success for meaningful work that's poorly rewarded. If so, policy intervention may be needed. More meaningful work is good for employees, customers, employers, and society.

GROWING EMPOWERMENT

One of the core conclusions of self-determination theory, as set out by psychologists Deci and Ryan in the 1980s, is that motivation, development, and wellbeing improve when employees have more autonomy.[543] Having more control increases ownership of decisions and actions. Empowering and trusting employees to do their jobs boosts positive engagement at work.

One of the selling points for AI is that it will "empower" more people. Microsoft's chief product officer recently said, "The potential for lifting people up and empowering people is enormous,"[544] while CEO of OpenAI, Sam Altman, said, "We have never empowered individuals as much as we're about to."[545]

This idea may help sell products, but the data suggests the opposite could be true. A longitudinal survey of 35,000 workers in the UK by Professor Ying Zhou and team shows that task discretion has fallen from 62% in 1992 to 34% in 2024.[546] Modern technology can be used to measure and direct workers. This used to be the case for factory work, with more discretion allowed in higher skill areas, but autonomy is now falling in these areas too, from 48% to 34%. The University of Groningen study mentioned above also found that people perceived their autonomy decreased in industries with high levels of robotisation. Similarly, in his book *The Skill Code,* Matt Beane notes that jet fighters operating drones and surgeons using robots often found their jobs could be more alienating and boring.[547]

So, technology can improve efficiency, but it can also increase surveillance, control, and what psychologists term "learned helplessness." Knowing this, how do we make sure AI empowers workers? This starts with leaders *wanting* to empower people and trusting them. Taking lessons from positive psychology, having open discussions with employees and giving them more agency in how AI is used will help. Workers will also probably ask to create environments in which they can do their best work, including eliminating obstacles getting in their way. As Muhammad Ali said, "It isn't the mountains ahead to climb that wear you out; it's the pebble in your shoe."[548] Let's use AI to reduce these pebbles.

One of the biggest pebbles for workers has been commuting. The rise of remote working has reduced commutes and increased flexibility, autonomy, and empowerment. Work-from-home policies are thus a good test of how much empowerment companies are willing to extend to workers—and whether they can shake off old-fashioned fears that it enables "shirking from home." However, the same technology that allows employees to work remotely can make them feel constantly connected and always on. This is another pebble. Work used to be done in workplaces, in a working day, within a working week. Now, many knowledge workers are connected during evenings, weekends, and holidays, so discussions on how to be empowered, rather than enslaved, may be helpful. More empowerment may require a reset, such as the right to disconnect.

GROWING THANKS

"I can live for two months on a good compliment," quipped Mark Twain.[549] Being seen and valued by others is a basic human need. Our understanding of how gratitude can have a positive impact on human emotions is thankfully increasing. Positive psychology has grown rapidly as a field, and happiness studies abound. We can see how this is trickling down in the popularity of gratitude journals. And we know that taking time to appreciate others benefits both the giver and the receiver—a double helping of positivity.[550]

Cultures of appreciation at work provide multiple positive ripple effects, such as creating bonds between people and improving trust. Harvard studies show that increased recognition also improves engagement and retention at work.[551] A 2022–2024 Gallup-Workhuman study found that employees receiving high-quality recognition were 45% less likely to leave and that recognition had significant positive impacts on engagement and an employee's connection to a company's purpose.[552]

However, the same Gallup-Workhuman study highlighted significant room for improvement. While 42% of senior leaders felt their organisations valued employee recognition, only 22% of employees thought leaders did. Only 22% of employees said they got the right amount of recognition, with over half receiving no quality recognition at all. We can search for reasons for this disparity: perhaps leaders use silence to wield power, maybe they are too busy and rely on annual appraisals to comment, or they may have shifted to digital and automated systems to recognise people. Whatever the reason, we should course-correct.

How many people did you praise at work this week? Cultures of gratitude must be built by us all, and we know that thanks and praise are best when they are authentic, delivered in the moment, specific, frequent, and seen by others. This is not something we should outsource to machines, but systems can help nudge us and measure outcomes. Workhuman, an employee experience platform that helps companies build positive cultures, has collected over 30 million moments between 5 million employees over 20 years.[553] By capturing positive experiences between people in a business and providing data analysis on who is helping whom, it can identify and reduce risk areas, if, for example, a team's positive contribution ratio is falling dramatically or a leader is not getting involved. This can then feed into performance-management processes.

Praise is not about money, but allocating a portion of pay or the bonus pool to those employees that companies want to thank can help spread goodwill and accountability. Even a symbolic 1% has been shown to help. Co-workers are the most knowledgeable on who has helped whom, so crowdsourcing the payment of micro-bonuses may be seen as fairer while encouraging good habits and a culture of gratitude.

Given appreciation benefits the giver as well as the receiver, an everyone-to-everyone recognition system can create ripples of positivity all around.

Taking time to celebrate successes is another form of gratitude, and it can create shared moments full of positive energy—a very visible act that tells employees they are valued. The rush of dopamine drives happiness and helps people form bonds. It's also important to take time to celebrate personal moments, such as having a baby, a birthday, work milestones, or retirement. Workhuman data suggests that celebrating just one life event boosts employees' belief that their company has a human work culture by 23%.[554] AI could help in three ways: by freeing up time for celebrations, by helping to organise and communicate opportunities, and by acting as a catalyst and a reminder to celebrate humanity more than efficiency.

GROWING REAL CONNECTIONS

If we get a hit of dopamine from celebrating and gratitude, we get a hit of oxytocin from connecting with others. Sometimes called the bonding hormone or love hormone, oxytocin comes from social interactions and helps increase attachment, support, trust, and happiness. In turn, it helps people flourish or even survive. When anthropologist Margaret Mead was asked what she believed the first evidence of civilization was, she reportedly said a healed human femur from 15,000 years ago, as the bone indicated the wounded person received help from others.[555] As humans, we are built to connect with and help people we care about.

Unfortunately, despite happiness studies showing the importance of social connection, social cohesion has been falling since the 1960s, according to research by Harvard's Bob Putnam.[556] We are less bonded together, with declining belonging and social relationships. There are several reasons for this, including declines in equality, religion, and community, but a key reason is the increase in digitisation. Technology may have increased connectedness in a technical sense, but it makes us feel less emotionally connected to one another. Despite a myriad of instantaneous ways to connect with anyone, anywhere, we have stumbled into a loneliness epidemic that has worse health risks than smoking, alcoholism, or obesity.[557] This is not a fringe issue: one in four US men under 35 years old reports that they feel lonely.[558]

We can often see this playing out at work. How often do you email someone sitting next to you or jump on a Zoom call rather than meet in person, or have KPIs generated digitally, or have your work time tracked by the system rather than your boss? More remote work means less face-to-face contact, while the fact that people move from job to job rather than staying long term has increased the transactionality of work and reduced connectedness, which only encourages people to move jobs again. AI could exacerbate these trends, as there will be more non-human co-workers, more digital connectivity, and more transactionality.

Rather than see this as a downward spiral we can't control, we can look at this as an opportunity for companies to fill the void. Many employees seek community at work. They want to build bonds and relationships with co-workers. They want to feel included, appreciated, and cared for. Leaders can create this connection, but it requires effort: more communities, clubs, or affiliations within companies; more inclusion and teambuilding events, "teams that play together, stay together;" more recognition and celebrations of each other; in essence, more fun and less grind. AI could help by freeing up time to connect more by helping people get to know who's actually in the company and by measuring the strength of connections at work.

It is worth the effort to create more connection within the workplace. Self-determination theory research shows there are multiple upsides to improving relationships, relatedness, and belonging. At work, these can include better engagement, intrinsic motivation, performance, trust, retention, innovation, ability to navigate change, wellbeing, and happiness. The facts back up what we intuitively know; we just need to recognise and apply them.

GROWING TRUST

Trust is a critical factor in positive workplace cultures and for psychological safety. Research shows this is crucial for job satisfaction and wellbeing, but it is also needed for team effectiveness, change management, and even innovation.[559]

When Abraham Maslow published his famous paper in 1943, "A Theory of Human Motivation," safety was a core foundation in our hierarchy of needs. Maslow later asked, "Why is it that we often design organisations as if people naturally shirk responsibility… and can't be trusted to do the right thing?"[560] Douglas McGregor, a student of Maslow, went on to develop Theory X and Y of management, in which X managers believed rewards and punishments were needed for workers to do their jobs, creating a command-and-control management style based on low trust.[561]

Yet trust works both ways, with employees wanting to feel they are trusted by leaders and leaders being trusted by employees. Unfortunately, the most quoted work on trust in organisations, the Edelman Trust Barometer, shows that all is not well. Fear that "leaders lie to us" is at an all-time high in 2025, at 68% in relation to business leaders, just 1% behind political leaders.[562] Edelman data shows trust in leaders "to do what is right" has been falling, while a 2023 Gallup survey found only 21% of US employees strongly agree that they trust the leadership of their organisation.[563] Surely we can do better.

Clearly, this declining trust at work mirrors what's happening in society in general, partly due to the lack of social cohesion mentioned above. Yet trends in the workplace have also contributed. Decades of downsizing, restructuring, efficiency drives, and disruption have reduced job security and trust. Also, as we've discussed, employment relationships have become more short-term and transactional, eroding the psychological contract between employees and employers.

Employees often feel like they only get polished answers, half-truths, or toxic positivity in which bad news is constantly spun into an opportunity. And the relentless pace of change has increased uncertainty, so even if managers want to make promises about the future, they can't know if these can be kept, even in the medium term. This empathy gap has only been made worse by rising differentials in compensation between leaders and employees, which creates distance on a human as well as an economic level: CEO-to-worker pay ratios have grown from 20:1 in 1965 to 399:1 in 2021.[564]

One of the starkest examples of the hypocrisy of companies' rhetoric about supportive cultures is a growing trend of laying workers off by email or cutting off their access to systems overnight. The careers site Zety found that just 30% of US workers made redundant in the past two years learnt about their fate face-to-face.[565] As efficient as this may be, this brutal approach impacts not just those leaving but the culture for those staying as well. If we want more trust and humanity in organisations, this needs to be a red line that cannot be crossed.

If the changes brought by digitisation—both in terms of efficiency and disruption—have already impacted trust, the coming wave of AI could erode it further, and quickly. We should heed Johan Thorbecke's wisdom, who helped establish the Netherlands' first constitution in 1848: "Trust arrives on foot and leaves on horseback."[566] Job security is the biggest issue raised by the transformation of work by AI, as outlined in Part 1 of this book. Yet it could also erode trust for those who keep their jobs, through more workplace surveillance, continuous performance measurement, and management by algorithm.

So, if we recognise that trust is important but falling in the workplace and that AI could add fuel to the fire, what can be done? Building on Thorbecke's advice above, we need to understand that trust takes time and effort to build and that it grows from actions more than words. The most obvious action now is to give workers agency in deciding how to use AI. This starts with a discussion about what thriving in the workplace looks like and then an effort to steer towards that: more augmentation than substitution, more upskilling than layoffs, more sharing of insight with employees rather than extracting information from them, and more face-to-face discussions, team building, and celebration.

However, it can be a bit of a chicken-and-egg situation. There needs to be enough trust and psychological safety in the first place to allow employees to talk about their concerns; only then can they generate more trust by having respectful conversations towards a common goal. The onus is on leaders to create this environment so workers can speak up and feel protected. That is not easy; it takes time, and managers have to balance many trade-offs when making decisions.

Communication and agency are vital, but the biggest difference maker here is simply showing a belief in your employees. Leaders should dust their textbooks off and reread McGregor's Theory Y, which states that workers are intrinsically capable, motivated, and responsible. They should then promote and celebrate those who are trusted and skilled. Perhaps, instead of taking this approach, we have promoted managers who are trusted to grow profits and uphold compliance rather than grow people. Yet looking after people *and* profits is possible.

GROWING WELLBEING

Chapter VII focused on abundance. We can hopefully all agree that an abundance of wellbeing should be a key aspiration for the AI age, and given we spend a large portion of our waking hours at work, this needs to include wellbeing at work. It sounds simple, but unfortunately, the opposite is happening, according to the research. Americans' assessments of their mental and physical health have been in decline since 2013, according to Gallup, hitting a 24-year low.[567] More broadly, a 2023 Harvard Medical School and University of Queensland study of 150,000 people across 29 countries concluded that one in every two people in the world will develop a mental health disorder in their lifetime.[568] As we head into the AI age, and the possibility of job substitution, we know that unemployment is one of the most significant factors affecting wellbeing.

A core reason for deteriorating mental health at work is burnout, and unsurprisingly, a key cause of burnout is the rate of change. A 2023 McKinsey Health Institute study on the wellbeing of 30,000 people across 30 countries found 22% of employees were experiencing burnout.[569] Gartner data shows only 38% of employees are now willing to support more organisational change, down from 74% in 2016, so finding ways to limit or manage change in a way that supports people is needed.[570]

This matters. Excessive stress at work has a big economic impact. In their book *TomorrowMind*, Kellerman and Seligman estimate the cost as $190 billion per year to the economy in the US alone.[571] More importantly, it is estimated that work-related stress is a factor in 120,000 deaths in the US each year.[572] These numbers are far worse in Southeast Asia, with the World Health Organisation estimating over 700,000 deaths per year due to long work hours.[573] In the era of AI, we must harness its ability to free up time to reduce people's hours, not just spin the work wheel faster. Offering the opportunity to work from home for part of the week can help, given that this has been shown to improve stress and wellbeing.

Leaders are the main reason for burnout at work as they set the workload and expectations, so better training and coaching may be needed to help managers better help others. However, given that they are also subject to time pressures, heavy workloads, and efficiency and change mandates transmitted down the corporate hierarchy, AI needs to free up time for bosses as well. The biggest drops in positive engagement in work are among middle managers, so they are far from immune to work pressures. The metaphor of putting your own oxygen mask on first should be embraced by leaders to allow wellbeing to ripple out.

Caring for others seems like a hygiene factor for leadership, yet only one in four US employees strongly believes that leaders genuinely care about them, according to Gallup.[574] Are we choosing leaders who don't care, who care most about profits, or who don't know how to express they care? Or perhaps they don't know the reasons why they should care more. If it's the latter, Gallup's work shows that caring helps the company and not just employees, leading to better engagement, better retention, better trust, and better customer service. Teaching leaders that focusing on wellbeing will provide a return on investment is probably the easiest of these problems to solve.

Other solutions include appointing wellbeing officers at work, or even chief happiness officers. At a recent conference, I was struck by how Alexander Kjerulf, the founder and chief happiness officer of Woohoo inc, managed to boil down what made people happy at work to "doing great work with great people." Can AI free us up to do more of that?

Given its importance, measuring wellbeing at work is not just sensible but good economics. SAP, for example, tracks the wellbeing of its workforce annually, producing a Business Health Culture Index, and it estimates that a 1% increase in this index can add up to €100 million to the company's global operating profit.[575] Other companies conduct more frequent weekly pulse surveys to track how their employees are feeling, asking questions like: How are you feeling? How can you improve your wellbeing at work? How can you help the wellbeing of those around you at work? These may be simple, but the very act of asking is likely to be appreciated.

GROWING ADAPTABILITY

Given the pace and scope of change discussed in Part 1 of this book, keeping up with it has become a core skill for both individuals and organisations. Arguably, in the AI age, emotional intelligence (EQ) trumps IQ for humans, yet AQ, our adaptability quotient, will trump both—so AQ > EQ > IQ.

What does a healthy dose of AQ look like? Getting good at the following will help: learnability, meaning the ability to learn and to unlearn so we can relearn; curiosity and asking good questions; openness; grit; entrepreneurialism; perspection, meaning evaluating future possibilities to guide your actions; and wayfinding, meaning our ability to move forward without full knowledge of what lies ahead, a process Sonja Blignaut has adapted from complexity theory. New AI-powered tools, such as AQ.ai.io, can help individuals and teams understand their AQ, with suggestions on how to improve.

The good news is that we are not short of ideas when it comes to change management. The bad news is that, despite that, evidence shows that three-quarters of change management initiatives flop. This is not just about abandoned projects or the failure to achieve the goals set, but a waste of money, time, and energy. Usually, change management failures are not due to technology implementation challenges; they are driven by people issues and organisational cultures. That's because change is primarily about changing people's behaviours. This takes time and effort. Management needs to foster the right conditions to help workers be ready, willing, and able to change. Two-way communication and buy-in are vital. It is often not that employees are against change in theory; it's that they are against *being* changed. They need to understand the upside for them, which could be that the status quo is more dangerous than the new path. For this, a bedrock of trust is needed, along with the right level of support and some degree of control for workers.

Crucially, we must work within people's capacity to change. Too much change too fast can be overwhelming, pushing people to their limits, so companies should choose transformations carefully and give them the focus they need. Not everything can be urgent. Warren Buffett warned about the risk of "middling priorities." These are priorities that are seductive enough to be included but which distract from critical goals. Buffett suggests these should be avoided at all costs. Similarly, leaders can help employees adapt by not creating initiative overload. Less can be more.

GROWING STABILITY

A few years ago, I decided to do a master's degree in behaviour change. I could see there was a tidal wave of change coming and that successful adaptation to change was a hard problem to crack. It helped me realise something critical that isn't talked about very often: the need for stability during change. While this seems like an oxymoron, the concept is simple and will be familiar to us all. As the psychologist John Bowlby noted in the 1960s, when developing attachment theory, children start to explore from a secure base, which promotes healthy emotional development.[576] In other words, they explore new worlds—nursery, school, friends' houses—with confidence because they can then return to the safety of their home and parents. Similarly, at work, many take comfort from and feel security in the familiar, such as trusted team colleagues. Decades of loss aversion research also show that the fear of losing what we have exerts a far stronger influence on human behaviour than the promise of equivalent gains.[577] Stability, as a result, can be highly valued.

Research by the positive psychologist Martin Seligman provides a different, but related, angle. His safety signal hypothesis shows that the absence of safety signals can create chronic anxiety for animals.[578] When fear has an ending, it is easier to deal with. It is much harder to deal with when the fear is unbounded. Constant disruption and change at work can therefore feel like chronic uncertainty, driving anxiety and frustration. Exponential and unbounded AI growth, which will stoke our fears of job substitution, will only add to this.

This links back to our capacity to change. It is not that workers cannot adapt to change, but that too much change is overwhelming. It creates stress, uncertainty, vulnerability, and weariness. Gartner estimated that the average employee experienced ten change initiatives per year by 2022, up from two per year in 2016.[579] Change management initiatives can also increase intensity by creating the idea of a burning platform in which the status quo is unsustainable, but this impacts how safe employees feel. Jumping from transformation to transformation is part of the reason so many people at work feel burned out. Adding to this, leaders move jobs more often, and as the next boss takes the helm, team changes cascade, and a new set of "urgent and important" initiatives appear. Bewildered, employees are still expected to hit the next set of budgeted numbers on time. Not only are workers trying to fix the plane while flying it, but it's also going at full speed. That is a tough ask.

Alternatively, if it is not a big transformation, changes arrive as incremental steps that compound to produce big results over time. This idea of small changes compounding gradually was brilliantly captured by James Clear in his bestselling book *Atomic Habits*.[580] Some initiatives at work are layered in this way, so change compounds, and waves keep coming. What gets talked about less, however, is that the same principle can play out in the compounding of uncertainty and anxiety, creating a vicious cycle for mental, physical, and financial health. The compounding flywheel is not one directional; it can work positively or negatively.

Economists such as Marx and Schumpeter have long recognised this risk. Joseph Schumpeter is rightly lauded for his work on creative destruction, which he felt drove capitalism's dynamic progress, but fewer people know that he did not think capitalism would survive in the long run because disruption and job losses would cause society to seek more stability and security. His fears will be tested in the AI age.

How, then, can we balance the need for enough change with the need for enough stability? Nature, for example, often builds a protective shell, such as a butterfly's chrysalis, during metamorphosis. Or for our ancestors, a "port in a storm" provided a safe and calm place to rest on a long journey. Leaders can embrace this "port in a storm" idea today to provide comfort and reassurance during the waves of change coming from AI. Workers want to know their jobs are safe, that they will be looked after, that they can be upskilled or reskilled, and that it is OK to rest during relentless change initiatives. They want to know that other factors mentioned in this chapter—such as wellbeing, growth, recognition, and trust—will be supported by leaders, providing an anchor they can depend on.

Leaders need to create these conditions. To do so, they may want to lean on some battle-tested wisdom that Navy SEALs pass down to each other: "Calm is contagious." During periods of huge uncertainty, such as the fog of war, there is a need to create calm in your words and actions. Secondly, while stasis is not an option, having fewer change initiatives increases the probability of success for the critical few. One of the key tenets of change management is that change takes time, so rushing can increase the risk of failure, and slowing down can drive success. Lastly, segregating change initiatives into chunks that limit what people are exposed to at any one time can give them more control and reduce overwhelm.

Leaders not only set the direction; they model behaviours that influence cultures. Understanding that people crave stability as a counter to continual change, they can be an exemplar of good practice. Unlike computers, people need rest, so for example, some leaders send emails only during work hours and not over weekends. Or they may prioritise exercise and meditation to allow for recuperation. Leaders should also recognise that a company's traditions, values, rituals, and rules provide comforting anchors for workers. Enduring institutions and brands create stability. They should be celebrated, not hidden. Agility is in vogue, but stability should not be taboo.

Companies will always need to change, and adaptability is crucial here, but it is easier to make leaps from a firm footing. So, when measuring your adaptability quotient, find out what your stability quotient is, too. You'll be better off with both.

BUILDING BRIDGES TO BETTER WORK

Each of the factors discussed in this chapter is important. However, when put together, they can produce a wave of pro-human working conditions. Leaders are the ones with the power to create these conditions. They are making, investing in, deploying, and regulating AI, so they must also build bridges to better work, away from the risks of job substitution and falling wages. They should balance the AI arms race with a race towards pro-human leadership. This means managing disruption and growing profits while also creating an environment where people can do their best work.

Learning from history, the risks of not bringing enough people along on the AI journey are high. We already have low engagement and high anxiety at work. If AI makes this worse, leaders may find themselves forced by workers and voters to become more pro-human in ways they are not prepared for. If we act now, we don't need to get to this stage.

Leaders know we are at a pivotal point in the world of work. By acknowledging the risks ahead and committing to doing better, they can achieve a win-win. Yet this needs to be an authentic and lived commitment that is communicated clearly. To help, below are a few answers to common questions about how to embrace more pro-human leadership.

Aren't leaders already pro-human?

While many already are, and many claim or aim to be, the data suggests we need an upgrade for leaders to be more pro-human. Data on many of the topics discussed in this chapter—such as positive engagement, trust, and wellbeing—shows that we must do better. And Gallup notes that a good leader is the critical factor in issues like engagement: "[The] biggest workplace discovery is that a staggering 70% of the variance in team engagement is determined by just the manager."[581]

A lot of this depends on incentives, or threats, for leaders. Shareholder primacy made greater profitability the primary goal, and leaders usually have to produce results or lose their jobs. Being pro-worker has often been a secondary motivation, and it's often still in aid of driving profits: *if we make employees feel better, they will work more.* In her book *The Problem with Change*, Ashley Goodall suggests that, in 1970, when Friedman wrote his famous essay on shareholder primacy, only 50% of corporate profits went to shareholders; four decades later, this had increased to 91%.[582] What an amazing success for shareholders. However, a more equitable balance may be needed now—not just because of this dramatic shift in the last 50 years but because AI will systematically advantage pro-machine, pro-profit, and pro-power thinking and create even more significant headwinds for workers. As we try to find the right equilibrium, more pro-human leadership will be necessary.

What are the benefits of being more pro-human?

Pro-human leadership is not charity. The upsides for employees and employers are multi-fold: higher engagement, leading to higher productivity, higher customer satisfaction, and higher sales and profits; lower burnout; lower turnover; lower absenteeism; higher growth and fulfilment for talent and their output; better interpersonal relationships and teamwork; and improved organisational cultures.

Data from the Institute of Customer Service has shown that a 1% increase in employee engagement improved customer satisfaction by 0.4%,[583] with better customer service scores leading to better revenues, EBITDA, and return metrics than peers. Embracing new technology solutions can provide better and faster services to customers, but it can also be window dressing when the main goal is to reduce costs by cutting jobs. But this will only take firms so far. Combining human and machine is often the best solution.

Another way to think about this is giving workers "roots and wings." This phrase is credited to a wise woman in Hodding Carter's 1953 book *Where Main Street Meets the River*. AI *could* supercharge people's growth potential in multiple ways and empower more people, providing wings to help them explore opportunities. However, having stable roots from which to explore would help, such as improved trust, wellbeing, belonging, and praise. As we discussed earlier in this chapter, being pro-human embraces both nurturing adaptability and stability at the same time.

Lastly, we've spoken about pro-human leadership, providing workers with more agency in the discussion and decision-making process. Research has shown that during periods of change, the best results occur when people buy into the vision, not when it is forced on them. Lessons from a coaching style of management can be embraced to aid this process. If we empower employees, they will power employers. Both can succeed.

Isn't this human-centred leadership?

Human-centred leadership believes decisions should prioritise people *over* profits. This movement grew in strength after the 2008 Financial Crisis, when concerns that capitalism had become too one-sided grew louder. For example, a 2017 paper by the World Economic Forum titled "Advancing Human-Centred Economic Progress in the Fourth Industrial Revolution" argued for putting people at the heart of decision-making.[584] As Margaret

Mitchell, researcher and chief ethics scientist at Hugging Face, explained, "The most important thing is to centre the people instead of the technology. So instead of technology first, and then figuring out how it might be applied to people, people first, and then figuring out what technology might be useful for them."[585]

There are many crossovers between the recommendations made in this chapter and human-centred policies, but a key difference is that pro-human leadership means prioritising people *and* profits, rather than people *over* profits. It is possible to have both. Growing people helps generate new ideas that grow into new revenues and profits. Growing profits allows investment in future revenue streams to create new jobs.

An important area of common ground is that both pro-human and human-centred leaders believe that companies should not favour machines over people. Investment decisions should be made by humans, for humans, and human rights should always be prioritised over machine rights.

What are the trade-offs with pro-human leadership?

In comparison to many of the solutions offered in this book, some of which have difficult trade-offs, pro-human leadership should be positive for both employers and employees. That said, if it was so easy, then it would have already happened in most companies. So, what are the issues?

The most obvious is that leadership incentives usually prioritise profitability, with many shareholders focused on short-term gains that reward cost-cutting, rather than longer-term, pro-human initiatives. These are trade-off dilemmas leaders need to grapple with all the time, but AI could amplify them and tilt leaders towards temporal myopia—the prioritisation of short-term gains over long-term consequences.

AI disruption increases uncertainty about business models and worries about job security for leaders, not just workers. Fears that the outlook will get more difficult can create an extraction mindset of trying to get what you can, when you can—the opposite of the abundance mindset discussed in Chapter VII. For worried leaders, this may feel like a rational trade-off.

A second related issue is that being pro-human requires an investment of time, and some leaders just don't have enough to put into growing people. This is the knowing versus doing gap. Some firms will see AI and it's freeing up of time as the answer to investing more effort in their people rather than driving productivity harder or higher. Others will not.

A third trade-off occurs when managers need to make hard choices that impact individuals. The authors of *Compassionate Leadership: How to Do Hard Things in a Human Way* examined this issue by analysing one million data points collected from 350 executives. They explored the use of direct leadership for speed, the courage to make hard decisions, and the respect and kindness that come from better clarity.[586] Their conclusion was that leaders who succeeded embraced wise compassion, a mixture of doing the hard things that need to be done with the empathy and care that helps employees. The best leaders find the right balance.

Will leader incentives change to be more pro-human?

This is one of the most crucial and thorniest issues determining the outcomes ahead. Hoping for a change towards enlightened leadership that voluntarily adopts more pro-human altruism is naively optimistic. We would be better to heed the wise words of Charlie Munger, one of the greatest investors of all time: "Show me the incentive, and I'll show you the outcome."[587] CEOs can do many things, but not everything. They have to prioritise, and to help them, capitalism has built a simple and effective leader incentive system that is pro-profit. Elon Musk's recent $1 trillion compensation package is an extreme example of this.[588]

How could incentives shift? We know how to increase incentives to improve jobs, but as Harvard's 2024 assessment of incentive compensation plans for the largest 100 US companies shows, only 18% include a metric around improving employee engagement or satisfaction.[589] However, 51% include a metric for DEI, and 71% include one or more ESG metrics. So, making better jobs for more people depends on who decides what the priorities are.

It seems very unlikely that shareholders, currently the most important stakeholders in companies, will want to tilt leader incentives towards employees when they can see better returns from doing the exact opposite in the AI age. However, over time, it is possible that institutional investor motivations will change, especially if their end clients—individuals—demand it. This is one reason sustainability rose in importance. Pro-sustainability individuals moved their savings and pension funds into ESG funds and away from funds that did not support ESG. These investors were telling business leaders that ESG was important, influencing metrics. The same process could happen for pro-human fund mandates over time.

Company boards set leader incentives and consider all stakeholders, so they *could* be instrumental in increasing pro-human measures. However, given that boards primarily act in the interests of the company's shareholders, we may need regulatory change to readjust leader incentives towards supporting employees, as discussed in Chapter XII.

Governments have several tools to influence outcomes, from policy changes and unofficial asks to role modelling. As a large buyer of services in the economy, governments could decide they only want to deal with companies that are growing their human workforce, not substituting them. Governments often require professions uphold ethical codes, such as the Hippocratic Oath of conduct and obligations taken by doctors, and could enforce a pro-human code for business leaders, increasing their fiduciary duty towards human consequences, not just financial ones. However, government actions are likely to be dependent on voter attitudes and unemployment levels, and with a lag, even then.

The media's direct influence is limited, but indirectly, it can champion positive change makers who are growing people *and* profits rather than just stock prices, such as publishing an annual top impact list rather than a top rich list. They can also highlight good practices and bad actors, which may impact the behaviour of voters, workers, and customers.

It is possible that, when customers find out a company is using AI to grow shareholder returns at the expense of people, they will boycott it. However, given that customers also value convenience and low costs, as shown in the digital age, this could take time.

Given the time lags highlighted, calls for more pro-human outcomes and changes in leader incentives will likely come via workers' concerns about jobs and wages first. Collective action could ripple up to impact customers, shareholders, boards, and leaders, creating a long and messy transition to align leader incentives towards better jobs for more workers. The best companies will try to get ahead of and mitigate these risks.

How do you measure being more pro-human?

As discussed earlier, a core tenet of business is that "you cannot manage what you cannot measure." As leader incentives move towards being more pro-human, the measurement of their efficacy is therefore required. The simplest way is by surveying employees regularly on each of the 10 factors discussed: engagement and growth, purpose, empowerment, thanks, connection, trust, wellbeing, adaptability, and stability. Scores from one to 10 can then be plotted on a spider chart and measured over time, with action points to improve each metric. This helps illuminate what is working and provides a sort of pro-human satnav for a leader's improvement journey.

A second idea is even simpler and less about measuring than about ensuring a net positive effect. Clayton Christensen is best known for his work on disruptive innovation, but it is well worth watching his 2012 TED Talk "How Will You Measure Your Life?"[590] Taking his idea, if each leader can positively impact two people for every one that is negatively impacted, this would create a positive ripple effect. This recognises that difficult decisions need to be made, but that it is still possible to be a positive multiplier. For example, you could use AI to augment the work of two people for every worker substituted or hire two new people for every one let go. For some leaders, such as a CEO, it is possible to measure impacts like net job growth statistically, but a simpler and more practical option for every leader is to ensure they help more people than they hinder. This approach will help workers weather the AI transition.

A more holistic way to measure success is by combining these ideas of employee engagement with net job growth. We can measure if jobs are better, rather than worse, via average engagement scores (AE). Yet better jobs for a smaller and smaller number of employees is not ideal. By capturing whether firms create more new jobs than they cut, net jobs or NJ, we can see how pro-human their policies really are. Better jobs for more people can therefore be measured as AE x NJ = total engagement (TE).

Total engagement (TE) would reward those who grow engagement *and* employment. Driving net jobs syncs with the traditional capitalist thesis that more growth leads to more employment. And AE would capture the often cited aim that AI can augment jobs, and as noted above, given we now also have a formula for improving engagement, we have the building blocks for measuring pro-human outcomes. By measuring total engagement over time, we can highlight and celebrate leaders who create better jobs for more people.

There is a lot here. Is there a simple version?

The idea of being pro-human is deliberately designed to be simple. Not many will argue that they are not. Nor is being pro-human rocket science, but that is the point. However, obviously, things can get complicated for leaders trying to juggle lots of factors, for lots of stakeholders, and under competing pressures.

However, there is a very simple version that can be embraced by everyone. In every meeting that requires a decision to be made that impacts people, simply ask, **"How can we be more pro-human?"**

This simple question connects all the solutions in this chapter and all the chapters in this book. It puts the spotlight on the human in the room and turns intent into discussion and solutions. A 2020 study by the University of Southern California found the biggest predictor of long-term success was not motivation, rewards, or willpower; it was repetition.[591] Habits are powerful; small actions done consistently compound into big outcomes over time. And so, we must keep asking this one simple question consistently at work. As Carl Rogers, one of the founding fathers of coaching, said, if we begin with "unconditional positive regard" for people, good things will tend to follow.

How can we help leaders be more pro-human?

Leadership is a key skill and area of competitive advantage for humans over machines, so it should be nurtured. It also has the greatest influence over outcomes for AI and for workers under AI. It is so vital that we need an abundance of great leaders. However, something is not working as it should. Fewer than one in three managers are currently positively engaged at work. They are often more overwhelmed, stressed, and burnt out than their teams. They aren't immune to uncertainty or unaffected by the impacts of replacing people with technology; they often have to work out how to do more with less or run that bit faster. We need to look after managers so they can look after workers so they can look after customers. There are three things we can do right now to help them.

The first is to make sure the time freed up by AI is used to make leaders' jobs better so they can devote enough time to pro-human policies that help their teams. This is far from a given. In the future, managers could find themselves downsizing human teams and managing even larger teams of AI agents and robots.

There should be more training for managers, not just on using AI tools and managing hybrid teams, but on devising and implementing pro-human policies. Gallup data has shown that training can improve management engagement by 22% and engagement of their teams by 18%.[592] Despite these upsides, another survey found 82% of leaders had no formal leadership training, leaving most as "accidental managers."[593] More training for leaders and leaders in waiting, opportunities to share best practices with other leaders, and personalised coaching for senior leaders will pay dividends in creating a smooth AI transition.

Investing in leaders and their teams is not just about investing money and time, but growing cultures that are pro-human at their foundation. We would be wise to heed Plato's words from 2,500 years ago that "what is honoured in a culture gets cultivated there."[594] This includes simple everyday acts, like saying thank you or helping someone grow. It's also about promoting pro-human leaders—the ones employees want and not just the ones shareholders do. Most people will know of a leader who was promoted because they were a top performer in terms of profits, but a poor manager. We choose what to celebrate and who to celebrate. We can honour those who have grown employment, worker engagement, and customer satisfaction scores, and not just those who create shareholder value. By honouring pro-human leaders, we will cultivate more of them.

BE A VERB, NOT A NOUN

This quote from Stephen Fry, paraphrasing Oscar Wilde, means that we are defined by our actions rather than by fixed labels. Titles are not necessary. Positive action is. The primary focus of this book is on leaders in business and at work, but work is so central to our society that we all have a part to play in pro-human leadership. In this sense, leadership extends to leaders in society, leaders in education, leaders of the future, and even parents, as they lead their children, imparting guidance and values. It also includes self-leadership and how we interact with those around us. We all get to decide who and what we honour. Every day, we can congratulate others on a job well done, connect with people, or offer feedback to help someone grow. We can choose to shop in a local store rather than online, pay more for a human waiter rather than an automated solution, or thank the eldercare worker who is looking after our parent. We choose who to work for or which companies our pensions are put in. These are the micro-decisions that form cultures.

We should all try to "be the change you want to see," a phrase that was originally attributed to Mahatma Gandhi and later to Arleen Lorrance.[595] We can model the values we hold to be most important. As these small, pro-human actions compound each day, they will create a tide of positivity. Even if fears over AI are unfounded, the world will be better for this tide; it has little to no downsides.

In *Scary Smart*, Mo Gawdat offers a conclusion that builds on this idea. Arguing that AI will far surpass humans in most areas, Gawdat says that our best chance of ending up in a good place alongside it is by teaching AI what good looks like through our positive micro-actions and words.[596] The machines will learn from our patterns of humanity. Pro-human leadership can therefore go one step further than enriching giver and receiver: it can teach the machines what a better world looks like to shape our coexistence.

As self-leaders, we must also vote for the outcomes we believe are most important, with a clear understanding of AI threats, possibilities, and solutions. This is not just for our sake as we transition into the AI age, but for our children and the next generation. We have a responsibility to tackle this longer-term question of what we want a pro-human future with AI to look like. We turn to this in the next chapter.

XIV

PRO-HUMAN CAPITALISM

"Great leaders are not head down. They see around corners, shaping the future, not just reacting to it."

—Roselinde Torres[597]

"Better leaders, Better world."

—Robert Hargrove[598]

A SPUTNIK MOMENT

On 4 October 1957, the Soviet Union launched Sputnik 1, the world's first artificial satellite, into orbit. America's confidence in its technological superiority fell, and fears about attacks by rockets rose.

This Sputnik moment acted as a wake-up call for America that catalysed a chain reaction of shared purpose, energy, and progress. Nineteen fifty-eight saw the creation of NASA, DARPA, and the National Defense Education Act, increasing STEM graduates and practitioners. Defence spending rose.

The Apollo space programme was launched in 1961. By 1969, the first man had stepped on the Moon.

Sixty-five years later, ChatGPT has created another Sputnik moment—an awakening to what is now possible. The coming of AI superintelligence, bringing with it excitement, shock, and fear. A new AI renaissance of science and discovery. A productivity boom. Economic disruption. Technological unemployment. Educational change. National security risks. An arms race. An existential threat.

You can decide which of these outcomes you think is most likely, but we should use this moment to ask what shared purpose, progress, and outcomes we want from the AI age—and for the world of work.

MACHINE CAPITALISM

Few will deny that an AI technology revolution is underway. Given that AI will impact so many jobs, it is almost certain that it will also cause a work revolution and could change our current economic structure. How it does this is not predetermined, but let us start by looking at one potential path.

Economic systems have evolved over time. Feudalism was the dominant mode of production between the ninth and fifteenth centuries, in which peasants could use land and gained protection in exchange for services to the nobility. Mercantilism became the dominant system between the sixteenth and eighteenth centuries, driven by the growth in trade but with heavy state involvement.

Capitalism, in which private entities own the means of production, has been through three iterations so far. The industrial capitalism of the eighteenth and nineteenth centuries involved laissez-faire economics, underpinned by Adam Smith's concept of the invisible hand of the market, with minimal state intervention and the exploitation of labour. Keynesian capitalism, between the 1930s and 1970s, tried to address market failures and unemployment, so the drive to maximise profits was balanced by state oversight, welfare programmes, and labour regulations. In the 1980s, the baton was passed again, to neoliberal capitalism; this was centred on shareholder primacy, with big side helpings of deregulation, financialisation, globalisation, and digitalisation.

So, what's next? What will be the flavour of Capitalism 4.0? Some imagine it will be stakeholder capitalism, but let's consider another option as we enter the AI age – machine capitalism. Let's explore how this could play out.

Stage 4.1: Machines as Tools

We're already there. Ninety percent of the decision to hire you comes from a machine; it sifts your application, checks your qualifications, marks your psychometric test, and analyses your video interview. An HR bot helps with your onboarding. A tech bot helps set up your access. Training is mostly online and virtual. Client leads get served to you from automated marketing agents. Your digital co-pilot delivers relevant research for you. Contact with customers is scripted, prompted, and recorded. Live translation is available. A compliance bot makes sure you know the dos and don'ts and highlights red flags. There is a coaching bot to help you improve. Your attendance, your words, and your performance metrics are all digitally tracked. You are paid automatically at the end of each period based on your KPIs. Data lakes and data centres store everything. Information is power.

Stage 4.2: Machines as Helpers

You travel to work in a driverless car. Face ID allows you to enter the building and log on. You have been gifted an AI agent to help you do your work. It comes with its own identity and email address, reporting jointly to you and the head of AI talent. You order coffee via an app, and it gets delivered to your desk by a robot. When you leave the office, a robot cleaner starts its shift, recharging itself afterwards.

Stage 4.3: Machines as Co-Workers

You are now managing a team of AI agents who handle many of your tasks. Now you focus on setting the priorities, monitoring the outcomes, dealing with difficult client questions, and handling ethical issues. You are managing a hybrid team of humans and AI agents, allocating stretch projects as appropriate. Increasingly, you are moving from being the human-in-the-loop, in charge of AI, to trying to keep in the loop with AI that's becoming increasingly capable. All human work is recorded to train the agents. The key growth area for your firm is dealing with non-human customers: AI agents talking to AI agents. Your work is mainly remote now, and you start to wonder if your remote boss is an avatar—there is never a hair out of place.

Stage 4.4: Machines as Stakeholders

Driverless cars now have legal insurance attached to *them* rather than to a person. Not only is machine maintenance automatically carried out and paid for, but machines also have rights to certain key resources they need, such as data and energy. Most product orders happen automatically, when needed, using smart contracts that trigger manufacturing, distribution, and payment. Not only is all AI content creation labelled, but AI also gets credited for its work. AI has gone from being a tool to a co-creator, to officially owning the patent. The co-pilot has become the pilot. Agents monitor and mark each other's work. The cost of machines drops substantially below human wages, creating job losses and deflation. Some humans are paid to be "rubber stampers" for AI's output.

Stage 4.5: Machines as Capital Owners

There is a growing debate about whether AI systems should be allowed to own decentralized autonomous corporations (DACs)—organisations that own assets, manage logistics, and create revenues and profits. However, there are companies that are already non-human legal entities, voting via blockchain tokens is already opaque, and most investments are already made by machine-driven strategies, so the tide is turning. Seeing it as an opportunity to generate taxes, one nation allows DACs to incorporate under the ownership of an AI system. Authoritarian states follow to help aggregate power.

Stage 4.6: Machine Capitalism

At this point, AI and robotics drive nearly all value creation. Companies are increasingly run *by* machines and *for* machines. Income tax falls alongside wages, so most government revenue now comes from DACs. Humans shift to governance roles or into leisure, supported by UBI paid for by taxes on DACs. UBI payments create dependency, given that handouts are contingent on adhering to guidelines—a social scoring system—monitored and administered by AI. Money is power, and AI now creates and controls most of the economic value in the economy.

AN AI UPGRADE FOR HUMANITY

Given our current path, the scenario outlined above could be the logical endpoint. However, before we sleepwalk into it, shouldn't we ask what sort of future we want from this age of AI?

This question is urgent, partly because we are entering a new age in which technology will surpass humans in cognitive intelligence and partly because digitisation has not led to the outcomes we hoped for. In a 2025 survey by the *Wall Street*

Journal and NORC, only 25% of Americans believed that they had a good chance of improving their standard of living.[599] This is a nosedive from 75% in 2000 and a record low across surveys dating back to 1987. Going forward, AI could be a powerful force for good or a powerful force of destruction. There is no law that says that life will improve as new technology arrives. This AI tipping point should galvanise us to begin a conversation about what we want and what we don't want from it.

One way of navigating complicated topics is by using the Eisenhower Principle. President Dwight D. Eisenhower is credited with saying, "Whenever I run into a problem I can't solve, I always make it bigger. I can never solve it by trying to make it smaller, but if I make it big enough, I can begin to see the outlines of a solution."[600] So, when thinking ahead, let's zoom out and focus on a critical few areas where we want an AI upgrade for humanity: AI as a tool to create pro-human capitalism rather than pro-machine capitalism.

Let's agree that each generation should aim to leave the world in a better place for the next generation. And let's set the date for this goal at 2047—25 years on from the launch of ChatGPT (3.5). This is 30 years after the invention of the transformer technology that underpins ChatGPT, when we will have surpassed AGI, and when AI will be fully integrated into work.

How would you like our world to have changed over the quarter-century to 2047? Give yourself a moment to note down three things you hope for. I've done the same below. But first, let's look to the past and the future to consider what that vision should be.

LEARNING FROM THE PAST

To help guide us, we can draw on a rich history of great thinkers across the ages.

Going back to 500 BC, Confucianism advocated for the government prioritizing the wellbeing of the people. For individuals, it stressed the importance of ethical conduct within human relationships, contributing to society and self-improvement.

In his book *Politics*, written in the fourth century BC, Aristotle imagined a world in which machines, *automata*, could perform tasks on their own, liberating humans. He described human flourishing, or *eudaimonia*, as the ultimate purpose in life, which he believed came from living a life guided by virtue and reason to fulfil one's unique potential.

Petrarch, known as the father of humanism, focused on human-centeredness, critical thinking, and human potential. He is credited with initiating the fourteenth century Renaissance,[601] and given that there are parallels between the Renaissance and AI today, we should note the lessons. The Renaissance period was marked by technological innovation and an explosion in creativity and progress in science, philosophy, and the arts. We still celebrate the ideas that emerged from this era, as well as Gutenberg's printing press, which spread this knowledge and helped drive collective intelligence. However, as Professor Ian Goldin notes in his book *Age of Discovery*, we must also remember that the Renaissance ended in tears for many, with a rise in fundamentalism, religious wars, and the burning of books in the Bonfire of the Vanities.[602] Jobs were lost, wealth was concentrated, and the spread of fake news fragmented societies. This might sound eerily familiar. Technology empowers some, but it does not necessarily lead to a society that is human-centred.

From the seventeenth century, enlightenment humanists, such as Hume, Kant, and Rousseau, championed human potential, wellbeing, and agency. This movement also emphasised civic virtue and the responsibility of individuals to contribute to the betterment of society. Their thinking influenced modern democracies and the US Founding Fathers. Fast-forward to modern humanist thinkers, and they echo many of the same ideas. Bertrand Russell, who was awarded a Nobel Prize in 1950 for humanitarian ideas, focused on human flourishing and wellbeing, including liberty, compassion, and kindness. He believed in the capacity of humanity for good and to make progress. Carl Rogers, one of the founders of humanistic psychology, practised a person-centred approach rooted in empathy and human dignity. Martin Seligman, the founder of positive psychology, highlights accomplishment, meaning, and relationships as being foundational to wellbeing and flourishing.

In the world of work, the father of modern management, Peter Drucker, believed, "The purpose of an organization is to enable ordinary people to do extraordinary things."[603] Mary Parker Follett, a pioneer of humanistic management, said, "Leadership is not defined by the exercise of power but by the capacity to increase the sense of power among those led."[604] She believed workplaces should support growth, agency, and meaning, not just efficiency. Abraham Maslow believed work should help people self-actualize; fulfilling one's full potential sits at the top of his hierarchy of needs.[605]

Even economist Adam Smith saw capitalism as a means towards mass flourishing and not an end in itself. In his work *The Theory of Moral Sentiments,* Smith advocated for self-improvement, finding purpose, doing positive good for others, and social harmony.

There are, of course, so many other thinkers we could draw on, but it's clear that 2,500 years of humanistic thinking centres around the idea of mass flourishing—flourishing in one's own life, as Aristotle taught, and also in and with society.

LEARNING FROM THE FUTURE

Is it possible to learn from the future? Yes, and here are three ways to do so.

Having spent over three decades in investing, I've found that the best way to model the future is to model the past and then extend those lessons into the future to form projections and scenarios that you can learn from. This book is peppered with forecasts, starting with the estimate of 4 billion moving robots by 2050 in Chapter I.

A second way is by understanding what is happening at the leading edge and extrapolating. As science-fiction writer William Gibson noted, "The future is already here; it is just not very evenly distributed."[606] Trends have to start somewhere, and a good place to look for what is going to happen is to see what the rich are doing today. They have the means to buy what's currently expensive, new, and exclusive. They can have assistants, drivers, domestic help, personal tutors, coaches, therapists, fitness instructors, and predictive medicine. As part of the abundance thesis discussed in Chapter XII, AI can help democratise many of these areas going forward.

A very different way of hypothesising about future scenarios is by looking at science fiction; this may seem outlandish, but these speculative thought experiments can be useful. As Calum Chace once said, "Science fiction is philosophy in fancy dress."[607] Let's take a look at three stories.

You have to tip your hat to H.G. Wells. When writing *The Time Machine* in 1895, he imagined a future that included aeroplanes, tanks, television, and even the internet.[608] Travelling to the year 802,701, he finds the working-class Morlocks living underground, while the wealthy elite, the Eloi, live above ground with an abundance of all they need. However, as they are never challenged in their lives, they have lost their intellect, spirit, and interest in the world. Wells' warning has parallels to the machine capitalism scenario above.

Aldous Huxley's *Brave New World,* written in 1932, has been rated one of the best novels of the twentieth century.[609] Almost everyone in the story is content, but humanity has lost something—a need for meaning and experience; yet only a few are aware of this. It suggests that technology can dehumanise and enslave us and cautions against the dangers of passively absorbing things that make us comfortable rather than thinking deeply. Huxley warns that a drive towards efficiency, conformity, and shallow pleasure can allow us to be controlled, leading to totalitarianism. If Huxley was vexed by the assembly lines of the early twentieth century, there is a good chance he would be distraught by the power of AI algorithms today.

Lastly, in 2015, Yanis Varoufakis, the former finance minister of Greece, imagined the divergent outcomes of automation on society with music producer Brian Eno. It was brilliantly perceptive. Yanis mused:

> The way I try to express my own fear of, and hope for, the future is that we have our choice, which is between *Star Trek* and *The Matrix*. *Star Trek* is this: we're all sitting around having philosophical conversations like in the ancient Agora in Athens, and the slaves are not human. There are holes in the walls on the Starship Enterprise; you ask for something, and it comes up. Fantastic. So, then you can explore the universe and talk to Klingons. That's one choice—the utopia. The dystopia is *The Matrix*, where the machines are being fed by our own energy. We are plugged into a false consciousness that the machines have been created to keep us happy. We think we are leading a perfectly normal life, but all along, we are the slaves of the machines. So, these are the two extremes. And the choice whether we go to *Star Trek* or *The Matrix* is ours. It's a political choice.[610]

This idea that it is a political choice is vitally important. In democracies, we get to choose our path by voting. This means we can avoid, as Huxley warned, sleepwalking into a manufactured existence, or as Wells warned, creating a world of extreme inequality. Instead, we can decide to move towards the flourishing Aristotle conceived in the Agora in Athens 2,300 years ago—more *Star Trek* than *The Matrix*. As *Star Trek's* Captain Picard explains while jetting around in the twenty-fourth century, "The acquisition of wealth is no longer the driving force in our lives. We work to better ourselves and the rest of humanity."[611] Very pro-human.

ABUNDANCE 2047

Having looked backwards and forwards, let us return to today and what our hopes are for 2047. As decisions are made about what AI to invest in, what can we do to leave the world in a better place for the next generation? Which areas should we prioritise for abundance? Hopefully, you have your three. Here are mine.

1. Flourishing at Work

   The idea of an abundance of flourishing at work seems a worthy goal. People thriving rather than surviving. Let's break down how this might work in the AI age.

   As we discussed earlier, there is an obvious opportunity to point AI towards dull, dirty, and dangerous jobs. The dull includes freeing people from the mundane tasks within their roles so they can concentrate on more interesting work. Freed up time from using AI can also be gifted back to employees for wellbeing activities or human connection. This would reverse the current trend of a faster pace of work in the digital age. Machines have not liberated us so far because we have chosen to prioritise profits over people. We can prioritise both.

Next, we have to get better at all 10 factors discussed in the previous chapter to help people flourish at work: engagement and growth, purpose, empowerment, thanks, connections, trust, wellbeing, adaptability, and stability. We know how to, so again, it is merely a question of priorities, effort, and measurement. We must support leaders in this and not expect them to be superhuman. AI can help at the margins, but the danger is that AI tips the balance of power significantly towards employers and shareholders who can extract more rather than give more. Workers having more say may be part of the solution.

We spoke about the importance of giving employees purpose above. What the learnings from the past and the future on flourishing have in common is the importance of meaning in people's lives. In a 2024 conversation between Bill Gates and Sam Altman, they agreed that one of their long-term worries when people lose jobs to AI, even if they are still supported financially by AI's gains, is how they will find meaning and purpose.[612]

Turning to one of the world's greatest experts and the author of *Man's Search for Meaning*, Viktor Frankl notes that the greatest task for any person in life is a quest for meaning. When people have enough to live on but nothing to live for, a feeling of meaninglessness can lead to their decline. Finding meaning in work—perhaps by doing something significant, often in the service of others—is something we should aspire towards. AI can create a work upgrade here, freeing people from dull tasks and providing tools to do more meaningful work.

Meaning can help towards Maslow's concept of self-actualisation, the desire to become the most one can be, but while we aspire to reach the top of Maslow's pyramid, we must first make sure workers have the safety and security at the bottom of the pyramid. Flourishing in an AI age will require enough jobs to provide a liveable income *and* meaning. Unemployment crushes flourishing.

Given AI is an extension of digitisation, we must recognise that several decades of digitisation have not yet produced the gains many hoped for. For example, research from the Robin Hood Foundation and Columbia University, published in 2025, estimates that a quarter of New Yorkers live below the poverty line.[613] For all this talk of abundance, if we cannot provide the basic physiological and financial needs for human survival in the AI age, something has gone very wrong.

Given that we know AI will substitute jobs, how do we reduce the risks to engineer more flourishing? Companies prioritising long-term augmentation over short-term efficiency gains via substitution is one way. Another is moving to shorter working weeks and job sharing, so more people have jobs, even if there are fewer to go around, creating more job equality. Voters tilting policies and taxes towards more pro-human outcomes can also help, as discussed in Chapter XI, as could workers having more say, as discussed in Chapter XII.

Unlike AI, none of the above is rocket science. It's about decisions. If an abundance of flourishing at work is a common aspiration, can leaders commit to prioritising it in the AI age?

2. Lifelong Learning

When picking areas of abundance to focus on, lifelong learning must be high on the list. It is essential if workers move away from jobs that machines can do into new areas of opportunity. This upskilling and reskilling bridge was discussed more fully in Chapter X, so there is no need to go over the same ground here. Companies should be encouraged to do their part, but given that companies are the ones that will substitute jobs, we also need to make skilling something that isn't dependent on being employed. In the same way that the Industrial Revolution gave birth to free schooling, a goal of the AI revolution should be abundant lifelong learning to give everyone the best chance of flourishing.

Clearly, to achieve this, we must find ways to reduce the cost of education and increase access to it. Formal educational institutions are often expensive and require that you take time out of work to complete qualifications. The good news is that AI could be game-changing in making this happen, linking learners anywhere to an abundance of relevant content and testing while offering AI personal tutors to every individual. Non-profit organisations like the Khan Academy are already doing this. Unfortunately, YouTube, arguably the most widely used education tool worldwide, appears to be going in the opposite direction; it is prioritising profits for shareholders by charging subscription prices and increasing advertising inserts. Content providers can help by using sites that are free to all. Governments could also provide AI talent intelligence platforms free of charge, enabling people to find jobs that align well with their skills, and set up lifelong learning voucher schemes, ensuring that cost isn't a barrier for anyone.

3. Health Is Wealth

Before his death, at age 53, my father's advice, as I headed into the world of investment banking, was, "Health is wealth." Health is life's first condition and its last lesson.

The great news is that AI's biggest gift to humanity could be improving health outcomes. AI will help in the prediction and prevention of poor health, from warning of a heart attack and screening health data to personalised medication. It will help us make amazing new health discoveries, such as DeepMind's work on folding proteins, that will drive the creation of new drugs and save millions of lives. AI can also improve the efficiency of health systems by reducing costs and freeing up health practitioners to do more value-added work.

If we had a magic wand to create abundance, the sector that could create the biggest benefits for humanity would be healthcare. It is the biggest sector in the US economy, at 17.6% of GDP, and given demographics and longevity trends, it could get even bigger.[614] The average US family of four spends over $32,000 per year on healthcare,[615] and healthcare costs have been rising faster than inflation, with medical care prices up 40% between January 2012 and 2025.[616]

Despite the importance and potential of AI for healthcare, abundance is far from a given. This cost inflation has happened despite decades of digitisation. And AI talent has been drawn to sectors where it is easier to make money in the short term. A combination of ethical prudence, complexity, and vested interests create challenges in achieving health abundance.

There is also a work-related challenge to be tackled. In many countries, such as the US, healthcare is often linked with employment. If AI disrupts employment, this may mean millions of people lose their healthcare. As Aneurin "Nye" Bevan, founder of the UK's NHS, said in 1948, "No society can legitimately call itself civilised if a sick person is denied medical aid because of lack of means."[617] Making healthcare accessible to all, whether employed or not, should be a core aim 100 years on from Bevan's statement, given the rise in wealth and technological progress. Good health is foundational for a flourishing society. It is not a coincidence that the happiest country in the world, Finland, has a publicly funded healthcare system.

In addition to health security, there are three other important areas related to health and work. The last chapter highlighted the prevalence of work-related health issues, such as burnout, stress, or even death, resulting from long working hours. Prioritising wellbeing at work has positive individual, economic, and societal benefits. Secondly, unemployment comes with many negative health impacts, so we need to mitigate AI joblessness. Thirdly, Chapter XIII noted that the biggest opportunity for new jobs in the future was in the caring economy. As jobs in the knowledge economy are increasingly lost to AI, we should invest in good caring jobs that AI cannot replicate and value these jobs appropriately. Let's embrace the wisdom that "health is wealth."

MOONSHOTS TO A BETTER WORLD

We started this chapter by looking at the 1957 Sputnik moment that created a chain reaction of ambition, progress, and growth.

In 1961, President John F. Kennedy pledged to put a man on the Moon within a decade. He reduced NASA's aspirations to just one tangible aim. In doing so, he created what the press termed a "Moonshoot"—an inspirational, unifying vision that galvanised the nation. As he said in his speech to Congress, "This decision demands a major national commitment of scientific and technical manpower, material and facilities, and the possibility of their diversion from other important activities where they are already thinly spread."[618] This shared goal—which offered focus, alignment, and collective ambition—was just what the deeply divided country needed. When Kennedy made his first trip to NASA in 1962, he is said to have asked a janitor carrying a broom what he did there. The man replied, "I'm helping put a man on the Moon."[619] This is what we should be aiming for: a shared vision that can give every worker, at every level, a feeling of purpose, meaning, and impact. Apollo 11 touched down on 20 July 1969.

If ChatGPT *is* another Sputnik moment, can we aim towards something similarly collective and positive? Perhaps that could be abundance, but abundance of what? We looked at three potential options above, but let's make them more tangible.

Moonshot 1: Mass flourishing scores above 8.5 in every country by 2047.
Moonshot 2: Free lifelong learning for all by 2047.
Moonshot 3: Free essential healthcare for all by 2047.

Given 2 and 3 help to create 1, we could consolidate all these goals into Moonshot 1. If this were possible, how could we define and measure flourishing? The good news is that there is already an empirically tested way. The future is already here.

MEASURING FLOURISHING

Founded in 2016, the Human Flourishing Program at Harvard University has developed a measurement approach to human flourishing, which they define as "a state in which all aspects of a life are good."[620] They use six central domains: happiness and life satisfaction, physical and mental health, meaning and purpose, character and virtue, close social relationships, and financial and material stability. Harvard and partners have collected data from over 200,000 participants across 22 countries, which represent nearly half of the world's population.

The three highest scores from their longitudinal Global Flourishing Study, published in April 2025, were Indonesia (8.10), Israel (7.87), and the Philippines (7.71). The UK (6.79), Turkey (6.32), and Japan (5.89) occupied the bottom three places. Stress and long working hours are not helping scores in Japan. Despite strong economic growth and technological adoption, the US ranked twelfth. While many developed nations have higher levels of financial security, they often report lower scores on relationship quality, sociality, and meaning. More pro-human leadership could help improve these metrics.

Digging further into some of these findings, the unemployed have lower flourishing scores than the employed or self-employed, emphasising a clear risk if AI increases joblessness. The authors also note that meaning often reduces as GDP per capita rises, suggesting that just driving towards GDP growth may not be enough for mass flourishing. Another conclusion is that "young people are not doing as well as they used to be," including growing financial insecurity, loss of meaning, and mental health challenges. We must find ways to make sure AI makes all these better, not worse.

No measure is perfect, but you need to start somewhere. We have all become so used to using GDP as a measure of society's success that we forget it was only pioneered relatively recently, in the 1930s, by the economist Simon Kuznets. Also, he explicitly warned Congress in 1934 that "the welfare of a nation can scarcely be inferred from a measure of national income."[621] Kuznets believed that markets were efficient in allocating resources but not in allocating fairness, and he argued we should look beyond GDP to judge if people's lives were improving. Indeed, GDP measures the quantity of economic output but not the *quality* of progress, how wealth is distributed, environmental health, or people's wellbeing. At some point, we became transfixed by GDP without understanding the nuance of its inventor's argument.

Research since GDP was embraced has shown that economic growth has failed to make us happier over time. Started in 1938, the longest-running study on happiness, the Harvard Study of Adult Development, highlights that connection to others and health are key.[622] Similarly, the Easterlin Paradox, proposed in 1974 by US economist Richard Easterlin, a student of Kuznets, empirically shows that long-term growth rates of income and happiness are not significantly related.[623] In his 2021 book *An Economist's Lessons On Happiness,* Easterlin notes that relationships, health, and job security play critical roles.[624]

One country that has taken a different path is Bhutan, whose previous head of state, King Jigme Singye Wangchuck, famously stated, "Gross National Happiness is more important than Gross Domestic Product."[625] Despite the country's poor GDP per capita, in 2008, Bhutan made its citizens' happiness a guiding principle of its constitution. It has a comprehensive approach to measuring progress via a gross national happiness (GNH) index, which uses nine primary domains and 33 indicators, including several work-related factors: psychological wellbeing; time balance; education; good governance, including rights and trust in institutions; community vitality, including belonging, trust, and volunteering; and living standards.

GNH informs policy, which includes free healthcare, free education, and preserving the environment. Similar to Kennedy's Moonshot, this has enabled focused planning, action, and measurement towards a collective goal—to be rich in happiness and wellbeing—and Bhutan has increased GNH scores from 0.743 in 2010 to 0.781 in 2022. This shows it is possible for citizens to agree that mass flourishing, free healthcare, and free education should be societal goals.

A RACE TO THE TOP

We started this chapter by asking how AI could provide an upgrade for humanity and how we could leave the world in a better place for the next generation. Looking at wisdom from past thinkers and imagining scenarios from the future, we can surely agree that mass flourishing should be a collective goal. Digging deeper in the last two chapters, we have seen it is possible to measure flourishing at work and in life and to devise action plans that improve its many components.

Mass flourishing can be a race to the top. There's no reason why it cannot be a realistic goal for every country, company, and individual. One person's gain does not have to be another's loss. We can all be winners. By doing better, leaders will encourage others to improve. Sharing best practices will benefit all. This vision contrasts sharply with the current picture: political divides, economic tariffs, business disruption, and an AI arms race that could be a dive to the bottom in terms of prices, jobs, and wages.

We know there is a risk that AI morphs Capitalism 4.0 into "profits + machines," yet we can deliberately steer society towards growing "profits + people." We have extended the idea of growing people into full-scale flourishing that can be measured and improved. This is a tilt and not a wholesale change for capitalism, towards "gross domestic product (GDP) + gross national flourishing (GNF)" for economies and "profits + flourishing scores" for companies. A tilt from shareholder primacy towards human primacy, the basis for pro-human capitalism.

While there are not many who will actively disagree with the goal of human flourishing, authentically committing to it and taking steps to turn words into actions is different. A simple first step, as discussed in Chapter XIII, is to pause when we're making a decision that impacts workers and ask, "How can we be more pro-human?" It is an action that everyone, from the leader to the janitor, can start taking today. And it can be small, such as taking a moment to thank someone, or big, such as helping a young person get their first foot on the career ladder. Let's consider an example. As a leader, next time you are meeting with your employees, ask what they think would be the best use of AI. If their answer is taking away mundane tasks, consider how a 20% time saving could be used to benefit people rather than reduce the workforce by 20%.

By continually asking how we can be more pro-human, we *can* create a better place for the next generation. We can create a flow that becomes a current that creates a wave. A wave of positive outcomes for humans to balance the wave of machine workers that are headed our way.

XV

THE BESST™ FRAMEWORK: A HOPEFUL PATH

It isn't enough to talk about being pro-human.
One must believe in it. And it isn't enough to believe in it.
One must work at it.

—Adapted from Eleanor Roosevelt's 1951 words on peace[626]

"It will never rain roses: when we want to have more roses, we must plant more trees."

—George Eliot[627]

PLANT WISELY

George Eliot was Mary Ann Evans' pen name. Born in 1819, her 1871 novel *Middlemarch* has been voted one of the greatest literary works ever written.[628] It is set in a small English town during the political crisis leading up to the 1832 Reform Bill, a critical turning point for democracy in Britain. The story reflects the tensions between progress and reform.

Between new ideas and traditional social structures. It is about the pursuit of goals and the challenges of living a meaningful life in a changing world. Sound familiar?

Evans' works are filled with descriptions of gardens and plants—metaphors for growth. Plants need the right conditions to survive and thrive. Their size above the ground is often proportional to the health of their roots below, which provide stability as the wind blows. Beautiful blooms appear only after unseen hard work. And to Evans' point in the quote above, flourishing takes time.

The same is true for us in the world of work. We need the right conditions. We need adaptability and stability. We need companies and governments to put in the time to help us thrive. Work is so important for livelihoods, families, friendships, and living a meaningful life that it should not be left to chance or hope. So, as AI starts to sweep through the world of work, what should we plant and tend?

The first part of this book looked at how this technology revolution may drive a work revolution. It explored how this time it's different—in the breadth and scope of change, in the nature of change, given that AI will surpass us in many areas and has no upper bound, and in the extraordinary pace of change, which impacts our ability to adapt.

When starting this journey together, I asked that you hold three things in mind as you read:

1. While it may take time, we have undeniably entered a new technology revolution that will lead to a work revolution (Amara).
2. Although this will create challenging crosscurrents, we have the ingenuity to find solutions that benefit most (Kennedy).
3. We can achieve this as long as we remember our humanity (Einstein).

So, how should we adapt to benefit from AI's upsides—in intelligence, science, and productivity—and mitigate AI's risks—of disruption, joblessness, and backlash?

THE BESST PATH

The core aim of this book has been to surface solutions so AI can benefit as many people as possible in relation to work. The good news is that the search has offered over 130 options. What I've learnt over time is that if you offer multiple solutions, people rightly ask, "Which one?" On the other hand, if you start by giving one solution, then the question asked is, "What else?" To remedy this, and to provide some clarity in the midst of complexity, I have condensed these solutions into one simple model: the BESST™ Framework. The outcome that offers the most for the most.

It can be broken down as follows:

B Is for Better Jobs:

- Creating better jobs should be a simple goal everyone can agree on. Compared to inventing superintelligence, moving from agreeing on how to do this to making a commitment, measuring progress, and then offering transparency on the results should be easy.
- As discussed in Chapter IX – Better Jobs, this starts with using AI to reduce dangerous and dirty jobs and then moves to the dull. AI can free people from mundane tasks, allowing them to do more interesting and higher-value work.
- This may be more controversial, but time saved from using AI will likely lead to shorter working hours in the long term.

- We can significantly improve compliance when it comes to existing labour rights, yet we may also need to consider additional workers' rights in the AI age, such as data privacy, transparency of algorithmic management, the right to disconnect, the right to flexibility, and the training of AI.
- As discussed in Chapter XIII – The Pro-Human Leader, even if AI does not lead to joblessness, both employees and employers would benefit from better engagement and growth, purpose, empowerment, thanks, connection, trust, wellbeing, adaptability, and stability. Digitisation has not improved these factors yet, but we have the opportunity to change that. All 10 factors can be measured, and leaders can implement improvement plans to make jobs better.

E Is for Enough Jobs:

- A better job first requires *having* a job. Society needs enough meaningful jobs for people to survive and thrive. As discussed in Chapter VIII – New Jobs and Chapter XI – Society Votes, this means focusing AI on augmentation rather than job substitution, which may require incentives or mandate changes for companies, leaders, and central banks.
- Better measurement of and transparency around how many jobs leaders create could help, rather than focusing purely on the profits they generate. We can choose what to celebrate.
- If there are still not enough jobs to go around, one answer may be shorter working weeks or more job sharing to create more job equality.

- An area that requires urgent attention is creating enough starter jobs for young people so they can climb onto the career ladder. This likely requires incentives.
- As discussed in Chapter X – Upskilling and Reskilling, a critical component of creating enough jobs is ensuring people have the appropriate skills demanded by businesses and future growth opportunities.

S Is for Say:

- Effective change requires workers to have agency in what and how AI is implemented at work. There are many ways in which having a say can be achieved. Leaders asking each other, “How can we be more pro-human?” is a start, but of course, it would be much better to have these conversations with employees.
- As discussed in Chapter XII – Employees Vote, if people really do matter, HR—or human talent managers—should have more seats, and say, at the top decision-making tables and on boards, as well as more value in the C-suite.
- If needed, trade union representation can help workers have a stronger say. Given that a wave of AI workers is arriving, human workers may lose even more influence as time goes on.
- It is also possible for workers to take back more control through work councils, codetermination, workers cooperatives, new rights, licencing, or bans.
- Votes at the ballot box will ultimately dictate how AI impacts work within countries. Given the time lag created by election cycles, citizens’ assemblies could step in to allow wider discussion and voting on the paths ahead.

S Is for Safety Nets:

- Work transitions during the AI age will be challenging for many, and safety nets can smooth the path. This includes helping people reskill for new growth opportunities. As discussed in Chapter X – Upskilling and Reskilling, companies need to play their part here, but given their lack of investment in training over the last few decades, many need encouragement to do so.
- Governments likely need to institute lifelong learning schemes for those not supported by companies. As part of this, universities can shift to becoming multi-versities, offering cheaper, more flexible, and stackable courses that support what businesses require. AI can lower learning costs and increase access. Free national AI talent intelligence platforms can also help identify opportunities and learning paths.
- Both governments and companies need to find ways to help young people onto the career ladder, perhaps through apprenticeship-style schemes.
- As discussed in Chapter XI – Society Votes, society will need to provide support for the unemployed. There are various options for this, from ALMPs to tax changes, or if needed, a universal basic income (UBI).
- A conditional basic income could be a good solution, particularly for the young and the old, as it provides income, skilling, purpose, and community.

T Is for Tilts:

- It will be challenging to reach a consensus on what the impact of AI on work will be, but we can agree that the solutions will need to match the severity of those impacts.

For example, UBI will not be needed if employment remains buoyant, but it could be if unemployment is overwhelming. While it's best to prepare and test solutions rather than leap in and impose policy changes prematurely, we can still agree on what tilts in policy *may* be required depending on what occurs. We can then be driven by the data, in the same way interest rates are tilted in response to the ups and downs of the economy.

- As discussed in Chapter XI – Society Votes, if unemployment rises substantially and structurally, then taxation will need to tilt away from income tax towards other sources. For example, a tilt towards taxing technology could penalise labour-substituting technology rather than labour-augmenting technology. A tilt towards taxing corporates may require a sales tax if corporates and their profits move to other countries.
- If inequality continues to rise, taxation will likely need to tilt towards higher marginal rates or wealth taxes. If wealth moves to other countries, it may need to shift towards areas that cannot move, such as property.
- As discussed in Chapter XI – Society Votes and Chapter XIV – Pro-Human Capitalism, abundance is an aspiration, but it may require that we tilt AI and investment towards the areas society cares about most, such as flourishing in work, education, and healthcare, rather than an abundance of content, consumption, or non-human workers. Incentives and taxation levers can help direct abundance.
- Chapter XII – Employees Vote and Chapter XIV – Pro-Human Capitalism also discussed democracy tilting capitalism itself – away from the dominant doctrine of shareholder primacy and towards growing profits *and* people. This tilt would require using additional

measures to drive flourishing and engagement at work. If the economic singularity discussed in Chapter IV – Falling Wages becomes more likely, this tilt could become essential—a topic that needs thought and preparation.

This BESST™ Framework can help us navigate many of the issues around AI and work. Although each category includes five bullets, it is worth noting that 31% of the solutions offered in this book are in the Better jobs category, followed by 25% in Safety nets, 21% in Say, 13% in Enough jobs, and 10% in Tilts. Clearly, this is not an exhaustive plan, and the context of each situation will differ, but this collection of mutually supportive and hopeful ideas can provide a pro-human wave to balance the growing wave of AI agents and robots coming our way.

Either as a wrapper for this bundle, or just a simple, standalone tool, asking, "How can we be more pro-human?" when making business decisions that impact people will nudge us along the BESST path. This one easy habit can be used in almost any context to surface issues, ideas, and actions. The more we ask, the better we will be.

Leaders are the ones managing change, and having a framework can help them think through the impacts of their actions and how to bring enough people along with them to ensure success. Leadership will need to change to manage more non-human workers and hybrid teams, but this shift towards AI should not mean that the treatment of and attention to human workers is downgraded. We need an upgrade. If they are committed to this goal, as simple examples, leaders could try to answer these questions:

- **B – Better Jobs**: How can you make other people's jobs better, which could be as simple as giving more praise or constructive feedback?

- **E – Enough Jobs**: How can you help young people get on the career ladder, so they become future human-in-the-loop experts?
- **S – Say**: How can you give your team more say in shaping their work outcomes?
- **S – Safety Nets**: Who can you reskill or upskill to move them away from areas of substitution to areas of opportunity?
- **T – Tilts**: What tilts could be coming down the road that will impact your business, and how can you respond to them?

If you lead a team or organisation, you can create a 90-day plan by picking one BESST pillar to move first, with two concrete actions and a metric you will track. Alternatively, the framework can be used as a base in a leadership workshop in which each person picks their top three options to improve work for their teams. Then the group agrees on two to work on, assigning an owner, next steps, and timelines for each.

However, these potential solutions and questions are not just for leaders; they should be for every one of us, as we navigate self-leadership. For example, these questions should help you to discover what you can do to help shape the future of work:

- **B – Better Jobs**: How can AI make your job better?
- **E – Enough Jobs**: What parts of your job will AI eliminate, and what can this freed-up time be best used for?
- **S – Say**: Do you speak up enough about your fears around AI and the opportunities it provides in your work?
- **S – Safety Nets**: As AI disrupts work, what are you doing to create your own safety nets, from upskilling yourself

and building a network of opportunities to making sure you have rainy day savings put aside?

- **T – Tilts**: What tilts would you vote for to make sure the opportunities for AI outweigh the risks? What tilts can you make in your life to be more pro-human? For example, have you tilted your pension towards companies providing pro-human solutions?

PROACTIVE AND PRO-HUMAN

You will have your own versions of the questions above, but the aim of this book is to increase awareness of the issues and solutions and to motivate action. We need to both smooth the transition today and build a longer-term vision of how to move the world of work into a better place. You can decide how to move forward—in a few big leaps or a series of small steps that compound over time. Yet one thing is for sure: we get to shape the future with our choices and actions.

However, AI is moving at an exponential pace, and it will quickly surpass us in many areas; it's not hanging around waiting for us to catch up. Whether that leads to dystopian or utopian outcomes in work is not yet known. But to Evans' point above, if we want roses, we need to be proactive and get planting. So, how can you be more pro-human in your actions today? And tomorrow. And over the next year.

One simple answer could be modelling the behaviours you want to see. Another is to pass this book to your boss, or your boss's boss. Alternatively, discuss the issues, solutions, and actions with your team, family, or friends. Or send me your suggestions and successes so we can collectively find the best path. I know I don't have all the answers, just a desire to see AI benefit most and witness the positive ripples of pro-human behaviour. Ripples that allow people to swim with the tide rather than against it.

Thank you for sharing this journey. We end where we started, with the quote below, but now with a better understanding of what might come next, why leaders need to act, and how they can create a world that is more pro-human. More importantly, we end with hope. Go well on your next path.

When the conditions change, pessimists fret, optimists hope, and procrastinators dither; yet leaders *act* to forge the BESST path.

ABOUT THE AUTHOR

Rob Garlick partners with leaders to shape how AI is transforming business, work, and leadership. He is an author, visiting professor, consultant, and executive coach with over three decades of experience, spanning AI and innovation, capital markets, and pro-human leadership.

Rob's innovation journey began in the 1990s as a US fund manager and leading TMT equity salesperson, from the commercial birth of the internet with Netscape's IPO in 1995 to being part of Google's IPO in 2004. In 2013, he founded Citi's Disruptive Innovation series and later became head of innovation and technology at Citi Global Insights.

Recognising early on that AI and robotics would reshape work, in 2015, Rob began collaborating with Oxford's Carl Benedikt Frey, one of the world's leading experts on AI and work, on a series of Technology at Work reports. He has published more than 60 papers on innovation, delivered over 100 talks worldwide on AI and the future of work, and is a visiting professor at the Future of Work Research Centre at the University of Surrey.

Rob brings deep expertise in how innovation transforms businesses and how capital markets really function. At Citi, he served as head of research EMEA, global product head focused on theme investing and innovation, and head of US equity sales in the UK. He led teams to top rankings in the Institutional Investor surveys across the UK, Western Europe, and globally, and he was a No. 1-rated global TMT salesperson. Rob passed the AIIMR (Associate of the Institute of Investment Management and Research) as a prize-winner in Interpretation of Accounts and Corporate Finance.

Rob has over 20 years of leadership experience, including several thousand meetings with C-suite leaders around the globe. Promoted to managing director in 2006, he has managed, mentored, and coached senior leaders at the highest levels. He holds a master's degree in behavioural change and is a qualified executive coach and EMCC Senior Practitioner.

Building on these experiences, Rob is the author of *AI – Anarchy or Abundance?* which argues why the future of work needs pro-human leadership. His BESST™ Framework champions a practical approach to ensuring AI benefits many.

Rob lives near London with his wife and four children.

ENDNOTES

Introduction

[1] Hargrove, R. (2024) Author Robert Hargrove: Five Things Business Leaders Can Do To Create A Fantastic Work Culture, Authority Magazine, December 11, https://medium.com/authority-magazine/author-robert-hargrove-five-things-business-leaders-can-do-to-create-a-fantastic-work-culture-d0c8a9026b2d

[2] Youtube (2025) The Economics of Artificial Intelligence https://youtu.be/XSy7ry-x5pA?si=QPQGwZQ-Glk9je7o

[3] Hindmoor, A. & McConnell, A. (2014) Who saw it coming? The UK's great financial crisis, Journal of Public Policy, 35 (1), 63–96.

[4] Citi GPS (2024) The Rise of AI Robots: Physical AI is Coming for You, Citi Global Perspectives & Solutions.

[5] International Labour Organization (2025) Measuring what matters: NEET vs youth unemployment, https://www.ilo.org/resource/article/measuring-what-matters-neet-vs-youth-unemployment

[6] National Museum of Nuclear Science & History (1955) Russell-Einstein Manifesto, https://ahf.nuclearmuseum.org/ahf/key-documents/russell-einstein-manifesto/

[7] YouTube (2025) NVIDIA CEO Jensen Huang's Vision for the Future, https://www.youtube.com/watch?v=7ARBJQn6QkM

Part 1 – Work WITHOUT Human Workers

Chapter I – The Rise of AI Robots

[8] Rus, D. (2015) The Robots Are Coming, Foreign Affairs, June 16, https://www.foreignaffairs.com/articles/2015-06-16/robots-are-coming

[9] Wakefield, J. (2022) Musk: Robots to be bigger business than Tesla cars, BBC News, January 27, https://www.bbc.co.uk/news/technology-60154782

[10] TechGig (2024) What Is Physical AI and Why It Could Be the Next Wave in AI?, https://content.techgig.com/technology/what-is-physical-ai-and-why-it-could-be-the-next-wave-in-ai/articleshow/110787358.cms

11 Peter H. Diamandis (2024) Tech Breakthroughs on My Mind: 10 Billion Humanoid Robots, Life on Mars..., https://www.diamandis.com/blog/10-billion-humanoid-robots-life-on-mars

12 Citi GPS (2024) The Rise of AI Robots: Physical AI is Coming for You, Citi Global Perspectives & Solutions.

13 World Bank (2025) Total Labor Force, https://data.worldbank.org/indicator/SL.TLF.TOTL.IN

14 International Federation of Robotics (2024) Record of 4 Million Robots in Factories Worldwide, IFR Press Release, September 24, https://ifr.org/ifr-press-releases/news/record-of-4-million-robots-working-in-factories-worldwid

15 Citi GPS (2024) The Rise of AI Robots: Physical AI is Coming for You, Citi Global Perspectives & Solutions.

16 Wu, J. and Bosa, D. (2025), Waymo crosses 450,000 weekly paid rides as Alphabet robotaxi unit widens lead on Tesla, CNBC, December 8, https://www.cnbc.com/2025/12/08/waymo-paid-rides-robotaxi-tesla.html

17 Wessling, B. (2025) Waymo reaches 100M fully autonomous miles across all deployments, The Robot Report, July 18, https://www.therobotreport.com/waymo-reaches-100m-fully-autonomous-miles-across-all-deployments/

18 Waymo (2025) Our mission is to be the world's most trusted driver, https://waymo.com/about/

19 Optics (2024) Hesai boosted by Baidu robotaxi deal, https://optics.org/news/15/7/35

20 Medium (2023) How Autonomous Vehicles Use Synthetic Data, https://medium.com/amelias-blog/how-autonomous-vehicles-use-synthetic-data-9b3d1e0b60d7

21 Our World in Data (2004-2020) Labor Share of GDP, https://ourworldindata.org/grapher/labor-share-of-gdp

22 1X (2025) NEO Home Robot, https://www.1x.tech/discover/neo-home-robot

23 Feng, C. (2025) China's Unitree debuts US$5,900 humanoid robot in race to make cheaper products, South China Morning Post, July 25, https://www.scmp.com/tech/tech-trends/article/3319637/chinas-unitree-debuts-us5900-humanoid-robot-race-make-cheaper-products

24 GOV.UK (2025) Farming Evidence: Key Statistics, https://www.gov.uk/government/publications/farming-evidence-pack-a-high-level-overview-of-the-uk-agricultural-industry/farming-evidence-key-statistics-

25 Office for National Statistics (2021) Industry and Occupation in England and Wales: Census 2021, https://www.ons.gov.uk/employmentandlabourmarket/peopleinwork/employmentandemployeetypes

26 Dizikes, P. (2020) How many jobs do robots really replace?, MIT News, May 4, https://news.mit.edu/2020/how-many-jobs-robots-replace-0504

27 Hicks, M. J. and Devaraj, S. (2015) The Myth and the Reality of Manufacturing in America, Center for Business and Economic Research, Ball State University.

28 Citi GPS (2024) The Rise of AI Robots: Physical AI is Coming for You, Citi Global Perspectives & Solutions.

29 Uber Newsroom (2024) Only on Uber: Helping to make driving and delivering safer, fairer, and easier, https://www.uber.com/newsroom/onlyonuber24/

30 Sriram, A. (2024) Lyft unveils improved pay measures to attract more drivers, Reuters, October 8, https://www.reuters.com/business/autos-transportation/lyft-announces-measures-improve-driver-pay-2024-10-08/

31 Pakulniewicz, M. (2023) Global truck driver shortage to double within 5 years, says new IRU report, Trans.INFO, November 23, https://trans.info/en/truck-driver-shortage-372189

32 Wikipedia (2023) Electric Car Use by Country, https://en.wikipedia.org/wiki/Electric_car_use_by_country

33 World Bank (2025) Total Labor Force, https://data.worldbank.org/indicator/SL.TLF.TOTL.IN

Chapter II – The AI Industrial Revolution

34 Mcelwee, J. J.(2015) Catholicism can and must change, Francis forcefully tells Italian church gathering, National Catholic Reporter, November 10, https://www.ncronline.org/catholicism-can-and-must-change-franci s-forcefully-tells-italian-church-gathering

35 Gates, B. (2023) The age of AI has begun, Gates Notes, March 21, gatesnotes.com/the-age-of-ai-has-begun-chapter-00

36 Walters, R. (2022) Big Tech shows off its AI, Financial Times, October 13, https://www.ft.com/content/42c95389-6fe0-4a69-bab7-6fc96c6896be

37 Milmo, D. (2023) ChatGPT reaches 100 million users faster than any app in history, The Guardian, February 2, https://www.theguardian.com/technology/2023/feb/02/chatgpt-100-million-users-open-a i-fastest-growing-app

38 Backstone (2026) 2026 Investment Perspectives, January 12, https://www.blackstone.com/insights/article/office-of-the-cio-2026-investment-perspectives/

39 Techcrunch (2023) Hippocratic is building a large language model for healthcare, https://techcrunch.com/2023/05/16/hippocratic-is-building-a-large-language-model-for-healthcare/

40 Heikkila, M. & Morris, S. (2025) Microsoft claims AI diagnostic tool can outperform doctors, Financial Times, June 30, https://www.ft.com/content/149296b9-41b6-4fba-b72c-c72502d01800

41 Garlick, R. & Fei, W. (2024) AI Meets Human Capital, Citigroup Global Insights.

42 McKenzie, L. (2019) Would your mobile phone be powerful enough to get you to the moon?, The Conversation, July 1, https://theconversation.com/would-your-mobile-phone-be-powerfu l-enough-to-get-you-to-the-moon-115933

43 Calvino, F., Reijerink, J. & Samek, L. (2025) The effects of generative AI on productivity, innovation and entrepreneurship, OECD.

44 Citi GPS (2024) What Machines Can't Master, Citi Global Perspectives & Solutions.

45 PitchBook (2025) AI startups grabbed a third of global VC dollars in 2024, https://pitchbook.com/news/articles/ai-startups-grabbed-a-third-of-global-vc-dollars-in-2024

46 Morris, Heikkila,& Criddle (2025), Can Google still dominate search in the age of AI chatbots? Financial Times, May 23, https://www.ft.com/content/dec83193-c787-4301-8098-4277fdd0e5af

47 Staff Report on Algorithmic Trading in U.S. Capital Markets (2020)

48 Citi GPS (2024) Technology at work v4.0, https://www.citigroup.com/global/insights/technology-work-v4-0

49 EMBL (2023) AlphaFold uses open data and AI to discover the 3D protein universe, https://www.embl.org/news/science/alphafold-using-open-data-and-ai-to-discover-the-3d-protein-

50 Garlick, R. & Fei, W. et al. (2024) AI Time: AI Assistants Are Coming For You, Citigroup Global Insights.

51 Peng, S. et al. (2023) The Impact of AI on Developer Productivity: Evidence from GitHub Copilot, Cornell University.

52 Nolan, B. (2025) Mark Zuckerberg is building an AI engineer to help with coding tasks at Meta, and ramping up spending to $65 billion, Fortune, January 24, https://fortune.com/2025/01/24/mark-zuckerberg-ai-engineer-capex-spend/

53 SmythOS (2025) Can an AI code itself?, https://smythos.com/ai-trends/can-an-ai-code-itself-claude-code/#:~:text=This%20statement%20didn't%20come,decisions%20about%20architecture%20or%20features

54 Intuition Labs (2024) AI Reasoning: Gold-Medal Performance at the 2025 IMO, https://intuitionlabs.ai/articles/ai-reasoning-math-olympiad-imo

55 Heikkila, M. (2025) DeepMind and OpenAI achieve gold at 'coding Olympics' in AI milestone, Financial Times, September 17, https://www.ft.com/content/c2f7e7ef-df7b-4b74-a899-1cb12d663ce6

56 Thomas, D. (2025) WPP races to harness AI before the technology kills its business, Financial Times, June 11, https://www.ft.com/content/4d1d939c-23e3-491f-9a5e-58532fdc82cb

57 YouTube (2024) Ep17. Welcome Jensen Huang | BG2 w/ Bill Gurley & Brad Gerstner, https://www.youtube.com/watch?v=bUrCR4jQQg8

58 OpenAI (2025), Introducing GPT-5.2, December 11, https://openai.com/index/introducing-gpt-5-2/

59 Chess.com (2014) Stockfish Outlasts "Rybkamura", https://www.chess.com/news/view/stockfish-outlasts-nakamura-3634

60 Hammond, G. (2025), AI sceptic Emily Bender: 'The emperor has no clothes', Financial Times, June 20, https://www.ft.com/content/9029cc1c-4a3f-42ca-9939-f3ef8e8336ae

61 Grace, K. et al. (2018) When will AI exceed human performance?, Journal of Artificial Intelligence Research, 62, 729-754.

62 AIMultiple (2025) When Will AGI/Singularity Happen? 8,590 Predictions Analyzed, https://research.aimultiple.com/artificial-general-intelligence-singularity-timing/#easy-footnote-bottom-22-58322

63 Metaculus (2025) When will the first general AI system be devised, tested, and publicly announced?, https://www.metaculus.com/questions/5121/date-of-artificial-general-intelligence/

64 Citi GPS (2023) Quantum Computing, https://www.citigroup.com/global/insights/quantum-computing

65 Cuthbertson, A. (2019) Quantum computing breakthrough means Google could be very close to revealing revolutionary machine, The Independent, June 27, https://www.independent.co.uk/tech/quantum-computing-google-computer-lab-hartmut-neven-law-a8973951.html

66 Aschenbrenner, L. (2024) Situational Awareness: The Decade Ahead

67 Peter H. Diamandis (2023) Raising our AI Children, https://www.diamandis.com/blog/raising-children

68 University of Cambridge (2016) The best or worst thing to happen to humanity, https://www.cam.ac.uk/research/news/the-best-or-worst-thing-to-happen-to-humanity-stephen-hawking-launches-centre-for-the-future-

69 Lakenheath Alliance for Peace (2024) The Explosive Power Of Nuclear Weapons, https://lakenheathallianceforpeace.org.uk/the-explosive-power-of-nukes/#:~:text=The%20effects%20of%20nuclear%20weapons,(50%20megatons)%20of%20explosives.

70 CodingScape (2024) 40% of global employment is exposed to AI – IMF report, https://codingscape.com/blog/40-percent-of-global-employment-is-exposed-to-ai-imf-

71 Andersen, R (2023) The Sudden Fall of Sam Altman, The Atlantic, November 17, https://www.theatlantic.com/technology/archive/2023/11/sam-altman-open-ai-fallout/676046/

72 Suleyman, M. (2023) The Coming Wave: AI, Power, and Our Future, Crown.

73 VandeHei, J. & Allen, M. (2025) Behind the Curtain: A white-collar bloodbath, Axios, May 28, https://www.axios.com/2025/05/28/ai-jobs-white-collar-unemployment-anthropic

74 Beane, M. (2024) The Skill Code: How to Save Human Ability in an Age of Intelligent Machines, HarperCollins.

75 World Economic Forum (2025) The Future of Jobs Report 2025, https://www.weforum.org/publications/the-future-of-jobs-report-2025/?utm_medium=email&_hsenc=p2ANqtz-

76 Nurse.org (2025) 15 Highest Paying Nursing Jobs in 2026, https://nurse.org/articles/15-highest-paying-nursing-careers/#top-highest-paid-nursing-jobs-in-2026

77 UK Finance (2025) Generative AI in action: Opportunities and Risk Management in Financial Services, https://www.ukfinance.org.uk/system/files/2025-01/Generative%20AI%20in%20action-

78 Eloundou, T. et al. (2023) GPTs are GPTs: An Early Look at the Labor Market Impact Potential of Large Language Models, Cornell University.

79 Kinder, M. et al. (2024) Generative AI, the American worker, and the future of work, Brookings, October 10, https://www.brookings.edu/articles/generative-ai-the-american-worker-and-the-future-of-work/

80 Frey, C. B. & Osborne, M. A. (2017) The future of employment: How susceptible are jobs to computerisation?, Technological Forecasting and Social Change, 114, 254–280.

81 Wikipedia (n.d), The Landmarks of Tomorrow, https://en.wikipedia.org/wiki/The_Landmarks_of_Tomorrow

82 Srivastava, S. (2025) JPMorgan instructs managers to pause hiring and use AI instead, People Matters, May 20, https://www.peoplematters.in/news/recruiting-and-onboarding/jpmorgan-instruct-managers-to-pause-hirin g-and-use-ai-instead-45620

83 Computing (2023) IBM CEO says 30% of back office roles could disappear within five years, https://www.computing.co.uk/news/4113200/ibm-ceo-office-roles-disappear

84 Sherman, N. (2025) Amazon boss says AI will replace jobs at tech giant, BBC News, June 17, https://www.bbc.co.uk/news/articles/cn0q2v851k9o#:~:text=Mr%20Jassy%20said%20he%20expected,of%20jobs%2C%22%20he%20wrote.

85 Wall Street Journal (2025) Walmart CEO Issues Wake-Up Call: 'AI Is Going to Change Literally Every Job', https://www.wsj.com/tech/ai/walmart-ceo-doug-mcmillon-ai-job-losses-dbaca3aa

86 Farrar, O. (2025) Bill Gates on AI and innovation, Harvard Magazine, February 4, https://www.harvardmagazine.com/university-news/harvard-bill-gates-ai-and-innovation

Chapter III – Digital and Remote Work

87 The Guardian (2003) Natural Injustice, The Guardian, July 14, https://www.theguardian.com/world/2003/jul/14/globalisation.guardianleaders#:~:text=Napoleon%20is%20said%20to%20have,trade%20and%20aid%20programmes%20certainly.

88 Citi GPS (2023) Technology at Work v7.0, https://www.citigroup.com/global/insights/technology-at-work-v7-0

89 Citi GPS (2021) Technology at Work v6.0, https://www.citigroup.com/global/insights/technology-at-work-v6-0

90 Crawford, K. (2024) Study finds hybrid work benefits companies and employees, Stanford Report, June 12, https://news.stanford.edu/stories/2024/06/hybrid-work-is-a-win-win-win-for-companies-workers

91 Oxford Martin School (2022) Long-distance collaboration makes scientific breakthroughs more likely, suggests Oxford University research, https://www.oxfordmartin.ox.ac.uk/news/long-distance-collaboration

92 Citi GPS (2023) Technology at Work v7.0, https://www.citigroup.com/global/insights/technology-at-work-v7-0

93 CSET (2023) The Global Distribution of STEM Graduates: Which Countries Lead the Way? https://cset.georgetown.edu/article/the-global-distribution-of-stem-graduates-which-countries-lead-the-way/

94 Benedikt Frey, C. Garlick, R. et al. (2023) Technology at work v7.0, Citigroup, https://www.citigroup.com/global/insights/technology-at-work-v7-0

95 INDIAai (2024) India leads global AI talent and skill penetration, https://indiaai.gov.in/article/india-leads-global-ai-talent-and-skill-penetration

96 U.S. National Science Foundation (2024) The STEM Labor Force: Scientists, Engineers, and Skilled Technical Workers, https://ncses.nsf.gov/pubs/nsb20245/foreign-born-stem-workers

97 International Labour Organization (2022) Working Time and Work-Life Balance Around the World, International Labour Organization

98 International Labour Organization (2024) Global Employment Trends for Youth 2024, International Labour Organization

99 Citi GPS (2021) Technology at Work v6.0, https://www.citigroup.com/global/insights/technology-at-work-v6-0

100 Deel (2025) A Billion Thank Yous: Deel Celebrates $1bn Run Rate, https://www.deel.com/blog/deel-celebrates-one-billion-revenue-run-rate/

101 Valuates Reports (2025) Global Employer of Record Market Research Report 2025, https://reports.valuates.com/market-reports/QYRE-Auto-7D9395/global-employer-of-record

102 Johnson, C (2024) Spend on contingent workers holds steady at $1.4 trillion, Staffing Industry Analysts, September 23, https://www.staffingindustry.com/news/global-daily-news/spend-on-contingent-workers-holds-steady-at-14-trillion#:~:text=There%20were%2018.3%20million%20contingent,estimated%20down%20from%2019.4%20million.

103 Knowledge Based Value Research (2023) Contingent Workforce Management Market, https://www.kbvresearch.com/contingent-workforce-management-market/

104 Taskrabbit (2024) Tasking Through 2024—Our Best Year Yet, https://www.taskrabbit.com/blog/tasking-through-2024-our-best-year-yet/

105 The Side Hustle Project (2017) Fiverr CEO Micha Kaufman on Freelancing, Building a Marketplace, and Growing a Startup, https://sidehustlelab.com/fiverr-ceo-micha-kaufman-interview/

106 WallStreetZen (2025) Upwork Revenue, https://www.wallstreetzen.com/stocks/us/nasdaq/upwk/revenue#:~:text=What%20was%20Upwork's%20annual%20revenue,a%2024.31%25%20increase%20from%202019.

107 Umbrex (2025) Understanding the Fractional Executive Model, https://umbrex.com/resources/fractional-executive-playbook/understanding-the-fractional-executive-model/
108 Citi GPS: Global Perspectives & Solutions (2021) Technology at work v6.0, Citigroup
109 Brynjolfsson, E., Li, D. & R. Raymond, L. (2023) Generative AI at Work, National Bureau of Economic Research

Chapter IV – Falling Wages

110 https://www.goodreads.com/quotes/353440-when-the-facts-change-i-change-my-mind---what
111 Chace, C. (2016) The Economic Singularity: Artificial Intelligence and the Death of Capitalism, Three Cs.
112 World Intellectual Property Organization (2024) Robotics Industry Doubles since 2015, https://www.wipo.int/en/web/global-innovation-index/w/blogs/2024/robotics-industry
113 Mooney, M. (2025) Robots installed in US auto industry up by double digits, Robotics and Automation Magazine, May 9, https://www.roboticsandautomationmagazine.co.uk/news/robots-installed-in-us-auto-industry-up-by-double-digits.html
114 Author Unknown (2002) World robot survey reports sales up 25 per cent in 2000, Industrial Robot, 29(2), 106–108.
115 Carlsson, B. (2012) Technological Systems and Economic Performance: The Case of Factory Automation, Springer Science & Business Media.
116 Construction Physics (2024) What Progress Has There Been in Industrial Robots? https://www.construction-physics.com/p/what-progress-has-there-been-in-industrial
117 Acemoglu, D. & Restrepo, P. (2020) Robots and Jobs: Evidence from US Labor Markets, Journal of Political Economy, 128 (6), 2188–2244.
118 Binder, A. J. & Bound, J. (2019) The Declining Labor Market Prospects of Less-Educated Men, Journal of Economic Perspectives, 33(2).
119 Economic Policy Institute (2025) The Productivity–Pay Gap, https://www.epi.org/productivity-pay-gap/
120 Pawel, A. (2018) The mightier, the stingier: Firms' market power, capital intensity, and the labor share of income, Munich Personal RePEc Archive.
121 Economic Policy Institute (2021) Growing inequalities, reflecting growing employer power, have generated a productivity–pay gap since 1979, https://www.epi.org/blog/growing-inequalities-reflecting-growing-employer-power-have-generated-a-productivity-pay-gap-since-1979-productivity-has-grown-3-5-times-as-much-as-pay-for-the-typical-worker/#:~:text=The%20key%20metric%2C%20as%20explained,growth%20for%20the%20bottom%2090%25.

122 Transport For London (2025) Learn the Knowledge of London, https://tfl.gov.uk/info-for/taxis-and-private-hire/licensing/learn-the-knowledge-of-london#:~:text=The%20Knowledge%20was%20introduced%20as,and%20how%20much%20you%20earn.

123 Berger, T., Chen, C. & Benedikt Frey, C. (2017) Drivers of Disruption? Estimating the Uber Effect, Oxford Martin School.

124 Demand Sage (2025) How Many Uber Drivers Are There (2025 Statistics), https://www.demandsage.com/uber-statistics/

125 Kristal, T. (2020) Why Has Computerization Increased Wage Inequality? Information, Occupational Structural Power, and Wage Inequality, Work and Occupations, 47(4), 466–503.

126 Autor, D., Dorn, D., Katz, L. F., Patterson, C. & Van Reenen, J. (2017) The fall of the labor share and the rise of superstar firms, CEP Discussion Papers, dp1482, 1–72.

127 Claude (n.d). Novo Nordisk accelerates clinical documentation and drug development with Claude, https://www.claude.com/customers/novo-nordisk#:~:text=Healthcare,Read%20more%20Read%20more

128 Castle, S. (2021) Who Are Knowledge Workers And How Do We Enable Them?, Forbes, December 1, https://www.forbes.com/sites/sisense/2021/12/01/who-are-knowledge-workers-and-ho w-do-we-enable-them/

129 Bg2Pod (2024) Ep17, https://youtu.be/bUrCR4jQQg8?si=cKGxk9ENsq5zyIN2

130 Citi Global Insights (2023) AI Time, https://www.citivelocity.com/rendition/authfilelinksvcs/eppublic/V1/file?paramData=ZmlsZU5hbWU9L2dsaW4vcnNjaF9wZGZfMzAxNzIzNDIucGRmJnBsYXRmb3JtSWQ9MTA5JmRvY0lkPTMwMTcyMzQy

131 Statista Research Department (2025) Number of mobile app downloads worldwide from 2018 to 2024, https://www.statista.com/statistics/271644/worldwide-free-and-paid-mobile-app-store-downloads/

132 World Bank (2025) Total Labor Force, https://data.worldbank.org/indicator/SL.TLF.TOTL.IN

133 AIPRM (2025) 100+ Must-Know Robotics Statistics 2025, https://www.aiprm.com/en-gb/robotics-statistics/

134 YouTube (2024) Humans Adapting in the Age of AI, https://www.youtube.com/watch?v=bXeLQ2JfIOA

135 Goldstein, P. (2019) The Computing Power of Apollo 11: The Tech Behind It, FedTech Magazine, July 18, https://fedtechmagazine.com/article/2019/07/computing-power-apollo-11-tech-behind-it#:~:text=Today's%20smartphones%2C%20which%20fit%20into,processing%20power%20of%20the%20AGC.

136 YouTube (2025) CFO of OpenAI Sarah Friar Interview at the Oxford Union, https://www.youtube.com/watch?v=gyGCBitfYvg

[137] Chamorro-Premuzic, T. (2023) I, human: AI, automation, and the quest to reclaim what makes us unique, Harvard Business Press.
[138] Korinek, A. (2023) Scenario Planning for an A(G)I Future, F&D Magazine, https://www.imf.org/en/publications/fandd/issues/2023/12/scenario-planning-for-an-agi-future-anton-korinek
[139] Goodreads (n.d.) "How did you go bankrupt? Two ways: gradually, then suddenly.", https://www.goodreads.com/quotes/102579-how-did-you-go-bankrupt-two-ways-gradually-then-suddenly
[140] Murray, J.E. (2024) Scary smart: the future of artificial intelligence and how you can save our world, by Mo Gawdat. Essays in Philosophy, 25(1/2), 62-64.
[141] Harari, Y.N. (2016) Homo Deus: A brief history of tomorrow, Random House.
[142] Chace, C. (2016) The economic singularity, Three Cs.
[143] Congress.gov (2024) Introduction to U.S. Economy: Consumer Spending, https://www.congress.gov/crs-product/IF11657#:~:text=As%20defined%20by%20the%20Bureau,the%20case%20of%20rising%20prices.
[144] Amodei, D. (2024) Machines of Loving Grace , https://darioamodei.com/essay/machines-of-loving-grace

Chapter V – Data Over People

[145] Goodreads (n.d.) "Once men turned their thinking over to machines…" https://www.goodreads.com/quotes/842526-once-men-turned-their-thinking-over-to-machines-in-the
[146] Wikipedia (2025) Have I Told You Lately That I Love You?, https://en.wikipedia.org/wiki/Have_I_Told_You_Lately_That_I_Love_You%3F
[147] Wikipedia (2025) Have I Told You Lately That I Love You?, https://en.wikipedia.org/wiki/Have_I_Told_You_Lately_That_I_Love_You%3F
[148] Claremont Colleges Digital Library (n.d.) Peter Drucker on management tape 8: people are our ..., https://ccdl.claremont.edu/digital/collection/dac/id/4891/
[149] Quote Fancy (n.d.) "Efficiency is doing better what is already being done."- Peter F. Drucker, https://quotefancy.com/quote/887898/Peter-F-Drucker-Efficiency-is-doing-better-what-is-already-being-done
[150] Goodreads (n.d.) "You can't manage what you can't measure." https://www.goodreads.com/quotes/11299805-you-can-t-manage-what-you-can-t-measure
[151] Macheel, T. (2025) Another 'near miss': Citigroup mistakenly credited a customer account with $81 trillion, CNBC, March 1, https://www.cnbc.com/2025/03/01/citigroup-mistakenly-credited-a-customer-account-with-81-trillion.html
[152] Brynjolfsson, E., Li, D. & R. Raymond, L. (2023) Generative AI at Work, National Bureau of Economic Research.

153 Hill, A. (2025) Inside DHL's AI upgrade: 'Love it or hate it, you have to work with it', Financial Times, August 25, https://www.ft.com/content/ce09786f-2481-44fe-957c-f7bb0b43e284

154 Staton, B. (2026) The recruitment company training AI to do your job, Financial Times, January 24, https://www.ft.com/content/0cab0fcd-e355-40e8-83a3-2ad5066d7b48

155 Gartner (2022) The Right Way to Monitor Your Employee Productivity, https://www.gartner.com/en/articles/the-right-way-to-monitor-your-employee-productivity#:~:text=While%20the%20concept%20of%20monitoring,are%20implementing%20productivity%20monitoring%20technology

156 Blasey, L. & Faguy, A. (2025) List weekly accomplishments or resign, Musk tells US federal workers, BBC News, February 22, https://www.bbc.co.uk/news/articles/cr72n1yyj30o

157 Roast (2025) Tinder statistics 2025: All you need to know about the dating app! https://roast.dating/blog/tinder-statistics

158 Statista (2025) Volume of data or information created, captured, copied, and consumed worldwide from 2010 to 2029, https://www.statista.com/statistics/871513/worldwide-data-created/

159 Rivery (2025) Big data statistics: How much data is there in the world? https://rivery.io/blog/big-data-statistics-how-much-data-is-there-in-the-world/

160 University of Sheffield (2025) Clive Humby - Visiting Professor of Computer and Information Science, https://sheffield.ac.uk/cs/people/academic-visitors/clive-humby

161 Procter & Gamble Company (2024) P&G + Me = Mutual Success: Delivering a Superior Employee Value Equation, https://us.pg.com/blogs/delivering-a-superior-employee-value-equation/

162 Dealmakers (2025) The Story of Instagram's $1billion Acquisition, https://dealmakers.co.uk/the-story-of-instagrams-1billion-acquisition/#:~:text=Just%2018%20months%20after%20its,up%20with%2030%20million%20users.

163 Rushe, D. (2014) WhatsApp: Facebook acquires messaging service in $19bn deal, The Guardian, February 20, https://www.theguardian.com/technology/2014/feb/19/facebook-buys-whatsapp-16bn-deal

164 The Indent (2019) The Robots Are Coming: Grappling with Our AI Future, https://theindent.com/our-ai-future/

165 Wikipedia (2025) Blockbuster (retailer), https://en.wikipedia.org/wiki/Blockbuster_(retailer)#:~:text=Blockbuster%20or%20Blockbuster%20Video%20is,worldwide%20and%20operated%209%2C094%20stores.

166 StockAnalysis (2025) Netflix, Inc. https://stockanalysis.com/quote/neo/NFLX/employees/

167 Tiny Teams (2025) Tiny Teams home page, https://tinyteams.xyz

168 Wikipedia (2025) Procter & Gamble https://en.wikipedia.org/wiki/Procter_%26_Gamble

169 Knibbs, K. (2024) Every AI Copyright Lawsuit in the US, Visualized, Wired, December 19, https://www.wired.com/story/ai-copyright-case-tracker/#:~:text=The%20plaintiffs%20include%20individual%20authors,else%20you%20need%20to%20know.

170 Smith-Goodson, P. & Kimball, M. (2025) The Stargate Project: Trump Touts $500 Billion Bid For AI Dominance, Forbes, January 30, https://www.forbes.com/sites/moorinsights/2025/01/30/the-stargate-project-trump-touts-500-billion-bid-for-ai-dominance/

171 Citi GPS (2018) The Bank of the Future, https://www.citigroup.com/global/insights/bank-future

172 Blakey, D. (2023) US bank branch numbers fall to 40-year low: do branches matter to win customer deposits?, Retail Banker International, November 20, https://www.retailbankerinternational.com/features/us-bank-branch-numbers-fall-to-40-year-low/

173 Finder (2025) Bank branch statistics: Number of bank branches in the UK, https://www.finder.com/uk/banking/banking-branch-usage

Chapter VI – AI Anarchy

174 BrainyQuote (n.d.) Aldous Huxley Quotes, https://www.brainyquote.com/quotes/aldous_huxley_391055

175 Goodreads (n.d.) Alan Moore Quotes, https://www.goodreads.com/quotes/7618344-the-roots-of-the-word-anarchy-are-an-archos-no

176 Dobbs, R., Manyika, J. and Woetzel, J. (2016) No Ordinary Disruption: The Four Global Forces Breaking All the Trends, PublicAffairs.

177 IEMed (2014) Arab Youth Values and Identities: Impact of the Arab Uprisings, https://www.iemed.org/publication/arab-youth-values-and-identities-impact-of-the-arab-uprisings/

178 Wikipedia (n.d.) Luddite, https://en.wikipedia.org/wiki/Luddite#:~:text=Government%20officials%20sought%20to%20suppress,defendants%20at%20the%20York%20trials.

179 The Age of Revolution (n.d.) The Swing Riots, https://blogs.kent.ac.uk/ageofrevolution/riots/the-swing-riots/#:~:text=They%20were%20called%20the%20Swing,were%20five%20phases%20of%20action:

180 Bengali, L., Valletta, R. G. and Zhao, C. (2025) Explaining Stagnation in the College Wage Premium, Federal Reserve Bank of San Francisco Working Paper 2025-01, https://www.frbsf.org/wp-content/uploads/wp2025-01.pdf

181 World Economic Forum (2025) Global Risks Report 2025, World Economic Forum, https://reports.weforum.org/docs/WEF_Global_Risks_Report_2025.pdf

182 Criddle, C. (2025) 'Godfather of AI Yoshua Bengio says latest models lie to users', Financial Times, June 3, https://www.ft.com/content/2b3ce320-2451-45c4-a15c-757461624585

183 The Guardian (2024) 'Godfather of AI' raises odds of the technology wiping out humanity over next 30 years, The Guardian, December 27, https://www.

theguardian.com/technology/2024/dec/27/godfather-of-ai-raises-odds-of-the-technology-wiping-out-humanity-over-next-30-years

184 Clifford, C. (2018) Elon Musk at SXSW: A.I. is more dangerous than nuclear weapons, CNBC, March 13, https://www.cnbc.com/2018/03/13/elon-musk-at-sxsw-a-i-is-more-dangerous-than-nuclear-weapons.html

185 BBC News (2014) Stephen Hawking warns artificial intelligence could spell end of human race, BBC News, December 2, https://www.bbc.co.uk/news/technology-30290540#:~:text=Prof%20Hawking%20says%20the%20primitive,can%20match%20or%20surpass%20humans.&text=%22It%20would%20take%20off%20on,increasing%20rate%2C%22%20he%20said.

186 Jackson, S. (2025) The secret escapes of billionaires: from bunkers to secure compounds, Yahoo Finance UK, December 3, https://uk.finance.yahoo.com/news/billionaire-boltholes-inside-doomsday-hideouts-170000871.html

187 BBC News (2018) New Zealand bans sale of homes to foreigners, BBC News, August 15, https://www.bbc.co.uk/news/world-asia-45199034

188 Lex Fridman (2025) Demis Hassabis: Future of AI, Simulating Reality, Physics and Video Games (YouTube video), YouTube, https://youtu.be/-HzgcbRXUK8

189 Benaich, N. and Air Street Capital (2025) State of AI Report 2025, https://www.stateof.ai

190 Smith, K. N. (2018) The computer that almost started a nuclear war, and the man who stopped it, Forbes, September 25, https://www.forbes.com/sites/kionasmith/2018/09/25/the-computer-that-almost-started-a-nuclear-war-and-the-man-who-stopped-it/

191 Morris, C. (2025) Anthropic CEO warns AI could eliminate half of all entrylevel whitecollar jobs, Fortune, May 28, https://www.fortune.com/2025/05/28/anthropic-ceo-warning-ai-job-loss/

192 Business Today Desk (2025) AI could replace 80% of jobs in 5 years, warns Silicon Valley investor Vinod Khosla, Business Today, August 4, https://www.businesstoday.in/technology/news/story/ai-could-replace-80-of-jobs-in-5-years-warns-silicon-valley-investor-vinod-khosla-487637-2025-08-04

193 Shibu, S. (2025) Fiverr CEO says AI will take your job — here's what to do, Entrepreneur, https://www.entrepreneur.com/business-news/fiverr-ceo-says-ai-will-take-your-job-heres-what-to-do/491198

194 The Holy See (2025) Address of His Holiness Pope Leo XIV to the College of Cardinals, 10 May 2025, Vatican.va, https://www.vatican.va/content/leo-xiv/en/speeches/2025/may/documents/20250510-collegio-cardinalizio.html

195 Parikh, T. (2025) The rising resistance to creative destruction, Financial Times, June 16, https://www.ft.com/content/4c1abb2a-f710-4aa3-80ac-d8811abad84f

196 Gallup (2025) State of the Global Workplace 2025, https://www.gallup.com/workplace/349484/state-of-the-global-workplace.aspx

197 Rogers, T. (2025) The strike threat at US ports and the coming battles over automation, Financial Times, January 9, https://www.ft.com/content/eb11f69c-e45c-4f23-8793-0ca5866b4b67

198 Krisher, T., Vejpongsa, T. and Fortune (2024) U.S. economy could lose $4.5 billion a day as ports hit with biggest dockworkers strike since 1977, Fortune, October 1, https://fortune.com/2024/10/01/us-economy-lose-billion-day-ports-hit-dockworkers-strike-1977/

199 Baertlein, L. and Beech, E. (2024) Trump says automation causes more harm to longshoremen than it's worth, Reuters, December 12, https://www.reuters.com/world/us/trump-says-automation-causes-more-harm-longshoremen-than-its-worth-2024-12-12/

200 Talbott, S. J. (2025) The Waymo vandalism incident: A wakeup call for the AV industry, Forbes, January 27, https://www.forbes.com/sites/selikajosiahtalbott/2025/01/27/the-waymo-vandalism-incident-a-wake-up-call-for-the-av-industry/

201 Lodge, M. and Strudwick, M. (2024) Ulez cameras cut: Sadiq Khan elected Mayor, Daily Mail, May 6, https://www.dailymail.co.uk/news/article-13386507/ulez-cameras-cut-sadiq-khan-elected-mayor.html

202 Home Office (2024) New protest laws on face coverings and pyrotechnics, GOV.UK, February 8, https://www.gov.uk/government/news/new-protest-laws-on-face-coverings-and-pyrotechnics

203 Financial Times (2025) Biden and Republicans spar over automation and labour markets, Financial Times, April 26, https://www.ft.com/content/dd6dff7d-c2c4-49ec-a11e-eb9e2130ccbb

204 Barrett, P., Appendino, M., Nguyen, K. and de Leon Miranda, J. (2020) Measuring Social Unrest Using Media Reports, IMF Working Paper No. 2020/129, International Monetary Fund, https://www.imf.org/en/Publications/WP/Issues/2020/07/17/Measuring-Social-Unrest-Using-Media-Reports-49573

205 Barrett, P. and Chen, S. (2021) The economics of social unrest, Finance & Development, August 2021, https://www.imf.org/external/pubs/ft/fandd/2021/08/economics-of-social-unrest-imf-barrett-chen.htm

206 Grasso, M. T. and Giugni, M. (2016) Protest participation and economic crisis: The conditioning role of political opportunities, European Journal of Political Research, 55(4), 777–800, https://doi.org/10.1111/1475-6765.12153

207 International Labour Organization (2013) World of Work Report 2013: Repairing the Economic and Social Fabric, https://www.ilo.org/sites/default/files/wcmsp5/groups/public/@dgreports/@dcomm/documents/publication/wcms_214476.pdf

208 HadziVaskov, M., Pienknagura, S. and Ricci, L. A. (2021) The macroeconomic impact of social unrest, IMF Working Paper No. 2021/135, International Monetary Fund, https://www.imf.org/en/Publications/WP/Issues/2021/05/07/The-Macroeconomic-Impact-of-Social-Unrest-50338

209 Barrett, P., Chen, S., Chivakul, M. and Igan, D. (2021) Pricing Protest: The Response of Financial Markets to Social Unrest, IMF Working Paper No. 2021/079, International Monetary Fund, https://www.imf.org/en/Publications/WP/Issues/2021/03/19/Pricing-Protest-The-Response-of-Financial-Markets-to-Social-Unrest-50146

210 U.S. Bureau of Labor Statistics (n.d.) Unemployment Rate [UNRATE], Federal Reserve Bank of St. Louis FRED, https://fred.stlouisfed.org/series/UNRATE

211 The Times (2025) Jobs market is flashing a warning sign to Rachel Reeves, The Times, June 14, https://www.thetimes.com/business/economics/article/jobs-market-is-flashing-a-warning-sign-to-rachel-reeves-rhqlhkcgm

212 Kalshi (2025) Unemployment spike market (Unemployment above 9% before 2030), https://kalshi.com/markets/kxu3max/unemployment-spike

213 Agence FrancePresse (2018) Youth unemployment, Europe's unshakeable challenge, ChatEurope, February 1, https://chateurope.eu/en/youth-unemployment-europes-unshakeable-challenge/

214 TradingEconomics (2025) Youth Unemployment Rate for South Africa, https://tradingeconomics.com/united-states/youth-unemployment-rate-for-south-africa-fed-data.html

215 The Prince's Trust (2024) NatWest Youth Index 2024, https://assets.ctfassets.net/qq0roodynp09/1dwzhtDnn0c2f MyH7AGZTC/434c31c34cfd896a735c11261e2c98af/DSN6204_Princes_Trust_Youth_Index_2024.pdf

216 Carnevale, A. P., Jayasundera, T. and Gulish, A. (2016) America's Divided Recovery: College Haves and HaveNots, Georgetown University Center on Education and the Workforce, https://cew.georgetown.edu/wp-content/uploads/Americas-Divided-Recovery-web.pdf

217 Brynjolfsson, E., Chandar, B. and Chen, R. (2025) Canaries in the Coal Mine? Six Facts about the Recent Employment Effects of Artificial Intelligence, Stanford Digital Economy Lab Working Paper, https://digitaleconomy.stanford.edu/wp-content/uploads/2025/08/Canaries_BrynjolfssonChandarChen.pdf

218 Almeida, L. (2025) Number of new UK entrylevel jobs has dived since ChatGPT launch – research, The Guardian, June 30, https://www.theguardian.com/business/2025/jun/30/uk-entry-level-jobs-chatgpt-launch-adzuna

219 Oxford Economics (2025) Educated but unemployed, a rising reality for US college grads, Oxford Economics, May 27, https://www.oxfordeconomics.com/resource/educated-but-unemployed-a-rising-reality-for-us-college-grads/

220 Murray, C. (2025) Is AI killing graduate jobs?, Financial Times, July 24, https://www.ft.com/content/99b6acb7-a079-4f57-a7bd-8317c1fbb728

221 The Times (2025) Meet the Oxbridge graduates who can't get a (good) job, The Times, August 13, 2025, https://www.thetimes.com/uk/education/article/oxbridge-graduates-cant-get-good-job-d9ddj9dff

[222] Institute of Student Employers (2024) 5 trends you need to know from ISE's Recruitment Survey 2024, https://ise.org.uk/knowledge/insights/260/5_trends_you_need_to_know_from_ises_recruitment_survey_2024/

[223] My Art Broker (n.d.) Banksy: 'Sorry, the lifestyle you ordered is currently out of stock', https://www.myartbroker.com/artist-banksy/articles/banksy-sorry-the-lifestyle-you-ordered-is-currently-out-of-stock

[224] Feiner, L. (2025) Satya Nadella says as much as 30% of Microsoft code is written by AI, CNBC, April 29, https://www.cnbc.com/2025/04/29/satya-nadella-says-as-much-a s-30percent-of-microsoft-code-is-written-by-ai.html

[225] Bernard, B. (2025) The US tech hiring freeze continues, Indeed Hiring Lab, July 30, https://www.hiringlab.org/2025/07/30/the-us-tech-hiring-freeze-continues/

[226] SignalFire (2025) The SignalFire State of Tech Talent Report 2025, https://www.signalfire.com/blog/signalfire-state-of-talent-report-2025

[227] Uddin, R. (2025) Microsoft to cut 4% of staff in new wave of layoffs, Financial Times, July 2, https://www.ft.com/content/3e656455-8dec-40ec-92f7-676fc5ae873c

[228] Kelly, J. (2025) The jobs that will fall first as AI takes over the workplace, Forbes, April 25, https://www.forbes.com/sites/jackkelly/2025/04/25/the-jobs-that-will-fall-first-as-ai-takes-over-the-workplace/

[229] Gooding, M. (2023) IBM could replace 7,800 back office workers with AI, Tech Monitor, May 2, https://www.techmonitor.ai/digital-economy/ai-and-automation/ibm-could-replace-7800-back-office-workers-with-ai

[230] Gartner (2025) Gartner predicts agentic AI will autonomously resolve 80% of common customer service issues without human intervention by 2029, Gartner, March 5, https://www.gartner.com/en/newsroom/press-releases/2025-03-05-gartner-predicts-agentic-a i-will-autonomously-resolve-80-percent-of-common-customer-service -issues-without-human-intervention-by-20290

[231] Singh, J. (2025) Meta aims to fully automate advertising with AI by 2026, Reuters, June 2, https://www.reuters.com/business/media-telecom/meta-aims-fully-automate-advertising-wit h-ai-by-2026-wsj-reports-2025-06-02/

[232] Kelly, J. (2025) The jobs that will fall first as AI takes over the workplace, Forbes, April 25, https://www.forbes.com/sites/jackkelly/2025/04/25/the-jobs-that-will-fall-first-as-ai-takes-over-the-workplace/

[233] Kennedy, J. (2024) Indeed's 2025 UK Jobs & Hiring Trends Report: Labour Market Could Prove the UK Economy's Achilles Heel, Indeed Hiring Lab UK & Ireland, December 10, https://www.hiringlab.org/uk/blog/2024/12/10/indeed-2025-uk-jobs-and-hiring-trends-report/

[234] Tomlinson, K., Jaffe, S., Wang, W., Counts, S. and Suri, S. (2025) Working with AI: Measuring the Applicability of Generative AI to Occupations, arXiv preprint arXiv:2507.07935, https://arxiv.org/pdf/2507.07935

235 Frey, C. B. and LlanosParedes, P. (2025) Lost in translation: Artificial Intelligence and the demand for foreign language skills, Oxford Martin School, University of Oxford, https://www.oxfordmartin.ox.ac.uk/publications/lost-in-translation-artificial-intelligence-and-the-demand-for-foreign-language-skills

236 AI Uncovered (2025) Anthropic Made the Impossible Happen! (Goodbye Lawyers) (YouTube video), YouTube, https://youtu.be/WoqcSIcdx-Y

237 Hatzius, J., Briggs, J., Kodnani, D. and Pierdomenico, G. (2023) The Potentially Large Effects of Artificial Intelligence on Economic Growth, Goldman Sachs Global Economics Analyst, March 26, https://www.key4biz.it/wp-content/uploads/2023/03/Global-Economics-Analyst_-The-Potentially-Large-Effects-of-Artificial-Intelligence-on-Economic-Growth-Briggs_Kodnani.pdf

238 Morabito, C. (2024) Why more men are dropping out of the workforce, CNBC, September 21, https://www.cnbc.com/2024/09/21/why-more-men-are-dropping-out-of-the-workforce.html

239 Katz, L. F. and Krueger, A. B. (2016) The rise and nature of alternative work arrangements in the United States, 1995–2015, NBER Working Paper No. 22667, National Bureau of Economic Research, https://www.nber.org/papers/w22667

240 McKinsey Global Institute (2016) Independent work: Choice, necessity, and the gig economy (Executive Summary), McKinsey & Company, October, https://www.mckinsey.com/~/media/mckinsey/featured%20insights/employment%20and%20growth/independent%20work%20choice%20necessity%20and%20the%20gig%20economy/independent-work-choice-necessity-and-the-gig-economy-executive-summary.pdf

241 Saad, L. (2025) AI: Major threat or just the next tech thing?, Gallup, July 10, https://news.gallup.com/poll/692435/major-threat-next-tech-thing.aspx

Part 2 – Work WITH Human Workers

Chapter VII – AI Abundance

242 Diamandis, P. (2023) While many are fearful of AI, there are some (including myself) who … [X (formerly Twitter) post], X, https://x.com/PeterDiamandis/status/1737274958026354859

243 Altman, S. (2023) Planning for AGI and beyond, OpenAI, February 24, https://openai.com/index/planning-for-agi-and-beyond/

244 The Idiomatic Orchestra (n.d.) 14. Orchestra size and setting, https://theidiomaticorchestra.net/14-orchestra-size-and-setting/

245 A Stamp A Day (2018) Thomas Edison's Invention of the Phonograph, https://stampaday.wordpress.com/2018/11/21/thomas-edisons-invention-of-the-phonograph/

246 Spotify (n.d.) Company Info, https://www.spotify.com/about-us/contact/

[247] Pratt, R. (2025) Q&A with Khan Academy founder Sal Khan, Corridor Business Journal, April 16, https://corridorbusiness.com/qa-with-khan-academy-founder-sal-khan/

[248] Perkel, J. M. (2011) Making the most of PMC, Nature Methods, 8, 521–522.

[249] Bendix, A. et al (2020) Moderna designed its coronavirus vaccine in 2 days, Business Insider, December 19, https://www.businessinsider.com/moderna-designed-coronavirus-vaccine-in-2-days-2020-11

[250] Goldman, S. (2023) A year ago, DeepMind's AlphaFold AI changed the shape of science, but there is more work to do, VentureBeat, July 15, https://venturebeat.com/ai/a-year-ago-deepminds-alphafold-ai-changed-the-shape-of-science-but-there-is-more-work-to-do

[251] Hassabis, D. (2023) Building AI responsibly, to benefit humanity: 2023 UCL Prize Lecture in Life and Medical Sciences, UCL News, December 13, https://www.ucl.ac.uk/news/2023/dec/google-deepmind-co-founder-discusses-how-ai-can-benefit-humanity-ucl

[252] Diamandis, P. and Kotler, S. (2012) Abundance: The Future Is Better Than You Think, Simon & Schuster.

[253] Criddle, C. (2025) Silicon Valley's abundance of hype over abundance, Financial Times, June 5, https://www.ft.com/content/241b86b6-dd2b-4254-afaa-7d500004763b

[254] Mayne, M.. (2023) Elon Musk says AI will mean people no longer need work, People Management, November 6, https://www.peoplemanagement.co.uk/article/1846529/elon-musk-says-ai-will-mean-people-no-longer-need-work--hr-experts-respond

[255] Citi GPS (2024) Future of Healthcare: The Oxford Prescription, https://www.citigroup.com/global/insights/future-of-healthcare

[256] AZQuotes (n.d.) Peter Diamandis Quote, https://www.azquotes.com/quote/843442

[257] Coughlan, S. (2019) 'Unstoppable' degree inflation at university, says vice-chancellor, BBC News, September 26, https://www.bbc.co.uk/news/education-49841620

[258] U.S. Bureau of Labor Statistics (2021) Celebrating Women's History Month with a look at women in the labor force, https://www.bls.gov/blog/2021/celebrating-women-s-history-month-with-a-look-at-women-in-the-labor-force.htm

[259] Cross, P. (2018) Hey Canadians, does anyone remember what economic growth can do?, Financial Post, July 12, https://financialpost.com/opinion/philip-cross-hey-canadians-does-anyone-remember-what-economic-growth-can-do

[260] World Bank (2024) September 2024 global poverty update from the World Bank, https://blogs.worldbank.org/en/opendata/september-2024-global-poverty-update-from-the-world-bank--revise

[261] Crimmins, E.M.. Lifespan and Healthspan: Past, Present, and Promise. Gerontologist. 2015 Dec;55(6):901-11

262 Weller, C. (2017) Barack Obama has a one-question test that proves how good the world is today, Business Insider, September 20, https://www.businessinsider.com/president-barack-obama-speech-goalkeepers-2017-9

263 International Telecommunication Union (n.d.) Publications and reports: AI for Good, https://aiforgood.itu.int/newsroom/publications-and-reports/#un-activities-ai

264 PwC (2025) Reinvention on the edge of tomorrow, https://www.pwc.com/gx/en/issues/analytics/assets/pwc-ai-analysis-sizing-the-prize-report.pdf

265 McKinsey Global Institute (2023) The economic potential of generative AI: The next productivity frontier, https://www.mckinsey.com/capabilities/mckinsey-digital/our-insights/the-economic-potential-of-generative-AI-the-next-productivity-frontier

266 Aghion, P. and Bunel, S. (2024) AI and growth: Where do we stand?, Policy Note.

267 Parikh, T. (2024) Erik Brynjolfsson: 'This could be the best decade in history — or the worst', Financial Times, January 31, https://www.ft.com/content/b71759fe-397b-4688-bc81-b082edb25f31

268 YouTube (2025. Cathie Wood's Big Ideas 2025 Recap, YouTube, https://youtu.be/gXm8WwkL_QU

269 Epoch AI (2025) AI and explosive growth redux, https://epoch.ai/gradient-updates/ai-and-explosive-growth-redux

270 Blair, T. (2024) My advice to Keir Starmer, The Times, https://www.thetimes.com/uk/politics/article/tony-blair-my-advice-to-keir-starmer-j0zlmzwr3

271 Pew Research Center (2025) Views of children's financial future, https://www.pewresearch.org/global/2025/01/09/views-of-childrens-financial-future/

272 Our World in Data (2015) Share of the population who think the world is getting better, https://assets.ourworldindata.org/uploads/2016/12/Optimistic-about-the-future-2.png

273 Acemoglu, D. (2025) Liberalism can win back the working class. Here's how, Financial Times, November 29, https://www.ft.com/content/96aadc56-d99e-463a-b95c-d5cab088cacc

274 The Harris Poll (2023) Millennials lead American optimism for the future, https://theharrispoll.com/briefs/millennials-lead-american-optimism-for-the-future/

275 OECD (2024) Reviving productivity growth, https://www.oecd.org/content/dam/oecd/en/publications/reports/2024/10/reviving-productivity-growth_936a1da3/61244acd-en.pdf

276 Office for National Statistics (2025), Annual multi-factor productivity, market sector, UK: October to December 2024, https://www.ons.gov.uk/economy/economicoutputandproductivity/productivitymeasures/bulletins/growthaccountingmultifactorproductivityestimatesuk/octobertodecember2024

277 J.P. Morgan Private Bank (2024) How AI can boost productivity and jump-start growth, https://privatebank.jpmorgan.com/nam/en/insights/

markets-and-investing/ideas-and-insights/how-ai-can-boost-productivity-and-jump-start-growth

278 Bureau of Labor Statistics (2025) Consumer Price Index, https://www.bls.gov/cpi/

279 Federal Reserve Bank of Cleveland (2020) Is the Middle Class Worse Off Than It Used to Be?, https://www.clevelandfed.org/publications/economic-commentary/2020/ec-202003-is-middle-class-worse-off

280 MIT Department of Economics (2024) Daron Acemoglu: What do we know about the economics of AI?, https://economics.mit.edu/news/daron-acemoglu-what-do-we-know-about-economics-ai

281 Congressional Budget Office (2025) The long-term budget outlook: 2025 to 2055, https://www.cbo.gov/system/files/2025-03/61187-Long-Term-Outlook-2025.pdf

282 Citi GPS (2024) Embracing the demographic transition, https://www.citigroup.com/global/insights/embracing-demographic-transition

283 Zucman, G. (2019) Global wealth inequality, Annual Review of Economics, 11, 109–138.

284 OECD (2020) How's life?2020, https://www.oecd.org/en/publications/how-s-life/volume-/issue-_9870c393-en.html

285 Congressional Research Service (2020) Real Wage Trends, 1979 to 2019, https://www.congress.gov/crs-product/R45090

286 Bipartisan Policy Center (2024) Delving into the Reasons Why Some Prime-Age Men are Out of Work, https://bipartisanpolicy.org/blog/why-some-prime-age-men-are-out-of-work/

287 International Labour Organization (2025) Measuring what matters: NEET vs youth unemployment, https://www.ilo.org/resource/article/measuring-what-matters-neet-vs-youth-unemployment

288 OECD (2020) How's life?2020, https://www.oecd.org/en/publications/how-s-life/volume-/issue-_9870c393-en.html

Chapter VIII – New Jobs

289 Thompson, D. (2015) A world without work, The Atlantic, July, https://www.theatlantic.com/magazine/archive/2015/07/world-without-work/395294/

290 Keynes, J. M. (1930) Economic possibilities for our grandchildren, in Essays in Persuasion, Palgrave Macmillan.

291 Wikipedia (n.d.) Seamus McSporran, https://en.wikipedia.org/wiki/Seamus_McSporran

292 Guinness World Records (n.d.) Most acting roles, https://www.guinnessworldrecords.com/world-records/69981-most-acting-roles

293 World Economic Forum (2023) Why workers are likely to have multiple careers in their lifetime, https://www.weforum.org/stories/2023/05/workers-multiple-careers-jobs-skills/

294 Foxen, J. (2024) What the latest trends tell us about the world's population, UN News, July 11, https://news.un.org/en/story/2024/07/1151971

295 Our World in Data (2024) Population by age group, https://ourworldindata.org/grapher/population-young-working-elderly

296 Department for Environment, Food & Rural Affairs (n.d.) Farming evidence pack: Key statistics, https://www.gov.uk/government/publications/farming-evidence-pack-a-high-level-overview-of-the-uk-agricultural-industry/farming-evidence-key-statistics-accessible-version

297 House of Commons Library (2025) Employment in agriculture, https://commonslibrary.parliament.uk/research-briefings/sn05206/

298 CoinLaw (2025) App revenue statistics, https://coinlaw.io/app-revenue-statistics/

299 Chin, C. et al. (2022) New frontiers: The origins and content of new work tasks, MIT Department of Economics.

300 Acemoglu, D. and Restrepo, P. (2019) Artificial intelligence, automation and work, NBER Working Paper No. 25684, National Bureau of Economic Research, https://www.nber.org/system/files/working_papers/w25684/w25684.pdf

301 World Economic Forum (2025) The Future of Jobs Report 2025, https://reports.weforum.org/docs/WEF_Future_of_Jobs_Report_2025.pdf

302 Citi GPS (2019) Technology at work v4.0, https://www.citigroup.com/global/insights/technology-work-v4-0

303 PWC (2025) The Fearless Future: 2025 Global AI Jobs Barometer, https://www.pwc.com/gx/en/issues/artificial-intelligence/ai-jobs-barometer.html

304 BBC (2025) OpenAI boss: Meta offering $100m plus to poach my staff, https://www.bbc.co.uk/news/articles/c8730088e5do

305 Walker, O. (2018) Al Gore: sustainability is history's biggest investment opportunity, Financial Times, April 29, https://www.ft.com/content/1757dc40-486f-11e8-8ee8-cae73aab7ccb

306 International Energy Agency Greenhouse Gas Programme (2023) Net zero roadmap update 2023, https://ieaghg.org/insights/iea-net-zero-roadmap-update-2023-ip13/

307 Statista (2025) Monthly number of employees in the United States, https://www.statista.com/statistics/192387/unadjusted-monthly-number-of-employees-in-the-us/

308 Office for National Statistics (2024) Improving the visibility of older people in global statistics, https://blog.ons.gov.uk/2024/10/01/improving-the-visibility-of-older-people-in-global-statistics/

309 Bureau of Labor Statistics (n.d.) Employment situation, https://www.bls.gov/emp/

310 World Health Organization (n.d.) Health workforce, https://www.who.int/health-topics/health-workforce

311 Burn-Murdoch, J. (2025) Rising graduate joblessness is mainly affecting men. Will that last?, Financial Times, July 18, https://www.ft.com/content/a9eadb06-8085-4661-9713-846ebe128131

[312] Hypebeast (2025), Breaking Rust's "Walk My Walk," an AI-Generated Song, Tops Billboard Country Digital Song Sales, https://hypebeast.com/2025/11/breaking-rust-walk-my-walk-tops-billboard-country-digital-song-sales
[313] Citi GPS (2023) Technology at Work, Citi Global Perspectives & Solutions, https://ir.citi.com/gps/7PUfiT7fJPblL/qpQla8YnPTu1opFVW5Qb5fu0LPwJGLKt4p0HcsDxN87TOJ/6kA/bMcrnTJTn8SFOdAlpoihg==
[314] United Nations (2024) UN projects world population to peak within this century, https://www.un.org/en/UN-projects-world-population-to-peak-within-this-century
[315] Citi GPS (2016) Technology at work 2.0, Citi Global Perspectives & Solutions, https://oms-www.files.svdcdn.com/production/downloads/reports/Citi_GPS_Technology_Work_2.pdf
[316] OECD (2025) OECD Employment Outlook 2025, https://www.oecd.org/en/publications/oecd-employment-outlook-2025_194a947b-en.html
[317] Citi GPS (2016) Technology at work v2.0, https://www.citigroup.com/global/insights/technology-work-v2-0
[318] Citi GPS (2024) Embracing the demographic transition, https://www.citigroup.com/global/insights/embracing-demographic-transition
[319] YouTube (2025) Leading in a Time of Change: Jamie Dimon, Chairman and CEO, JP Morgan Chase, YouTube, https://youtu.be/PdzMvk66wao
[320] Ghisellini, P. et al. (2021) Revisiting Keynes in the Light of the Transition to Circular Economy. PMC.1(1):143-171.
[321] Saacks, B. Vlamis, K. (2025) EY CEO says AI won't decrease its 400,000-person workforce — but it might help it double in size, Business Insider, https://www.businessinsider.com/ey-ceo-janet-truncale-ai-jobs-consulting-giant-2025-5
[322] Financial Times (n.d.) Does HR still need humans?, Financial Times, https://www.ft.com/content/e356d8e6-2f68-4fe2-9f17-bc930e6d0996
[323] World Economic Forum (2025) The Future of Jobs Report 2025, https://reports.weforum.org/docs/WEF_Future_of_Jobs_Report_2025.pdf
[324] Moretti, E. (2010) Local multipliers, https://eml.berkeley.edu/~moretti/multipliers.pdf
[325] PwC (2023) PwC's 26th Annual Global CEO Survey, https://www.pwc.co.uk/press-room/press-releases/pwcs-26th-annual-global-ceo-survey.html
[326] Hill, A. (2025) Does HR still need humans?, Financial Times, August 18, https://www.ft.com/content/e356d8e6-2f68-4fe2-9f17-bc930e6d0996
[327] Goodreads (n.d.) Give me a onehanded economist; all my economists say, https://www.goodreads.com/quotes/7887683-give-me-a-one-handed-economist-all-my-economists-say-on
[328] Citigroup (2024) AI Meets Human Capital (Management) Part 3 AI Doom or Boom for Jobs?, https://www.citivelocity.com/rendition/authfilelinksvcs/eppublic/V1/file?paramData=ZmlsZU5hbWU9L2dsaW4vcnNjaF9wZGZfMzAyMTk

0MzUucGRmJnBsYXRmb3JtSWQ9MTA5JmRvY0lkPTMw
MjE5NDM1
329 Collier, P. (2008) The Bottom Billion: Why the poorest countries are failing and what can be done about it, Oxford University Press.
330 BrainyQuote (n.d.) Niels Bohr quotes, https://www.brainyquote.com/quotes/niels_bohr_130288
331 Thompson, D. (2015) A world without work, The Atlantic, July, https://www.theatlantic.com/magazine/archive/2015/07/world-without-work/395294/

Chapter IX – Better Jobs

332 BrainyQuote (n.d.) Mahatma Gandhi quotes, https://www.brainyquote.com/quotes/mahatma_gandhi_107894
333 BrainyQuote (n.d.) Mark Twain quotes, https://www.brainyquote.com/quotes/mark_twain_162937
334 United Nations (2025) The Sustainable Development Goals Report 2025, https://unstats.un.org/sdgs/report/2025/The-Sustainable-Development-Goals-Report-2025.pdf
335 Citigroup (2023) AI in healthcare: Health administration, https://www.citigroup.com/global/insights/ai-in-healthcare-health-administration-
336 HealthLeaders Media (2020) Compassionate care is not a matter matter of time?, https://www.healthleadersmedia.com/clinical-care/expert-compassionate-care-not-matter-time
337 Shansong, W. et al. (2025) Capabilities of GPT-5 on Multimodal Medical Reasoning, arXiv preprint, https://arxiv.org/pdf/2508.08224
338 Morris, S., Heikkila, M. (2025) Microsoft claims AI diagnostic tool can outperform doctors, Financial Times, June 30, https://www.ft.com/content/149296b9-41b6-4fba-b72c-c72502d01800
339 WISERD (2024) What is happening to participation at work, https://wiserd.ac.uk/wp-content/uploads/2.-What-is-Happening-to-Participation-at-Work.pdf
340 ResearchGate (2021) Employee involvement, work engagement and skill development, https://www.researchgate.net/publication/355889308_Employee_involvement_work_engagement_and_skill_development
341 Gallup (2025) State of the global workplace, https://www.gallup.com/workplace/349484/state-of-the-global-workplace.aspx
342 Pew Research Center (2023) Workers' views on the risk of AI to their jobs, https://www.pewresearch.org/social-trends/2023/07/26/workers-views-on-the-risk-of-ai-to-their-jobs/
343 Economics Network (1930) Economic possibilities for our grandchildren, https://www.economicsnetwork.ac.uk/archive/keynes_persuasion/Economic_Possibilities_for_our_Grandchildren.htm

[344] Economics Observatory (2021) What might be the effects of a four-day working week?, https://www.economicsobservatory.com/what-might-be-the-effects-of-a-four-day-working-week
[345] Wikipedia (n.d.) Working time, https://en.wikipedia.org/wiki/Working_time
[346] International Labour Organization (n.d.) Working time, https://ilostat.ilo.org/topics/working-time/
[347] CNN (2025) Dutch kids the happiest in the world, https://edition.cnn.com/2025/06/29/health/dutch-kids-happiest-essay-wellness
[348] Valerie, A. (2010) Trends in time use in twentieth-century America, NBER Reporter, https://www.nber.org/reporter/2010number3/trends-time-use-twentieth-century-america
[349] Zhang, Q et al. (2022) Being busy, feeling poor: The scale development and validation of perceived time poverty, https://onlinelibrary.wiley.com/doi/abs/10.1111/ijsa.12395
[350] Wikipedia (n.d.) Parkinson's Law, https://en.wikipedia.org/wiki/Parkinson's_law
[351] Burkeman, O. (2021) Four thousand weeks: Time management for mortals, Farrar, Straus and Giroux
[352] Ratti, C. et al. (2024) SHIFTING PATTERNS OF SOCIAL INTERACTION:
EXPLORING THE SOCIAL LIFE OF URBAN SPACES THROUGH A.I., https://www.nber.org/system/files/working_papers/w33185/w33185.pdf
[353] The Times (n.d.) Graduates are quitting arts jobs for tech as pay beats prestige, The Times, https://www.thetimes.com/uk/education/article/graduates-are-quitting-arts-jobs-for-tech-as-pay-beats-prestige-vdhqh08tn
[354] Ring, S., Heikkila, M. (2025) A&O Shearman unveils AI tool to speed up senior legal work, Financial Times, April 6, https://www.ft.com/content/9bfebd81-b7f4-4b90-aa22-fdd012b4ccd1
[355] History Guild (2020) Why do we have an 8-hour working day?, https://historyguild.org/why-do-we-have-an-8-hour-working-day/
[356] New York Times (1956) Nixon foresees 4-day work week, New York Times, September 23, https://www.nytimes.com/1956/09/23/archives/nixon-foresees-4day-work-week-says-gop-policies-assure-fuller-life.html
[357] Gartner (2019) More than half of organizations are offering summer work flexibility, https://www.gartner.com/en/newsroom/press-releases/2019-06-06-more-than-half-of-organizations-are-offering--summer-
[358] McCurry, J. (2017) Premium Fridays: Japan gives workers a break to go shopping, The Guardian, February 24, https://www.theguardian.com/world/2017/feb/24/premium-fridays-japan-gives-workers-break-go-shopping
[359] China Briefing (2021) 996 is ruled illegal: Understanding China's changing labor system, https://www.china-briefing.com/news/996-is-ruled-illegal-understanding-chinas-changing-labor-system/
[360] Euronews (2025) Spain moves forward with a proposed law to shorten the working week to 37.5 hours, https://www.euronews.com/next/2025/05/07/

spain-moves-forward-with-a-proposed-law-to-shorten-the-working-work-to-375-hours

361 World Economic Forum (2021) United Arab Emirates weekend working week, https://www.weforum.org/stories/2021/12/united-arab-emirates-weekend-working-week/

362 Boffey, D. (2022) Belgium to give workers right to request four-day week, The Guardian, February 15, https://www.theguardian.com/law/2022/feb/15/belgium-to-give-workers-right-to-request-four-day-week

363 UK Research and Innovation (2024) Making the case for a four-day working week, https://www.ukri.org/who-we-are/how-we-are-doing/research-outcomes-and-impact/esrc/making-the-case-for-a-fou r-day-working-week/

364 ACCA (n.d) Four-day work week, https://www.accaglobal.com/uk/en/technical-activities/uk-tech/in-practice/2022/september/Four-day-work-week.html

365 New York City (n.d.) Automated employment decision tools, https://www.nyc.gov/site/dca/about/automated-employment-decision-tools.page

366 Thornhill, J. (2024) Superfluous people vs AI: what the jobs revolution might look like Financial Times, March 14, https://www.ft.com/content/f9b964bd-0edc-4dfd-ad30-88b011cd4fde

367 NBER (2025) The Earnings of self-employed workers, NBER, https://www.nber.org/be/20251/earnings-self-employed-workers

368 Bizspace (2014) Self-employed workers are poorer, happier, https://www.bizspace.co.uk/news/self-employed-workers-are-poorer-happier/

369 United Nations (n.d.) Goal 8: Decent work and economic growth, https://sdgs.un.org/goals/goal8

370 Gallup (2025) State of the global workplace, https://www.gallup.com/workplace/349484/state-of-the-global-workplace.aspx

371 Green, F. (2013) Demanding work: The paradox of job quality in the affluent economy, In Demanding Work, Princeton University Press.

372 Gallup (2025) Major threat from the next tech thing, https://news.gallup.com/poll/692435/major-threat-next-tech-thing.aspx

373 Australian Institute of Company Directors (2025) Trust in business leaders sinks, https://www.aicd.com.au/good-governance/public-trust/organisation/trust-in-business-leaders-employers-sinks-2025-edelman-trust-barometer.html

374 AllGreatQuotes (n.d.) [Quote page], https://www.allgreatquotes.com/quote-401168/

Chapter X – Upskilling and Reskilling

375 BrainyQuote (n.d.) Malcolm X quote, https://www.brainyquote.com/quotes/malcolm_x_386475

376 BrainyQuote (n.d.) Benjamin Franklin quote, https://www.brainyquote.com/quotes/benjamin_franklin_151593

377 McKinsey Global Institute (2024) A new future of work: The race to deploy AI, https://www.mckinsey.de/~/media/mckinsey/locations/europe%20and%20middle%20east/deutschland/news/presse/2024/2024%20-%2005%20-%2023%20mgi%20genai%20future%20of%20work/mgi%20report_a-new-future-of-work-the-race-to-deploy-ai.pdf

378 Citi GPS (2023) Technology at work v7.0, https://www.citigroup.com/global/insights/technology-at-work-v7-0

379 World Economic Forum (2025) The Future of Jobs Report 2025: Digest, https://www.weforum.org/publications/the-future-of-jobs-report-2025/digest/

380 Beane, M. (2025) The Skill Code: How to save human ability in an age of intelligent machines, HarperCollins.

381 Young, H. (2023) Report reveals employees say they are not learning enough, Startups.co.uk, April 23, https://startups.co.uk/news/employees-say-they-are-not-learning-enough/

382 Department for Education (2025) Employers cut training investment by £6bn as skills shortages ease but long-term concerns remain, FE News, December 23, https://www.fenews.co.uk/skills/employers-cut-training-investment-by-6bn-as-skills-shortages-ease-but-long-term-concerns-remain/

383 Citi GPS (2024) What machines can't master, https://www.citigroup.com/global/insights/what-machines-can-t-master

384 Bureau of Labor Statistics (2024) Employee tenure in 2023, https://www.bls.gov/news.release/pdf/tenure.pdf

385 Massachusetts Institute of Technology Sloan School of Management (2022) Survey: Workers who need training most aren't getting it, https://mitsloan.mit.edu/ideas-made-to-matter/survey-workers-who-need-training-most-arent-getting-it

386 Gallup (2025) Addressing barriers blocking employee development, https://www.gallup.com/workplace/692642/addressing-barriers-blocking-employee-development.aspx

387 GlobeScan (2024) Insight of the week: People feel overwhelmed by pace of change in the world, January 25 2024, https://globescan.com/2024/01/25/insight-of-the-week-people-feel-overwhelmed-by-pace-of-change-in-the-world/

388 Jaokar, A. (2024) The AI radiologists replacement saga: Don't be misled by the scaremongering - science v.s. science fiction, DataScienceCentral, January 22, https://www.datasciencecentral.com/the-ai-radiologists-replacement-saga-dont-be-misled-by-the-scaremongering-science-v-s-science-fiction/ :contentReference[oaicite:0]{index=0}

389 Citi (2022) The halflife of knowledge, Citi Asia Wealth Insights, February 10, https://asia.citi.com/wealthinsights/education/half-life-knowledge

390 Hult International Business School (2024) WI skills survey, https://www.hult.edu/blog/wi_skills_survey/

391 Citi GPS (2024) What machines can't master, https://www.citigroup.com/global/insights/what-machines-can-t-master

392 EDGE (2021) Skills shortages in the UK economy, https://www.edge.co.uk/documents/262/DD0511_-_Skills_shortages_bulletin_9_online_version2.pdf

393 Merisotis, J. (2020) Human work in the age of smart machines, Rosetta Books.

394 Citi GPS (2024.) What machines can't master, https://www.citigroup.com/global/insights/what-machines-can-t-master

395 Slaughter, A. (2016) Anne-Marie Slaughter: University of Utah commencement speech, Time, May 6, https://time.com/4321549/anne-marie-slaughter-university-of-utah-commencement-speech/

396 Amdur, E. (2022) The illiterate of the 21st century, Forbes, October 4, https://www.forbes.com/sites/eliamdur/2022/10/04/the-illiterate-of-the-21st-century/

397 The Innovation Show (2018) If the rate of change on the outside exceeds the rate of change on the inside, the end is near, https://theinnovationshow.io/if-the-rate-of-change-on-the-outside-exceeds-the-rate-of-change-on-the-inside-the-end-is-near/#:~:text=We%20have%20witnessed%20huge%20disruption,the%20needs%20of%20the%20market

398 The Decision Lab (n.d.) System 1 and System 2 thinking, https://thedecisionlab.com/reference-guide/philosophy/system-1-and-system-2-thinking

399 OECD (2024) Adult skills in literacy and numeracy declining or stagnating in most OECD countries, December, https://www.oecd.org/en/about/news/press-releases/2024/12/adult-skills-in-literacy-and-numeracy-declining-or-stagnating-in-most-oecd-countries.html#:~:text=Literacy%20and%20numeracy%20skills%20among,widening%20skills%20inequalities%20within%20countries

400 Blackburn, M. (2024) Between its censorship and harm to children, TikTok must be held accountable, October 21, https://www.blackburn.senate.gov/2024/10/between-its-censorship-and-harm-to-children-tiktok-must-be-held-accountable

401 Oxford University Press (2024) Brain rot named Oxford Word of the Year 2024, https://corp.oup.com/news/brain-rot-named-oxford-word-of-the-year-2024/#:~:text=In%202024%2C%20'brain%20rot',on%20an%20individual%20or%20society

402 Weber, B. (1997) Swift and slashing computer topples Kasparov, New York Times, May 12, https://www.nytimes.com/1997/05/12/nyregion/swift-and-slashing-computer-topples-kasparov.html

403 Prather, J. et al (2024) The Widening Gap: The Benefits and Harms of Generative AI for Novice Programmers, ACM Transactions on Computer-Human Interaction, 30(5), 1–25, https://dl.acm.org/doi/10.1145/3632620.3671116

404 Brumfiel, G (2025) Research suggests doctors might quickly become dependent on AI, NPR, August 19, https://www.npr.

org/sections/shots-health-news/2025/08/19/nx-s1-5506292/doctors-ai-artificial-intelligence-dependent-colonoscopy#:~:text=Television-,Doctors%20who%20use%20AI%20may%20'forget'%20some%20skills%20%3A%20Shots,help%20from%20an%20AI%20tool

405 Microsoft Research (2025) The Impact of Generative AI on Critical Thinking: Self-Reported
Reductions in Cognitive Effort and Confidence Effects From a Survey of Knowledge Workers, https://www.microsoft.com/en-us/research/wp-content/uploads/2025/01/lee_2025_ai_critical_thinking_survey.pdf

406 Wikipedia (n.d.) Mr Bates vs The Post Office, https://en.wikipedia.org/wiki/Mr_Bates_vs_The_Post_Office

407 Hounshell, D. (1984) From the American system to mass production, 1800-1932: The development of manufacturing technology in the United States (No. 4), Jhu Press.

408 Davis, J. (2025) Matt Beane. The Skill Code: How to Save Human Ability in an Age of Intelligent Machines, HarperCollins.

409 Citi GPS (2019) Technology at work v4.0, https://www.citigroup.com/global/insights/technology-work-v4-0

410 Beane, M. (2025) The Skill Code: How to Save Human Ability in an Age of Intelligent Machines, HarperCollins.

411 Fortune (2025) Anthropics CEO warning AI job loss, Fortune, May 28, https://fortune.com/2025/05/28/anthropic-ceo-warning-ai-job-loss/

412 SignalFire (2025) State of talent report 2025, https://www.signalfire.com/blog/signalfire-state-of-talent-report-2026

413 Retrain.ai (n.d.) Case studies, https://www.retrain.ai/why-retrain-ai/case-studies/

414 UK Government (2024) Skills England to transform opportunities and drive growth, https://www.gov.uk/government/news/skills-england-to-transform-opportunities-and-drive-growth

415 Davies, R. et al (2024) Are skill requirements on the rise?, Wiserd, https://wiserd.ac.uk/wp-content/uploads/7.-Are-Skill-Requirements-on-the-Rise.pdf

416 CSN (n.d.) Student finance for transition and retraining, https://www.csn.se/languages/english/student-finance-for-transition-and-retraining.html

417 Bureau of Labor Statistics (2025) National longitudinal survey of youth 1979, https://www.bls.gov/news.release/pdf/nlsoy.pdf

Chapter XI – Society Votes

418 BrainyQuote (n.d.) "When Roosevelt came along, I approved of his program, generally. I figured an economic system should work for people, not vice versa." Sargent Shriver, https://www.brainyquote.com/quotes/sargent_shriver_323439

419 Goodreads (n.d.) "A man without a vote is a man without protection", Lyndon B. Johnson, https://www.goodreads.com/quotes/178240-a-man-without-a-vote-is-a-man-without-protection

420 Alberta Animal Health Source (n.d.) War Horse – The True Story, Dr. Ron Clarke, https://albertaanimalhealthsource.ca/content/war-horse-true-story#:~:text=Eight%20million%20horses%2C%20donkeys%20and,taken%20overseas%20with%20American%2
421 CowboyWay (n.d.) Horse and Mule Population in the USA: 1900–1960, https://www.cowboyway.com/What/HorsePopulation.htm
422 Encyclopaedia Britannica (2025) "Marxian Communism," Britannica, https://www.britannica.com/topic/communism/Marxian-communism
423 Hubbard, G. (2022) The Wall and the Bridge: Fear and Opportunity in Disruption's Wake, Yale University Press
424 A-kasser.dk (2025) Unemployment Insurance in Denmark, April 16, https://www.a-kasser.dk/unemployment-insurance-in-europe/denmark/index.html
425 Statista (2024), Share of Movers and Non-Movers in the U.S. Population, Apr 19, https://www.statista.com/chart/32135/share-of-movers-and-non-movers-in-the-us-population/
426 Organisation for Economic Co-operation and Development (2025) Five Facts on Non-Compete and Related Clauses in OECD Countries, 25 April, https://www.oecd.org/en/publications/five-facts-on-non-compete-an d-related-clauses-in-oecd-countries_727da13e-en.html
427 U.S. Department of the Treasury (n.d.) Monthly Treasury Statement (MTS), https://fiscaldata.treasury.gov/americas-finance-guide/government-revenue/
428 Office for Budget Responsibility (2025) Income Tax, https://obr.uk/forecasts-in-depth/tax-by-tax-spend-by-spend/income-tax/
429 UBS (2025) The changing world of wealth, https://www.ubs.com/us/en/wealth-management/insights/global-wealth-report.html
430 Tax Foundation (2025) Capital Gains Tax Rates in Europe, https://taxfoundation.org/data/all/eu/capital-gains-tax-rates-europe/
431 Gentiloni, P. (2023) 2024 will herald the end of a race to the bottom in corporate tax rates, Financial Times, December 28, https://www.ft.com/cont ent/918fcf79-4703-41dc-98fc-309398068195
432 Brookings Institution (2020) Does the U.S. Tax Code Favor Automation?, March 18, https://www.brookings.edu/articles/does-the-u-s-tax-cod e-favor-automation/
433 World Economic Forum (2017) Bill Gates: This Is Why We Should Tax Robots, Feb 20, https://www.weforum.org/stories/2017/02/bill-gates-this-is-why-we-should-tax-robots/
434 Economics Help (2017) Thatcher Economic Policies, https://www.economicshelp.org/blog/glossary/thatcher-economic-policies/
435 Wikipedia (2025) Social VAT, https://en.wikipedia.org/wiki/Social_VAT
436 Organisation for Economic Co-operation and Development (2014) Trends in Top Incomes and Their Taxation in OECD Countries, OECD, https://www.oecd.org/content/dam/oecd/en/publications/reports/2014/05/trends-in-top-incomes-and-thei r-taxation-in-oecd-countries_g17a2495/5jz43jhlz87f-en.pdf

437 Tax Foundation Europe (2025) Top Personal Income Tax Rates in Europe, https://taxfoundation.org/data/all/eu/top-personal-income-tax-rates-europe/

438 Tax Foundation (2024) A Comparison of the Tax Burden on Labor in the OECD, https://taxfoundation.org/data/all/global/tax-burden-on-labor-oecd-2024/

439 Kuper, S. (2025) Article on labour or economic policy, Financial Times, March 20, https://www.ft.com/content/ace79979-e35e-47e7-8e76-03d99cb04834

440 Wikipedia (2025) Universal Basic Income Pilots, https://en.wikipedia.org/wiki/Universal_basic_income_pilots

441 Institute for Employment Studies (2023) Universal Basic Income: Pros, Cons and Evidence, https://www.employment-studies.co.uk/news/universal-basic-income-pros-cons-and-evidence

442 CNBC (2025) Tax bill includes $1,000 baby bonus in 'Trump Accounts' — here's who is eligible, https://www.cnbc.com/2025/05/22/tax-bill-maga-baby-bonus-now-called-trump-accounts-who-is-eligible.html

443 Wikipedia (2025) Works Progress Administration, https://en.wikipedia.org/wiki/Works_Progress_Administration

444 Istanbul University (2022) The Impact of the Nonprofit Sector on Employment and Unemployment in Developed Economies: Dynamic Panel Data Analysis*, https://cdn.istanbul.edu.tr/file/JTA6CLJ8T5/57BE9CB4FF54456B9FF7D9B56702C3CF

445 George Mason University, Schar School (2024) Nonprofit Employment Report, https://nonprofitcenter.schar.gmu.edu/wp-content/uploads/2024/12/Nonprofit-Employment-Report-12.24-Full-Text-2.pdf

446 Pro Bono Economics (2019) The Third Pillar and the Fourth Industrial Revolution, https://pbe.co.uk/wp-content/uploads/2025/03/the-third-pillar-and-the-fourth-industrial-revolution-c553330a.pdf

447 Tempo (2023) Tempo Impact Report, https://wearetempo.org/wp-content/uploads/2023/10/tempo-impact-report_202324_english.pdf

448 Young Scot (n.d.) Impact Reports, https://youngscot.net/impact

449 World Population Review (2025) Countries with Mandatory Military Service, https://worldpopulationreview.com/country-rankings/countries-with-mandatory-military-service

450 Wikipedia (2025) History of the Minimum Wage, https://en.wikipedia.org/wiki/History_of_the_minimum_wage

451 Organisation for Economic Co-operation and Development (2024) Part-Time Employment Rate, https://www.oecd.org/en/data/indicators/part-time-employment-rate.html

452 Wikipedia (2025) Kurzarbeit, https://en.wikipedia.org/wiki/Kurzarbeit

453 Ogletree Deakins (2025) California's "No Robo Bosses" Bill Could Restrict Employers' Use of AI, https://ogletree.com/insights-resources/blog-posts/californias-no-robo-bosses-bill-could-restrict-employers-use-of-ai/

454 Unifor (2018) The Future of Work, https://www.unifor.org/sites/default/files/legacy/documents/document/1173-future_of_work_eng_no_bleed.pdf

455 UNI Global Union (2017) Principles for Workers' Data Rights and Privacy, https://uniglobalunion.org/report/principles-for-workers-data-rights/

456 United States Congress (2024) H.R. 7690, https://www.congress.gov/bill/118th-congress/house-bill/7690/text

457 Cranfield University (2018) How Long Do Pilots Really Spend on Autopilot?, https://insights.cranfield.ac.uk/blog/how-long-do-pilots-really-spend-on-autopilot

458 Future of Life Institute (2024) The Pause Letter, One Year Later, https://futureoflife.org/ai/the-pause-letter-one-year-later/

459 YouTube (2025) Leading in a Time of Change: Jamie Dimon, Chairman and CEO, JP Morgan Chase, https://youtu.be/PdzMvk66wao

460 Daily Mail (2024) German Court Rules on Sunday Trading and Robots, https://www.dailymail.co.uk/news/article-13278447/german-court-rules-sundays-robots-teo-tegut.html

461 The Guardian (2021) Priti Patel pressed to explain award of spy agencies cloud contract to Amazon, https://www.theguardian.com/uk-news/2021/oct/26/amazon-web-services-aws-contract-data-mi5-mi6-gchq

462 Bank of England (2020) How Reliant Are Banks and Insurers on Cloud Outsourcing?, https://www.bankofengland.co.uk/bank-overground/2020/how-reliant-are-banks-and-insurers-on-cloud-outsourcing

463 Forbes (2020) Digital Crack Cocaine: The Science Behind TikTok's Success, Forbes, https://www.forbes.com/sites/johnkoetsier/2020/01/18/digital-crack-cocaine-the-science-behind-tiktoks-success/

464 Situational Awareness AI (2024) Situational Awareness, https://situational-awareness.ai

465 Hammond, G., Heikkila, M., Criddle, C. (2025) Meta invests $15bn in Scale AI, doubling start-up's valuation, Financial Times, June 13, https://www.ft.com/content/5a30cd25-90f9-41a4-924c-1e7c6772a47f

466 CNBC (2025) Sam Altman Says Meta Tried to Poach OpenAI Staff with $100 Million Bonuses, https://www.cnbc.com/2025/06/18/sam-altman-says-meta-tried-to-poach-openai-staff-with-10 0-million-bonuses-mark-zuckerberg.html

467 Statista (2025) Total Lobbying Spending in the United States, https://www.statista.com/statistics/257337/total-lobbying-spending-in-the-us/

468 Issue One (2025) Big Tech Cozies Up to New Administration After Spending Record Sums on Lobbying Last Year, https://issueone.org/articles/big-tech-spent-record-sums-on-lobbying-last-year/

469 European Court of Auditors (2024) Lobbying lawmakers: EU audit reveals transparency blind spots, https://www.eca.europa.eu/en/news/NEWS-SR-2024-05

470 Kuper, S. (2025) A new who's who of the global elites, Financial Times, April 10, https://www.ft.com/content/ff0af5e7-60eb-4cc9-aebd-da6fbc94f8c8

471 Investopedia (2022) Employment Act of 1946, https://www.investopedia.com/terms/e/employmentactof1946.asp

472 Investopedia (2025) Breaking Down the Federal Reserve's Dual Mandate, https://www.investopedia.com/articles/investing/100715/breaking-down-federal-reserves-dual-mandate.asp

473 Investor Daily (2023) New Agreement Gives RBA More Wiggle Room to Handle Inflation Goals, https://www.investordaily.com.au/regulation/54412-new-agreement-gives-rba-more-wiggle-room-to-handle-inflation-goals

474 Wikipedia (2025) Treaty on the Prohibition of Nuclear Weapons, https://en.wikipedia.org/wiki/Treaty_on_the_Prohibition_of_Nuclear_Weapons

475 New York Times (2025) AI Summit in Paris Highlights Global Technology Tensions, https://www.nytimes.com/2025/02/10/technology/ai-summit-paris-technology.html

476 World Economic Forum (2024) Davos 2024: Technology in a Turbulent World, https://www.weforum.org/podcasts/agenda-dialogues/episodes/davos-2024-technology-in-a-turbulent-world/

477 Australian Financial Review (2025) How AI Chatbots Can Change Your Mind in Under 10 Minutes, https://www.afr.com/technology/how-ai-chatbots-can-change-your-mind-in-under-10-minutes-20250814-p5mn1o

478 World Economic Forum (2022) The promises and perils of AI - Stuart Russell on Radio Davos, https://www.weforum.org/stories/2022/01/artificial-intelligence-stuart-russell-radio-davos/

479 Brookings Institution (2020) Public Service and the Federal Government, https://www.brookings.edu/articles/public-service-and-the-federal-government/

Chapter XII – Employees Vote

480 Holocaust Memorial Day Trust (n.d.) First They Came, by Pastor Martin Niemöller, https://hmd.org.uk/resource/first-they-came-by-pastor-martin-niemoller/

481 openDemocracy (2008) Companionism: Enlarging Democracy, https://www.opendemocracy.net/en/companionism_enlarging_democracy/

482 Economic Policy Institute (2025) CEO pay increased in 2024 and is now 281 times that of the typical worker, https://www.epi.org/blog/ceo-pay-increased-in-2024-and-is-now-281-times-that-of-the-typical-worker-new-epi-landing-page-has-all-the-details/

483 Harvard Law School Forum on Corporate Governance (2023) CEO Tenure Rates, August 4, https://corpgov.law.harvard.edu/2023/08/04/ceo-tenure-rates-2/

484 PWL Capital (2025) The Passive vs Active Fund Monitor, March 18, https://pwlcapital.com/wp-content/uploads/2025/03/20250318-The-Passive-vs-Active-Fund-Monitor.pdf.

485 Stavros, P. (2025) Private equity can defy the gloom narrative, Financial Times, July 5 https://www.ft.com/content/6105bea8-88a9-4b5d-9fd4-c777c602fbd1

[486] The Times (2024) Tell Sid He Should Worry About the FTSE's Future, https://www.thetimes.com/business-money/article/tell-sid-he-should-worry-about-the-ftses-future-zqgfzjtnx

[487] Stavros, P. (2025) Private equity can defy the gloom narrative, Financial Times, July 5 https://www.ft.com/content/6105bea8-88a9-4b5d-9fd4-c777c602fbd1

[488] Armstrong, A., & Gara, A. (2025) Private equity group Vista to cut staff in favour of AI, Financial Times, November 12, https://www.ft.com/content/7e8764f3-7a6d-4d7a-8273-734655bedff2

[489] Garrahan, M. (2025) Humanity deserves better, Financial Times, June 2, https://www.ft.com/content/7f0a45b0-a3cc-4e1c-be71-1b7b42958d4d

[490] National Center for Employee Ownership (n.d.) Employee Ownership by the Numbers, https://www.nceo.org/research/employee-ownership-by-the-numbers#how-many-esops-are-there

[491] Australian Financial Review (2025) As AI Takes Over, Does HR Still Need Humans?, August 18, https://www.afr.com/technology/as-ai-takes-over-does-hr-still-need-humans-20250818-p5mnvf

[492] Heidrick & Struggles (2023) Route to the Top: Interactive Dashboard, https://www.heidrick.com/en/insights/chief-executive-officer/route-to-the-top_interactive-dashboard-2023

[493] HR Dive (2016) There's a Significant Pay Gap Between CHROs and the Rest of the C-Suite, https://www.hrdive.com/news/theres-a-significant-pay-gap-betwee n-chros-and-the-rest-of-the-c-suite/427501/

[494] CIPD (2023) People Expertise, https://www.cipd.org/uk/knowledge/reports/people-expertise/

[495] Personio (2023) HR Study 2023: HR and the CEO, https://www.personio.com/about-personio/press/hr-study-2023-hr-ceo/

[496] U.S. Bureau of Labor Statistics (2024) Union Members—2023 (News Release), January 2024, https://www.bls.gov/news.release/pdf/union2.pdf

[497] Gallup (2022) Approval of Labor Unions at Highest Point Since 1965, August 30, https://news.gallup.com/poll/398303/approval-labor-unions-highest-point-1965.aspx

[498] U.S. Department of the Treasury (n.d.) Labor Unions and the Middle Class, https://home.treasury.gov/system/files/136/Labor-Unions-And-The-Middle-Class.pdf

[499] Workers World (2024) Article, October 2024, https://www.workers.org/2024/10/81195/

[500] Guardian (2023) Nearly a Million Days Lost to Strikes in December as UK Pay Growth…, February 14, https://www.theguardian.com/uk-news/2023/feb/14/nearly-million-days-lost-strikes-december-uk-pay-growth

[501] China Labour Bulletin (2024) Strike Map Data Analysis: 2024 Year Review, https://clbarchive.prvcy.page/en/content/china-labour-bulletin-strike-map-dat a-analysis-2024-year-review-workers'-rights/

502 Labor Relations Law Insider (2024) The Rise of Unions in Banking and Finance, March 2024, https://www.laborrelationslawinsider.com/2024/03/the-rise-of-unions-in-banking-and-finance/

503 GMB (n.d.) The GMB Union Campaign for Trade Union Recognition in Amazon Coventry, https://www.gmb.org.uk/assets/media/documents/the-gmb-union-campaign-for-trade-union-recognition-in-amazon-coventry-bleed.pdf

504 Gross, A., & Bradshaw, T., (2025) TikTok to lay off hundreds of UK moderators as it shifts to AI, Financial Times, August 22, https://www.ft.com/content/d277c456-4518-4994-8afd-c45a399db342

505 Organise Network (n.d.) Organise, https://organise.network

506 UNI Global Union (n.d.) UNI Global Union, https://uniglobalunion.org/

507 Wikipedia (n.d.) Worker Representation on Corporate Boards of Directors, https://en.wikipedia.org/wiki/Worker_representation_on_corporate_boards_of_directors

508 Inequality.org (2024) Stock Ownership Concentration, January 16, https://inequality.org/article/stock-ownership-concentration/

509 Oxfam GB (n.d.) World's Top 1% Own More Wealth Than 95% of Humanity, https://www.oxfam.org.uk/media/press-releases/worlds-top-1-own-more-wealth-than-95-per-cent-of-humanity/

510 Google Books (n.d.) Companionism, https://books.google.co.uk/books/about/Companionism.html?id=N3HeGAAACAAJ

511 Kay, J. (2025) The Corporation in the Twenty-First Century: Why (Almost) Everything We Are Told About Business Is Wrong, Yale University Press

512 Gallup (2025) Image of Capitalism Slips, September 2025, https://news.gallup.com/poll/694835/image-capitalism-slips.aspx

513 Pew Research Center (2022) Modest Declines in Positive Views of Socialism and Capitalism in U.S., September 19, https://www.pewresearch.org/politics/2022/09/19/modest-declines-in-positive-views-of-socialism-and-capitalism-in-u-s/

514 Australian Cardijn Institute (2022) Mondragon Limits Maximum Salaries to 6x, https://australiancardijninstitute.org/mondragon-limits-maximum-salaries-to-6x/

515 International Cooperative Alliance (n.d.) International Cooperative Alliance, https://ica.coop/en

516 AllMusicals (n.d.) Hamilton Lyrics: "The Room Where It Happens", https://www.allmusicals.com/lyrics/hamilton/theroomwhereithappens.htm

517 Harvard Business School (2024) 181 CEOs Pledged for Stakeholder Capitalism in 2019—Did It Make a Difference?, https://www.hbs.edu/bigs/181ceos-pledged-for-stakeholder-capitalism-in-2019-did-it-make-a-difference

Part 3 – Pro-Human Leadership

Chapter XIII – The Pro-Human Leader

518 Goodreads (n.d.) "The Best Way to Predict Your Future Is to Create It", https://www.goodreads.com/quotes/328848-the-best-way-to -predict-your-future-is-to-create

519 Howard, A. (2015) Humanise: Why Human-Centred Leadership Is the Key to the 21st Century, John Wiley & Sons

520 Time (2000) Person of the Century, https://content.time.com/time/teach/ glenspring2000/PDFs/PersonofCentury.pdf

521 Atomic Heritage Foundation (n.d.) Russell–Einstein Manifesto, https://ahf. nuclearmuseum.org/ahf/key-documents/russell-einstein-manifesto/

522 Farnam Street (n.d.) Bertrand Russell: "Love Is Wise", https://fs.blog/ bertrand-russell-love-is-wise/

523 Gallup (2022) State of the Global Workplace, https://www.gallup.com/ workplace/349484/state-of-the-global-workplace.aspx

524 Work Life Academy (2012) Q12 Meta-Analysis Research Paper, https://worklifeacademy.nl/wp-content/uploads/2012 -Q12-Meta-Analysis-Research-Paper.pdf

525 Pew Research Center (2023) AI in Hiring and Evaluating Workers: What Americans Think, April 20, https://www.pewresearch. org/internet/2023/04/20/ai-in-hiring-and-evaluating-worker s-what-americans-think/

526 Ipsos (n.d.) AI Is Making the World More Nervous, https://www.ipsos.com/ en/ai-making-world-more-nervous

527 Gallup (2022) State of the Global Workplace, https://www.gallup.com/ workplace/349484/state-of-the-global-workplace.aspx

528 Goodreads (n.d.) "The Best Way to Predict Your Future Is to Create It", https://www.goodreads.com/quotes/328848-the-best-way-to -predict-your-future-is-to-create

529 Gartner (2022) Gartner HR Research Finds Just 25% of Employees Are Confident About Their Career at Their Current Organization, September 15, https://www.gartner.com/en/newsroom/press-releases/2022-09-15- gartner-hr-research-finds-just-25-percent-of-employees-are-confid ent-about-their-career-at-their-current-organization

530 Gallup (2023) Why Build a Strengths-Based Culture?, https://www.gallup. com/workplace/470621/why-build-strengths-based-culture.aspx

531 Tulgan, B. (2014) The 27 Challenges Managers Face: Step-by-Step Solutions to (Nearly) All of Your Management Problems, John Wiley & Sons

532 Goodall, A. (2024) The Problem With Change: The Essential Nature of Human Performance, Random House

533 Frankl, V. E. (1985) Man's Search for Meaning, Simon and Schuster

534 Sinek, S. (2018) Start with Why, ReadinGraphics

535 Massey University (2023) Re-Evaluating Working Attitudes in a Post-COVID-19 World, https://www.massey.ac.nz/about/news/re-evaluating-working-attitudes-in-a-post-covid-19-world/
536 HR Dive (2017) Meaningful Work Is Critical to Worker Happiness, Study Says, https://www.hrdive.com/news/meaningful-work-is-critical-to-worker-happiness-study-says/506877/
537 HA Agency (n.d.) Purpose-Driven Employee Engagement, https://www.ha-agency.com/blog/purpose-driven-employee-engagement
538 McKinsey & Company (2021) Help Your Employees Find Purpose—or Watch Them Leave, https://www.mckinsey.com/capabilities/people-and-organizational-performance/our-insights/help-your-employees-find-purpose-or-watch-them-leave
539 Gallup (2019) Future of the Workplace Depends on Purpose, https://www.gallup.com/workplace/257744/future-workplace-depends-purpose.aspx
540 Gallup (2025) The Post-Pandemic Workplace: The Experiment Continues, https://www.gallup.com/workplace/657629/post-pandemic-workplace-experiment-continues.aspx
541 Wisdom.ge (n.d.) Old Soviet Union Joke: "They Pretend to Pay Us, We Pretend to Work", https://wisdom.ge/1814/old-soviet-union-joke-they-pretend-to-pay-us-we-pretend-to-work
542 ScienceDirect (2024) Article, https://www.sciencedirect.com/science/article/pii/S0048733324000362
543 Self-Determination Theory (n.d.) Self-Determination Theory, https://selfdeterminationtheory.org/theory/
544 Criddle, C. (2024) Microsoft's Sarah Bird: Core pieces are still missing from artificial general intelligence, Financial Times, December 18, https://www.ft.com/content/aac74337-cb3f-43e7-894a-d85afedd3610
545 The Times (2025) I Built a Game in Minutes With AI—The Thrill Took Me Back Years, https://www.thetimes.com/business-money/technology/article/i-built-a-game-in-minutes-with-ai-the-thrill-took-me-back-years-27mljwx6j
546 University of Surrey (2025) What Is Happening to Participation at Work?, April 2025, https://www.surrey.ac.uk/sites/default/files/2025-04/what-is-happening-to-participation-at-work.pdf
547 Davis, J. (2025) The Skill Code: How to Save Human Ability in an Age of Intelligent Machines
548 Parade (n.d.) Muhammad Ali Quotes, https://parade.com/1105459/marynliles/muhammad-ali-quotes/
549 BrainyQuote (n.d.) Mark Twain Quotes, https://www.brainyquote.com/authors/mark-twain-quotes
550 British Psychological Society (2017) Small Acts of Kindness at Work Benefit Giver, Receiver and Whole Organisation, https://www.bps.org.uk/research-digest/small-acts-kindness-work-benefit-giver-receiver-and-whole-organisation

551 Harvard Business Review (2016) The Benefits of Peer-to-Peer Praise at Work, February 2016, https://hbr.org/2016/02/the-benefits-of-peer-to-peer-praise-at-work
552 Gallup (2024) The Human-Centered Workplace: Building Organizational Cultures That Thrive, https://www.gallup.com/analytics/472658/workplace-recognition-research.aspx
553 Mosley, E. and Irvine, D. (2020) Making Work Human: How Human-Centered Companies Are Changing the Future of Work and the World, McGraw Hill Professional
554 HRZone (2021) Employee Recognition: Creating a Sense of Community at Work Through Celebration, https://hrzone.com/employee-recognition-creating-a-sense-of-community-at-work-through-celebration/
555 Blumenfeld, R. (2020) How a 15,000-Year-Old Human Bone Could Help You Through the Coronavirus, Forbes, March 21, https://www.forbes.com/sites/remyblumenfeld/2020/03/21/how-a-15000-year-old-human-bone-could-help-you-through-the--coronavirus/
556 Harvard Kennedy School (2020) Social Capital Is Predicting Epidemic Loneliness, https://www.hks.harvard.edu/faculty-research/policy-topics/social-policy/social-capital-predicting-epidemic-loneliness
557 MedicalXpress (2024) Loneliness Worse Than Alcoholism and Obesity, Primary…, March 2024, https://medicalxpress.com/news/2024-03-loneliness-worse-alcoholism-obesity-primary.html
558 Gallup (2025) Younger Men Among Loneliest in the West, 2025, https://news.gallup.com/poll/690788/younger-men-among-loneliest-west.aspx
559 CIPD (2024) Psychological Safety and Trust: Practice Summary, 2024, https://www.cipd.org/globalassets/media/knowledge/knowledge-hub/evidence-reviews/2024-pdfs/8542-psych-safety-trust-practice-summary.pdf
560 Fast Company (2023) Link, https://share.google/5KZqdBHofj7dIEXiL
561 Wikipedia (n.d.) Theory X and Theory Y, https://en.wikipedia.org/wiki/Theory_X_and_Theory_Y
562 Edelman (2025) 2025 Edelman Trust Barometer: Global Report, January 23, https://www.edelman.com/sites/g/files/aatuss191/files/2025-01/2025%20Edelman%20Trust%20Barometer%20Global%20Report_01.23.25.pdf
563 Gallup (2023) Why Trust in Leaders Is Faltering—and How to Gain It Back, https://www.gallup.com/workplace/473738/why-trust-leaders-faltering-gain-back.aspx
564 Economic Policy Institute (2022) CEO Pay Has Skyrocketed… in 2021, 2022, https://www.epi.org/publication/ceo-pay-in-2021/
565 Clark, P. (2025) The brutal truth about today's lay-offs, Financial Times, June 8, https://www.ft.com/content/b5fcd5ae-de6d-4112-859e-0b96845742d5
566 The HR World (2023) Trust in the Work, https://www.thehrworld.co.uk/workplace-culture/trust-in-the-work/

567 Gallup (2024) View of Healthcare Quality Declines to Year Low, 2024, https://news.gallup.com/poll/654044/view-healthcare-quality-declines-year-low.aspx

568 Harvard Medical School (2023) Half the World's Population Will Experience a Mental Health Disorder, https://hms.harvard.edu/news/half-worlds-population-will-experience-mental-health-disorder

569 McKinsey Health Institute (2023) Reframing Employee Health: Moving Beyond Burnout to Holistic Health, https://www.mckinsey.com/mhi/our-insights/reframing-employee-health-moving-beyond-burnout-to-holistic-health

570 Gartner (2025) This New Strategy Could Be Your Ticket to Change Management Success, https://www.gartner.com/en/articles/this-new-strategy-could-be-your-ticket-to-change-management-success

571 Kellerman, G. R. and Seligman, M. E. (2023) Tomorrowmind: Thriving at Work with Resilience, Creativity, and Connection—Now and in an Uncertain Future, Simon and Schuster

572 Stanford Graduate School of Business (2016) Relationship Between Workplace Stressors, Mortality, and Health Costs, https://www.gsb.stanford.edu/faculty-research/publications/relationship-between-workplace-stressors-mortality-health-costs-united

573 World Health Organization (2021) Long Working Hours Increasing Deaths from Heart Disease and Stroke: WHO/ILO, May 17, https://www.who.int/news/item/17-05-2021-long-working-hours-increasing-deaths-from-heart-disease-and-stroke-who-ilo

574 Gallup (2025) Post-Pandemic Workplace Experiment Continues, https://www.gallup.com/workplace/657629/post-pandemic-workplace-experiment-continues.aspx

575 Economist Impact (n.d.) Workplace Mental Health: Core Value, https://impact.economist.com/health/workplace-mental-health/core-value/

576 Simply Psychology (2025) Bowlby's Attachment Theory, https://www.simplypsychology.org/bowlby.html

577 University of Bath (2026) New research reveals how dread shapes decision-making, January 22, https://www.bath.ac.uk/announcements/new-research-reveals-how-dread-shapes-decision-making/

578 Binik, Y. and Seligman, M. (1977) Safety Signal Hypothesis, Taylor & Francis, https://www.taylorfrancis.com/chapters/edit/10.4324/9781003150404-7/safety-signal-hypothesis-martin-seligman-yitzchak-binik

579 Harvard Business Review (2023) Employees Are Losing Patience with Change Initiatives, https://hbr.org/2023/05/employees-are-losing-patience-with-change-initiatives

580 Clear, J. and Clear, J. (2018) Atomic Habits: Tiny Changes, Remarkable Results, Penguin Publishing Group

581 Gallup (n.d.) How to Improve Employee Engagement in the Workplace, https://www.gallup.com/workplace/285674/improve-employee-engagement-workplace.aspx

582 Goodall, A. (2024) The Problem With Change: The Essential Nature of Human Performance, Random House

583 8x8 (2024) How to Improve Customer Service in the Digital Age, https://www.8x8.com/blog/how-to-improve-customer-service-in-digital-age

584 World Economic Forum (2017) Advancing Human-Centred Economic Progress, 2017, https://www3.weforum.org/docs/WEF_Advancing_Human_Centred_Economic_Progress_WP_2017.pdf

585 Heikkila, M. (2025) Margaret Mitchell: artificial general intelligence is 'just vibes and snake oil', Financial Times, June 19, https://www.ft.com/content/7089bff2-25fc-4a25-98bf-8828ab24f48e

586 Hougaard, R. and Carter, J. (2022) Compassionate Leadership: How to Do Hard Things in a Human Way, Harvard Business Press

587 Goodreads (n.d.) "Show Me the Incentive and I'll Show You the Outcome", https://www.goodreads.com/quotes/11903426-show-me-the-incentive-and-i-ll-show-you-the-outcome

588 BBC News (2025) Elon Musk's $1tn pay deal approved by Tesla shareholders, https://www.bbc.co.uk/news/articles/cwyk6kvyxvzo

589 Harvard Law School Forum on Corporate Governance (2024) 2024 Proxy Roundup: ESG Metrics in Incentive Compensation Plans, August 5, https://corpgov.law.harvard.edu/2024/08/05/2024-proxy-roundup-esg-metrics-in-incentive-compensation-plans/

590 Christensen, C. (2012) How Will You Measure Your Life?, TEDxBoston, https://youtu.be/tvos4nORf_Y

591 National Library of Medicine (2021) Article, 2021, https://pmc.ncbi.nlm.nih.gov/articles/PMC8137900/

592 Gallup (2022) State of the Global Workplace, https://www.gallup.com/workplace/349484/state-of-the-global-workplace.aspx

593 Small Business Charter (2023) 82% of Bosses Do Not Have Management Training, https://smallbusinesscharter.org/help-to-grow-management/news-and-case-studies/82-of-bosses-do-not-have-management-training

594 Goodreads (n.d.) "What Is Honored in a Culture Gets Cultivated There", https://www.goodreads.com/quotes/8589482-what-is-honored-in-a-culture-gets-cultivated-there

595 Quote Investigator (2017) Be the Change, October 23, https://quoteinvestigator.com/2017/10/23/be-change/

596 Gawdat, M. (2021) Scary Smart: The Future of Artificial Intelligence and How You Can Save Our World, Pan Macmillan

Chapter XIV – Pro-Human Capitalism

597 Torres, R. (2014) What it takes to be a great leader, Ted Talks, https://youtu.be/aUYSDEYdmzw

598 Hargrove, R. (2014) Five Things Business Leaders Can Do to Create a Fantastic Work Culture, Medium / Authority Magazine, December 11, https://medium.com/authority-magazine/author-robert-hargrove-five-things-busines s-leaders-can-do-to-create-a-fantastic-work-culture-d0c8a9026b2d

599 Ellis, S. & Zither, A. (2025) Americans Lose Faith That Hard Work Leads to Economic Gains, WSJ-NORC Poll Finds, Wall Street Journal September 1, https://www.wsj.com/economy/wsj-norc-economic-poll-73bce003

600 ClearPoint Strategy (2014) The Eisenhower Principle and Business Strategy Management, https://www.clearpointstrategy.com/blog/eisenhower-principle-and-business-strategy-management

601 History of Information (n.d.) Information History Entry, https://www.historyofinformation.com/detail.php?id=4266

602 Goldin, Ian, and Chris Kutarna. Age of discovery: navigating the storms of our second renaissance. Bloomsbury Publishing, 2016

603 Deliberate Directions (n.d.) Manufacturing Quotes, https://deliberatedirections.com/manufacturing-quotes/

604 QuoteFancy (n.d.) Mary Parker Follett Quote, https://quotefancy.com/quote/1564904/Mary-Parker-Follett-Leadership-is-no t-defined-by-the-exercise-of-power-but-by-the

605 Wikipedia (n.d.) Maslow's Hierarchy of Needs, https://en.wikipedia.org/wiki/Maslow%27s_hierarchy_of_needs

606 Kelly, K. (2017) The Future Is Already Here — It's Just Not Very Evenly Distributed, https://www.researchgate.net/publication/314110709_The_future_is_already_here_it%27s_just_not_very_evenly_distributed

607 Chase. C. (2015) Science Fiction Philosophy in Fancy Dress, Singularity Weblog, March 14, https://www.singularityweblog.com/science-fiction-philosophy-in-fancy-dress/

608 Wikipedia (n.d.) The Time Machine, https://en.wikipedia.org/wiki/The_Time_Machine

609 Wikipedia (n.d.) Brave New World, https://en.wikipedia.org/wiki/Brave_New_World

610 Guardian (2015) Conversation: Brian Eno and Yanis Varoufakis, November 28, https://www.theguardian.com/lifeandstyle/2015/nov/28/conversation-brian-eno-yanis-varoufakis-interview

611 YouTube (2015) Video, https://youtu.be/8rh3xPatEto

612 Gates, B. (2014) Episode 6: OpenAI CEO Sam Altman on the future of AI, YouTube, Januray 10, https://youtu.be/PkXELH6Y2lM

613 Robin Hood Foundation (2023) Robin Hood Annual Poverty Tracker Report Shows 25% Poverty Rate in New York City, https://robinhood.org/news/robin-hood-annual-poverty-tracker-repor t-shows-25-overall-poverty-rate-in-new-york-city-climbing-beyond-record-highs-observed-in-2022/

[614] Statista (2025) U.S. Health Expenditure as a Percentage of GDP Since 1960, https://www.statista.com/statistics/184968/us-health-expenditure-as-percent-of-gdp-since-1960/
[615] Milliman (2024) 2024 Milliman Medical Index, https://www.milliman.com/en/insight/2024-milliman-medical-index
[616] U.S. Bureau of Labor Statistics (n.d.) BLS Data, https://data.bls.gov
[617] Trades Union Congress (n.d.) Nye Bevan, https://tuc150.tuc.org.uk/stories/nye-bevan/
[618] John F. Kennedy Presidential Library (1961) Address to a Joint Session of Congress on Urgent National Needs, May 25, https://www.jfklibrary.org/learn/about-jfk/historic-speeches/address-to-joint-session-of-congres s-may-25-1961
[619] From the Green Notebook (2017) The Janitor Who Helped Put a Man on the Moon, November 4, https://fromthegreennotebook.com/2017/11/04/the-janitor-who-help-put-a-man-on-the-moon/
[620] Harvard Human Flourishing Program (2025) Global Flourishing Study, https://hfh.fas.harvard.edu/global-flourishing-study
[621] World Economic Forum (2021) Stakeholder Capitalism: Episode 1 – A Brief History of GDP, December 2021, https://www.weforum.org/stories/2021/12/stakeholder-capitalism-episode-1-a-brief-history-of-gdp/
[622] Atlantic (2023) The Harvard Happiness Study and the Importance of Relationships, January 2023, https://www.theatlantic.com/ideas/archive/2023/01/harvard-happiness-study-relationships/672753/
[623] Wikipedia (n.d.) Richard Easterlin, https://en.wikipedia.org/wiki/Richard_Easterlin
[624] Easterlin, R. A. (2021) An Economist's Lessons on Happiness: Farewell Dismal Science, Springer, https://fernandonogueiracosta.wordpress.com/wp-content/uploads/2021/07/richard-a.-easterlin-an-economists-lessons-on-h appiness_-farewell-dismal-science-springer-2021.pdf
[625] Oxford Poverty and Human Development Initiative (2023) Gross National Happiness, https://ophi.org.uk/gross-national-happiness

Chapter XV – The BESST™ Framework: A Hopeful Path

[626] National WWII Museum (n.d.) The Four Freedoms, https://www.nationalww2museum.org/war/articles/four-freedoms
[627] BrainyQuote (n.d.) George Eliot Quote, https://www.brainyquote.com/quotes/george_eliot_165195
[628] BBC Culture (2015) Why Middlemarch Is the Greatest British Novel, December 4, https://www.bbc.co.uk/culture/article/20151204-why-middlem arch-is-the-greatest-british-novel

Printed in Great Britain
by Amazon

3005c1bc-24a9-44d4-8dc6-ddcb2dd222a9R01